I0814324

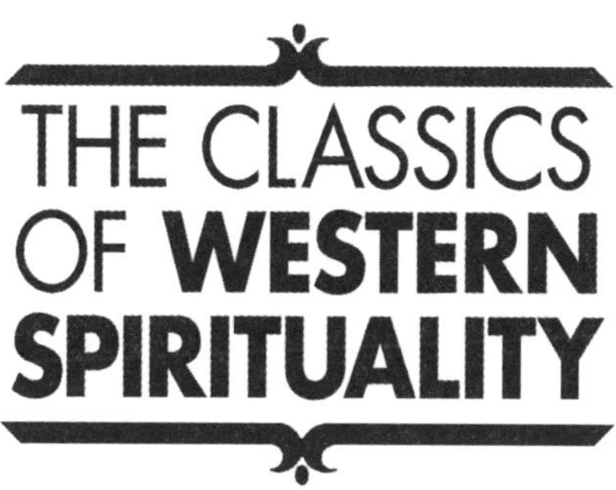
THE CLASSICS
OF WESTERN
SPIRITUALITY

THE CLASSICS OF WESTERN SPIRITUALITY
A Library of the Great Spiritual Masters

NARSAI

SELECTED SERMONS

Introduced and Translated by
Andrew Younan

Foreword by
Adam Becker

Paulist Press
New York / Mahwah, NJ

Caseside image: Manuscript from the Chaldean Catholic Church, Diocese of Alqush, Iraq, provided by the Hill Museum & Manuscript Library, Saint John's University, Collegeville, Minnesota.

Caseside design by Sharyn Banks
Book design by Lynn Else

Library of Congress Cataloging-in-Publication Data
Names: Narsai, approximately 413-503, author. | Younan, Andrew, 1979– translator.
Title: Narsai: selected sermons / introduced and translated by Andrew Younan; foreword by Adam Becker.
Other titles: Sermons. Selections. English
Description: New York; Mahwah, NJ: Paulist Press, [2024] | Series: The classics of Western spirituality | Includes bibliographical references. | Summary: "A collection of sermons by the Chaldean Christian Mar Narsai (AD 413–503), selected and translated for the first time for a wider audience"—Provided by publisher.
Identifiers: LCCN 2024007404 (print) | LCCN 2024007405 (ebook) | ISBN 9780809106721 (hardcover) | ISBN 9780809188123 (ebook)
Subjects: LCSH: Sermons, Syriac. | Sermons, Syriac—Translations into English. | Sermons, Early Christian.
Classification: LCC BR65.N377 E5 2024 (print) | LCC BR65.N377 (ebook) | DDC 252—dc23/eng/20240708
LC record available at https://lccn.loc.gov/2024007404
LC ebook record available at https://lccn.loc.gov/2024007405

ISBN 978-0-8091-0672-1 (hardcover)
ISBN 978-0-8091-8812-3 (ebook)

Published by Paulist Press
997 Macarthur Boulevard
Mahwah, New Jersey 07430
www.paulistpress.com

Printed and bound in the
United States of America

CONTENTS

CONTENTS

FOREWORD

At this point, a religious author has finally "made it" when their work has been included in this series. The Classics of Western Spirituality long ago outgrew the plain meaning of its name. Many of the works in the series may be classics in their particular tradition, but it is their placement in this series that makes them classics for most people. "Western," of course, is a relative term and "Eastern" Christian texts (along even with indigenous American texts, among other traditions) have become staples in this series. And what do we do with "spirituality"? Like its kin, "mysticism," we know now that it is a term that often hides as much as it reveals. Spiritual ideas, mindful meditations, and theological arguments require bodies practiced in cultivated habits. The texts in this series are not just spiritual but reflective of deeply embodied traditions.

One of those traditions is the Syriac Christian tradition of which Narsai is a major author. I should use scare quotes when I refer to the "Syriac Christian tradition." Many scholars such as myself use this appellation, but this is a modern scholarly invention that prioritizes one language to identify the ethno-religious cultures of multiple churches in which over the centuries numerous languages have been spoken (including Syriac, various Iranian languages, Arabic, Malayalam, Dutch, Swedish, and English). Narsai was more specifically a member of the Church of the East, the dominant *ecclesia* of late antique Iraq and Iran. In the modern period this church fractured, resulting today in several churches, the most significant being the Assyrian Church of the East and the Chaldean Catholic Church. Together they form part of an Assyro-Chaldean tradition that continues to look to Narsai as an authoritative church father.

NARSAI

Narsai lived in the borderlands between the later Roman Empire and the Sasanians, the last of the great pre-Islamic Persian Empires. Originally from Persian territory in what is now northern Iraq, he spent several decades studying and then teaching in Roman Edessa, modern Urfa in southeastern Turkey, before his flight back to the Sasanian realm after the so-called "School of the Persians" at Edessa was shut down due to its alleged theological heterodoxy. He settled in Nisibis, a major commercial center on the Sasanian side of the frontier, and together with the bishop of the city founded the School of Nisibis, an institution that would become the preeminent Christian intellectual center of late antique Mesopotamia. Until his death in 503 CE, Narsai served as the first head exegete at this school, which maintained a regimented hierarchy of instructors and its curriculum of Christian learning at least into the seventh century. (Nisibis would be known as, among other titles, the "mother of learning" for centuries to come.) Narsai's extant works, composed in Edessa and Nisibis, consist of over eighty poetical sermons (or metrical homilies) written in Syriac, the literary dialect of Aramaic, which is used until today by several ancient churches.

Narsai's works are smart, dense, heavy-handed, self-conscious, meditative, didactic, and exhortative. He writes on theology, exegesis, and ethics, often engaging in the direct address typical of the Syriac homiletical poetry of his day and pointing to a divine Creator who is himself an educator. He is an intellectual poet who at times beats the Syriac dialect until it reveals the pulp of the Semitic verbal root system. He also develops his own distinct vocabulary, a patois of technical terms for the ritual and narrative of Christian life. Due to all this, Narsai's works must be read in the original to grasp fully everything taking place in them. The next best thing—for life is short and study is long—is something that this series has always offered its readers and what Fr. Andrew Younan has produced: a lucid and learned translation that brings the reader into what is fundamentally a foreign idiom.

Fr. Younan has a particular kind of access to Narsai's idiom: he is also a speaker of Neo-Aramaic by familial descent, and a Chaldean priest, who, like Narsai, does more than think and meditate on spiritual issues. As a member and administrator of the Body of Christ, he reads Narsai in closer ways than a philologist like myself can, and that is one of the many virtues of this volume.

Adam H. Becker
New York University
June 2023

ACKNOWLEDGEMENTS

I am grateful, first, to Narsai's own Church and living tradition, in all its branches: the Chaldean Catholic Church, the Assyrian Church of the East, the Assyrian Apostolic Church of the East, and the Malabar Catholic Church. Many of its members have been extremely supportive of this project, beginning from my own Bishop Emanuel Shaleta to my brother priests and beloved faithful in the Chaldean and Assyrian communities in America and around the world. I am especially grateful to Bishop Sarhad Yawsip Jammo for his mentorship, to Bishop Ibrahim Ibrahim for my ordination, and to Bishop Bawai Soro for his friendship.

I am also extremely thankful for the small but growing community of Narsai scholars throughout the world. In particular I would like to thank Robert Kitchen, Aaron Butts, and Kristian Heal for welcoming my contributions to the Complete Narsai Translation project and their enthusiasm for this book. Similarly, I owe an enormous debt of gratitude to them as well as to Adam Becker and James Walters for their warm encouragement and learned comments on the manuscript, and especially to Adam for his kind Foreword to this volume.

Finally, I would like to dedicate this book to my parents, who brought and often dragged me to church.

INTRODUCTION

Narsai (d 503 CE), called by ancient sources both "the Tongue of the East" and "the Harp of the Spirit,"[1] was a brilliant Middle Eastern Christian poet who composed *memre*[2] or metrical sermons on various theological, scriptural, and spiritual topics. Indeed, Narsai's spirituality is found everywhere in his writings—from his scriptural commentaries to his understanding of human nature to his Christology and trinitarian theology to his understanding of the Christian life's good works and prayer. His memre and other poetic writings have been sung for centuries in the liturgical services of the Church of the East—most notably the beautiful Memra 16, On Human Nature—and have influenced the spirituality of that tradition since the time of their composition. The selection of the twelve memre in this volume attempts to give an overview of his spiritual thought:

Memra 62: On the Order of Creation, and the *Qnome* of the Trinity

Memra 49: On the Forming of Adam and Eve, and the Breaking of the Command

Memra 3: On Abraham

Memra 14: On Jonah

Memra 5: On the Incarnation (with *Soghyth*)

Memra 7: On Epiphany John the Baptist

Memra 21: On the Temptation of Christ

Memra 37: On the Thief

Memra 16: On Human Nature

Memra 81: On Christology
Memra 44: On the New Creation
Memra 13: On Prayer

The first four memre selected are a representative example of Narsai's thought on creation, nature, and the revelation given to the patriarchs and prophets. The next four are about Christian salvation history, which for Narsai centers around the life of Christ. The final four focus more particularly on Narsai's understanding of theology and spirituality.

Narsai lived in a time, place, and ecclesiastical context that should be fascinating to an average reader in the West today. Living in fifth-century Persia, near the border between the Roman and Persian Empires, in a Christian church that was defined, among other things, as being outside the Roman Empire, Narsai offers us a perspective unique to his own tradition. Indeed, this is precisely one of the reasons why we should read him: because human history is larger than the twenty-first century, civilization more than the Roman Empire and its remnants, and Christianity more than Europe. Narsai can be a window into a wider world. His spirituality is one of challenging boundaries and understanding the limitations of human categories. This is true from beginning to end: his church is one that exceeds the lines of our normal conceptions. His understanding of God, in the end, is one of a Mystery beyond our comprehension.

On the other hand, Narsai knows what "the West," in the sense of the Roman Empire, is. He was influenced by Theodore, a Greek-speaking[3] bishop of Mopsuestia, a diocese well within the Roman Empire; he is quite sensitive to the concerns of the Council of Nicaea; the school system that he cofounded was interested in Greek philosophy and later became a center of translation from Greek to Aramaic,[4] without which it is unlikely that Aristotle's works, for example, would have easily reached Arab philosophers centuries later.

Moreover, Narsai reads more or less the same Bible, sees the same creation, and makes use of the same power of reason that the rest of us do. He is a human being aware of the beauty of the world and the fallenness of the human race, a thinker with a penetrating but practical analysis of the scriptures, and a poet with an exquisite expressiveness. Narsai's world, therefore, overlaps with our own just enough to be comprehensible, but goes beyond it far enough to be both challenging and fascinating.

HISTORICAL CONTEXT

If Narsai is "the Tongue of the East," it is worth defining what exactly "the East" is. This is not a mere matter of geography, although the border between the empires of Rome and Persia in the ancient world, more or less around the Euphrates River, is a rough dividing line. Understanding the particular characteristics of the Church of the East in relation to and in distinction from the various churches of the West is important in order to situate Narsai within his immediate ecclesiastical context. After this, I will give a basic timeline of Narsai's life, though it will be difficult to separate legend from fact.

The Church of the East

The Acts of the Apostles mentions as present at Pentecost "residents of Mesopotamia,"[5] among others. According to venerable tradition, it was St. Thomas the Apostle, as well as Mar[6] Addai (now popularly called St. Jude Thaddeus) and Mar Mari who first evangelized in the "land between the rivers," then the epicenter of the great Persian Empire, now more or less the country of Iraq. Thomas, some legends say, proceeded through Mesopotamia and continued to India,[7] while Addai established a Church in Edessa, whose King Abgar the Black was miraculously healed by an image of Christ, and Mari moved south toward historical Babylon, building a church and commissioning an icon of Our Lady.[8] Addai and Mari are credited also with composing the anaphora or eucharistic prayer most used in the Church of the East, whose branches are now the Chaldean Catholic Church, the Assyrian Church of the East, the Ancient Apostolic Assyrian Church of the East, and the Syro-Malabar Catholic Church. This eucharistic prayer has recently become a focus of intense study, as it is arguably the oldest in continuous use in

Christianity and was declared to be valid by the Catholic Church despite not containing the Narrative of Institution.[9]

The history of this church is sometimes neglected and its tradition dismissed as "Nestorian," but it has survived terrible persecutions, and despite them, or because of them, its missionary activity had reached across Asia, with dioceses and monasteries well established for centuries in mainland China.[10] Moreover, in part because of Narsai himself, this church had an extensive system of religious schools beginning in the late fifth century that had no comparison in the West at the time and was even emulated there later.[11] Little of this has survived, due to various eras of violence throughout the ages on the continent, and the once glorious and expansive Church of the East now makes up a tiny proportion of Christianity, both in its Middle Eastern roots and in the diaspora.[12] And yet the people of this church still struggle against all odds, whether against persecution in their homeland or absorption into other cultures in the West.

By "Church of the East," then, we do not mean the Byzantine or even the Antiochian Churches, since in their history these traditions lived within the boundaries of the Roman Empire. "East," again, means "East of the Roman Empire," not "the Eastern part of the Roman Empire." This is a more significant designation than one might initially assume. One representative example of the significance of the Church of the East's location in the Persian Empire is the aftereffects of the conversion of Constantine and the Edict of Milan, which decreed Roman tolerance of the Christian religion. For the church in the Roman Empire, the Edict was a source of celebration or, at the very least, relief from persecution. The opposite result occurred for the Church of the East, since after the Roman Empire eventually made Christianity the official state religion, the Magi (priests of the Zoroastrian religion) took the opportunity to accuse Christians in Persia of being spies for the Roman Empire and disloyal citizens. This influence led to the bloody persecution of Shah Shabur II, which lasted decades and helped earn the Church of the East the title "the Church of the Martyrs."[13]

Though the times of persecution were not constant, the uneasy peace between them meant, at the very least, a different conception of the relation between church and state as the Church of the East grew. Under Persian rule, and similarly later under Arab, Mongolian, or Turkish rule, Christianity was not always persecuted, but it was never the official state religion. This often meant second-class social status and relative poverty, and sometimes discomfort, extra taxes, dislocation, or harassment. In such a context, building enormous glorious church buildings, or developing music or the iconographic arts,[14] was a precarious investment at best, since even modest structures could be, and often were, eradicated within a few generations. On the other hand, a glance at its liturgies even today, despite some stumbling attempts at modernization, reveals not only a lovely simplicity, but something approaching an ancient, pristine purity.[15]

Because of the geographical and historical distance between the modern West and the Church of the East in Narsai's time, it can be tempting to oversimplify the reality of his context. Combining the various, and varied, Eastern churches, each with its own intricate history, religious practice, and theology and generalizing them all into "the Eastern Church" or "Eastern Christianity" is one common oversimplification. The Church of the East has as little in common with, for example, a church from the Byzantine tradition as it does with the Anglican Church. It has much more in common, theologically speaking, with the Latin Church than it does with the Syriac Orthodox or Coptic Orthodox churches. The "East" and "West" categorization of churches is, therefore, of limited usefulness.

Similarly oversimplifying is the categorization of churches according to language, where traditions are mapped out in larger branches generally marked Latin, Greek, and Syriac. Like many generalizations, this has its legitimate uses, especially in academia, but it also has the tendency to erase or leave out legitimate traditions such as those of Ethiopia, and force others together that have little in common besides language. Again, the Christology of the Assyrian Church of the East today is much closer to that of Rome than it is to some of the other traditions within the "Syriac Church" category. Insofar as it is a useful category, one might suggest it be renamed "Aramaic" rather than "Syriac," to match the "Greek" and "Latin" traditions, which are named after full-fledged languages rather than dialects.[16] Traditionally, the different Aramaic ecclesial traditions were named "Jacobite" and "Nestorian," but scholars have rightly avoided these terms in more recent decades, preferring in most cases to call them "West Syriac" and "East Syriac." This designation is also far from ideal, since there was no time when the epicenter of the Church of the East was ever in Syria, and if the designation "East Syriac" is not referring to geography, then an entire Apostolic Christian Tradition is being named after a font.[17] Categorization is a useful and important activity of the human mind, but it always leaves things out and can often be more confusing than it is helpful. Especially here, where the particularity of the Church of the East is the topic, we should challenge ourselves to look beyond the generalizations of textbooks, which are often built more on scholarly convenience than anything else, and embrace particularity as it is in concrete reality.[18]

What we have in the Church of the East, then, is a non-Imperial Christianity[19] with, at least up till the time of Narsai, a Persian or, in many instances, Roman-Persian borderland, cultural backdrop, and a Semitic, specifically Aramaic, language. This, of course, is also a generalization, and among other things leaves out the important facts of the Church of the East's interaction with other churches and the Church Universal, and its incorporation of Greek literature. The Synod of Isaac is one important example before the time of Narsai of the Church of the East seeing itself as a self-governing body distinct from the "Western Church" of Antioch, but at the same time part of a larger universal church. During that synod in 410, the bishops made governing decisions for their own territory and designated the bishop of the Persian capital Seleucia-Ctesiphon as "Catholicos" (later named "Catholicos-Patriarch"). But they also incorporated into their legislation elements from the Council of Nicaea, which the bishops of the Church of the East could, in any case, not attend because it happened during a terrible Persian persecution. They also introduced liturgical advancements that were taught to them by Bishop Marutha, the envoy sent from the "Church of the West" in Antioch.[20]

The self-esteem of the Church of the East was also strong enough for it to incorporate particularly Western/Greek elements without fearing the loss of its identity. During Narsai's time and even before, there is strong evidence that Greek literature such as Aristotle's logical works[21] were incorporated into the curriculum of the School of Nisibis, and perhaps even earlier at the School of the Persians in Edessa, and it is clear that the works of Greek church writers, most prominently but not exclusively Theodore of Mopsuestia, were translated into Aramaic in a systematic way.[22] It is argued, I think correctly, that the Church of the East embraced and incorporated such thinkers in great part because it saw its own native thought well expressed in them.[23] Shortly after Narsai's time, Mar Abba the Great, a graduate of the School of Nisibis that Narsai helped found and a traveler to the great Christian centers of learning in the Roman Empire, redacted and introduced two Greek Anaphoras into the Church of the East's liturgy, as well as the Trisagion, "Holy God, Holy Mighty One, Holy Immortal One: have mercy on us."[24]

It is the Church of the East's incorporation of the thought and writings of Theodore of Mopsuestia that was the first catalyst of its eventual designation as the "Nestorian" Church.[25] Theodore was "the Interpreter," whose literal, though not literalistic, style of studying the scriptures became the model (or, again, represented an already strong tendency) of biblical interpretation for the entire Church of the East. His enormous influence on Narsai in particular, as well as on the School of Nisibis, is the subject of several studies, and it is debated among scholars whether Theodore or Ephrem had the biggest influence on Narsai, with Aphrahat being also arguably influential.[26] The *Cause of the Foundation of the Schools*, a text describing the history and meaning of the school system that grew from Edessa and Nisibis, describes Narsai as "mixing" the exegesis of Theodore with the distinct "tradition" of the School of the Persians in Edessa, likely including Ephrem, in his own thought.[27] Christologically, the influence of Theodore became a problem, since Theodore was also an influence on Nestorius, the bishop of Constantinople who objected to the use of the term "Mother of God" in reference to Mary, against the theology of Cyril, bishop of Alexandria. While there was a great deal of politics and personality involved in this debate, there was a theological issue at the core: the identity of Jesus Christ. If Christ is the Word made flesh, then he is God, and therefore Mary is the mother of God; on the other hand, Nestorius objected, Mary is not the mother of God the Father or the Holy Spirit; nor is she the cause of the existence of God the Son. Rather, she is the mother of the Man[28] Jesus Christ. This distinction of two natures in Christ, divinity and humanity, was uncomfortable to the Alexandrians, while the unity of Christ's Person was difficult to explain for Nestorius and his followers. There is, of course, much more to say about this christological controversy, and it will be taken up later in this Introduction, as well as in chapters 5 and 6.

Whatever the circumstances, the Church of the East eventually aligned itself with Theodore as well as Nestorius despite the latter's condemnation and his deposition, along with that of Cyril of Alexandria, at the Council of Ephesus in 431.[29] The rushed nature of the Council, as well as the very clear corrective validation of dyophysite ("two-nature") Christology during the Council of Chalcedon just twenty years later, must have created an atmosphere of unclarity, to say the least, and by the time Theodore was condemned by name in 553, over a century after his death, the Church of the East was already functioning independently, little concerned with churches in its neighboring empire that already condemned it as "Nestorian" for affirming the humanity of Christ.[30] In different ways during later centuries, and with the usual ecclesiastical politics in the background, the Church of the East has verified its orthodox Christology and various modes of unity with other churches, ranging from a large segment of the Church of the East now called the Chaldean Catholic Church uniting with the Roman Catholic Church to the Common Christological Declaration of 1994 (see note 9).[31]

The Church of the East is, therefore, not a static monolith, but a living and breathing complex entity that grew and developed and continues to do so in all its branches. It is the church of the *Pshyṭta*, the early Aramaic translation of the Bible; it is the church of Tatian's *Diatesseron*, the first "harmony" of the four Gospels that wove them into a single narrative; it is the Church of Aphrahat, the Persian Sage who wrote about the scriptures and Christ's redemption, some of the earliest proto-monastic communities, and the power of the priesthood to forgive sins (and even a "seal of confession") deep in Persia in the early fourth century; it is the church that existed in Nisibis, the city where St. Ephrem lived and wrote for most of his life, and one of the churches that has gratefully received and incorporated his beautiful poetry; it is the church of the Patriarch Timothy, who participated in and recorded the first public debate between a Christian and a Muslim; it is the church that first evangelized Central and East Asia and established dioceses and monasteries in China and had a Mongolian Patriarch; it is the church of the Martyrs, which faced periodic slaughter throughout the centuries from Persians, Arabs, Mongolians, and Turks, and which continues to face persecution in its own homeland and indifference internationally.

Narsai's Life

A harp needs to be well made and well tuned to be well played. The sixth-century author Barḥadhbshabba, whose works the *Ecclesiastical History* and *The Cause of the Foundation of the Schools* are the main ancient biographical sources for Narsai's life, presents "the Harp of the Spirit" in what appear to be semilegendary narratives. Whatever their historicity, they give us a picture of a holy and brilliant man who faced many tribulations. The actual years of the events of Narsai's life, including his birth and death, are not known with certainty, since the sources are unclear and at times even contradictory. Still, there is enough related in the sources to give us a picture of the memory that Narsai left with his contemporaries and immediate successors, and it is likely that much of the tradition is based in historical fact.

By any account, Narsai lived quite a long life, possibly as long as a century, but the approximations of the year of his death around 503 are better than that of his birth, which is calculated by counting backward and attempting to associate events of his early life with various Persian persecutions.[32] If his age is reckoned near or over a century, then his birth year would have been around 400; if there is exaggeration or misinterpretation in the reckoning, it would have been after 410. In any case, Barḥadhbshabba relates that at age seven, the remarkably virtuous young Narsai was sent to the catechetical school of his birth town of 'Ayn Dulba (modern Deleb) in the region of Ma'alta, in the northwestern part of Iraq/Kurdistan.[33] Within nine months, according to legend, the quick-witted Narsai had memorized the Psalter (an assignment given to elementary readers). While this might seem implausible, the Psalms were and are a large part of the daily liturgical prayer of the Church of the East, and an attentive youth would have heard them recited in an organized way at least twice a day without having to open a book. Parents of small children who have favorite songs might not be so surprised at their quick and thorough memorization.

Some time during his first year of study, "the Magi," that is, the Zoroastrian religious leaders, are said to have visited the school with the intent to convert the young Christian students. "The sword" is mentioned in this passage in the *Ecclesiastical History*, vaguely implying a wider context of physical persecution. Narsai's teacher, in response, took his class and fled to the mountains to wait for a safe time to return. We have no indication of how long this "gloom of the persecutors" lasted, whether hours or weeks or months, but our biographer notes that the young Narsai quoted psalms to strengthen his classmates against their fear. After their return, Narsai remained at this school for nine more years, that is, until his sixteenth year. Around this time, Narsai's parents died, and he went to live with his uncle Emmanuel, former student at the School of the Persians in Edessa and monastery abbot, who at the time was bishop of Amida (modern Diyarbakir). Emmanuel, noticing Narsai's intelligence, asked him to help with reading instruction at his local catechetical school. This Narsai did, but for less than a year, since by then he had heard of the renowned School of the Persians in Edessa and went there to continue his studies.[34]

From this point onward, the sources tell the story of a Narsai whose internal drive for learning and study was constantly embattled by calls for ecclesiastical service, persecution, or personal conflict. Whether as a student in Edessa or a schoolmaster in Nisibis, Narsai's preference was always the contemplative study for which he showed an aptitude even from a young age, but life always had other plans for him. Barḥadhbshabba paints the picture of a providential God "fine-tuning" Narsai by means of the tribulations he allowed in his life, for the sake of the students Narsai eventually taught and the *memre*, or metrical sermons, he eventually wrote.[35] This is shown through two thematic sections of his biographical chapter on Narsai's life: one from his first move to Edessa as a student until his appointment as the new head of the School of the Persians there, and the second from his expulsion from Nisibis by bishop Cyrus until his death. Each has its own implicit tripartite structure.

Having his uncle Emmanuel as the bishop of Nisibis had its drawbacks. Narsai being the age of a college freshman, he longed to be more than a reading instructor at a local catechetical school and so left for Edessa, where he studied for a decade. The "School of the Persians" in that city was possibly named so to distinguish it from schools of other groups there,[36] and one legend claims that it was founded by St. Ephrem.[37] At this school, Narsai would have continued his studies according to the curriculum there, reading scripture, Ephrem, and other Aramaic authors, and some of the works of Theodore and other writers, which by this time were already being translated from Greek.[38] It is also quite likely that a philosophical curriculum focusing on Aristotle's logical works and some Neoplatonic commentators was already there by the time of Narsai's studies, and that the translation movement commenced around this time.[39] What is certain, however, is that by the time of the composition of the *Cause of the Foundation of the Schools* later in Nisibis, Aristotelian philosophy—at least the formal study of Aristotelian logic—was commonplace among Narsai and his students.[40]

For a decade, Narsai enjoyed his studies in Edessa, but his uncle could not bear losing a useful worker in his diocese and sent a harsh decree asking him to return to Amida to teach again. He returned to three hundred monastic students, whom he taught for "a brief period" before he returned to Edessa again "due to the love of learning he possessed."[41] Here Barḥadhbshabba may be composing or skewing the facts, because he claims that the same events happened again in exactly the same way: Narsai spent *another* ten years in Edessa studying, and *again* was recalled by his uncle to Amida to teach. Whether or not this second ten-year stint as a student in Edessa happened will affect the calculation of his birth year. If it did happen, he was born around 400 and died at over a century old; if it did not, he was born after 410 and died in his nineties or younger.

It is possible that Barḥadhbshabba doubles Narsai's times as a student in Edessa as a poetic flourish, because the third part of this tripartite structure says that, after a year teaching again in Amida, Narsai returned yet again to Edessa, his uncle Emmanuel having died a few months before, after responsibly entrusting the work of teaching in Amida to one Gabriel. Narsai is now not only a student with a curious intellect but beginning also to take certain other responsibilities more seriously. In fact, some time after Narsai's purported third journey to Edessa, Rabbula, the head of the school, died, and Narsai was forced by popular demand to take on the headship of the School of the Persians. The passage in Barḥadhbshabba mentions that those calling for his instatement as head noted that by this time Narsai was a priest, an elegant speaker, and a humble and holy man. However, Narsai only accepted the nomination under the condition that others would be assigned to take over the lower instruction so that he could focus on interpreting the scriptures. The tension between the nature of the contemplative scholar and the demands of a hungry flock was thus somewhat resolved, and Narsai is said to have held this post for twenty years.[42]

After the depiction of three trips to the School of the Persians in Edessa, the second triad of events in Narsai's life painted by Barḥadhbshabba is of tribulations. In this second set of events, it is Narsai's writing that affects the people around him and particularly his persecutors. It is related, first, that Cyrus, the bishop of Edessa, spurred on by his miaphysite clergy and aided by the Roman Emperor Zeno, accused Narsai of heresy for being a student of Theodore and Nestorius. His clergy attempted to convert Narsai from his opinions to no avail. Barḥadhbshabba posits that one of the motivations for this accusation was a race-based (or, more precisely, empire-based) envy: "For they thought, 'How can a Persian man subdue Romans, this man, who is also foreign to the order of reason?'"[43] In the same vein, they added to heresy the accusation of espionage against the Roman Empire on the part of Persia, which would have led to his death by public burning. Rather than give in to their threats of violence and enticements, Narsai quoted several passages from St. Paul and vowed to imitate the saint's integrity. After a public accusation against him was made, Narsai fled Edessa at night, enlisting some Persians to help carry his books, which were "his whole treasure," to Nisibis, where his friend and fellow former student in Edessa, Barṣawma, was bishop. After his departure, Narsai's enemies slandered him even more to Cyrus, who was already regretting his actions, but Narsai wrote a letter to them which silenced their accusations and shamed them.[44]

Intending only to stop in Nisibis on his way deeper into Persia, Narsai was met by three priests who sent a message to Bishop Barṣawma, who in turn sent messengers asking him to enter the city. Narsai refused for a time, but after meeting with the archdeacon and ten priests, he was forced by social protocol to accept the bishop's invitation. The bishop, after all this, did Narsai the honor of coming out to meet him after he had entered the city, and proceeded with him into the church. Barṣawma's argument that Narsai should stay in Nisibis and teach referred to the city's proximity to both the Roman and Persian empires, positing that God in his providence had brought him to that place, at that time. Narsai agreed, and the bishop appointed him as Head Exegete of the School of Nisibis, supplanting the previous head, Simeon, who did not stand in Narsai's way. Almost immediately, Narsai's fame brought many new students to the school, and from a local catechetical school it became for the first time the landmark it was known as for centuries.[45] Its curriculum resembled that of Edessa described above, and is described in some detail in the *Cause for the Foundation of the Schools*, in Vööbus's famous work *History of the School of Nisibis*, and more recently in Adam Becker's *Fear of God and the Beginning of Wisdom*.[46] The canons governing student life there, attributed to Narsai, were edited by Vööbus.[47] Some time after Narsai's expulsion from Edessa, Cyrus closed the School of the Persians in Edessa, and the majority of its students joined Narsai in Nisibis.[48]

Things were not always peaceful, however, and Narsai's fame enflamed the jealousy of Barṣawma's wife, Mamai, who badgered the bishop for allowing someone else to become more prominent in his own diocese. This caused tension between Barṣawma and Narsai, and Narsai left his residence in Nisibis, which happened to be next door to Barṣawma's, and lived for six years in the monastery of Kephar Mari in Beth Zabdai. While there, he is said to have written two memre, on the misery of life and on the wickedness of women.[49] The second one he sent to Barṣawma, who read it publicly, and for the second time, Narsai's writings produced an effect in his adversaries, and Barṣawma sent to have Narsai brought back to Nisibis.

Having learned his lesson, Narsai chose to reside farther away from the home of Barṣawma and Mamai.[50]

At this point in the *Ecclesiastical History*, Barḥadhbshabba describes Narsai's austere lifestyle: one meal per day in the evening, a simple mat for a bed, constant vigils spent in meditation on the liturgy and scriptures, and an overall "angelic" way of life. In contrast to Narsai's simplicity, Barḥadhbshabba proceeds to describe the sugary eloquence of Narsai's theological rival, Jacob of Serug, who at this time had begun to write his famous metrical poetic sermons, which were drawing people away from the true faith by their false beauty.[51] Imitating King David, Narsai then began to write his own memre in response to Jacob's, with the intention that they should be sung. Barḥadhbshabba mentions twelve volumes of Narsai's memre, numbering over 360—one for each day of the year. If this is how much Narsai actually wrote, it is tragic that today we only have around a fourth that have survived, just over eighty.

Narsai's troubles were far from over. After shaming the priests of Cyrus in Edessa and touching the heart of Bishop Barṣawma of Nisibis, the third and final example of the converting power of Narsai's words has to do with the Sasanian King Peroz I.[52] After a military defeat caused by the king's pride, Narsai wrote a now lost memra that was harsh in tone, probably a chastisement against pride. Some of Narsai's rebellious students took this to the king's troops and reversed the accusation made against him by the priests of Cyrus: instead of being a Persian spy against Rome, now he was accused of being a Roman spy against Persia. Bystanders of this accusation went to Narsai and reported it, and he wrote another memra praising the Persian Empire, which was reportedly translated into Persian and read before the king. This changed the king's mind regarding Narsai, and again his accusers were ashamed and fled.[53]

Barḥadbshabba's hagiographic account of Narsai's life concludes by alluding to miraculous actions done by Narsai, such as predicting the death of a Persian emissary and healing a boy who had been possessed by a demon. The overall themes of his chapter on Narsai are not, however, typical saint stories, but a commentary on Narsai's deeply contemplative nature that drew him toward the scriptures, while God's providence drew him toward teaching, writing, and service to others. Narsai's childhood teacher, having no other recourse, fled to the mountains to protect his young students. Narsai, in contrast, faced the adversaries threatening him and his students and, through the power of his words, converted their hardness of heart.

Rough Timeline of Narsai's Life

400: Narsai is born in ʿAyn Dulba

407–416: Narsai studies at the village's school

416: Narsai's parents die, and Emmanuel takes him to Amida

416–426: Narsai's first stint in Edessa

426: Emmanuel takes him back to Amida

426–436: Narsai's second stint in Edessa

[431: Council of Ephesus]

436–437: Emmanuel takes him back to Amida a third time

437–457: Narsai's third stint in Edessa, now as Head of the School of the Persians

[449: "Robber Council" of Ephesus]

[451: Council of Chalcedon]

457: Narsai is expelled from Edessa by Cyrus and goes to Nisibis

457–463: Narsai leaves Nisibis for Kephar Mari and leads monastery school there

463–503: Narsai returns to Nisibis and leads the school for forty years

[484: Council of Beth Lapat]

[489: School of the Persians in Edessa closes]

496: Second set of Canons of the School of Nisibis composed by Narsai

503: Narsai dies

NARSAI'S THEOLOGY

Narsai's spirituality is revealed in every facet of his thought. His spirituality is utterly and deeply biblical, and in his readings of scriptural verses one senses a receptive and prayerful heart, a student learning at the feet of the Divine Teacher. His spirituality is grounded and humble—that is, human—and his reflections on human nature are the fruit of his prayerful consideration of both creation and revelation. His spirituality is rooted in the act of salvation accomplished by Christ and is therefore imbued with soteriology and Christology, two parts of theology that are inseparable to Narsai. His spirituality, therefore, is also trinitarian, especially in his stunned reverence before the unspeakable Mystery of the Father, Son, and Holy Spirit. His spirituality is revealed in his understanding of the life of good works and prayer expected of Christians and expressed in every syllable of his poetry. In understanding each of these aspects of Narsai's thought, we will therefore understand something of his spirituality.

Scripture and Divine Pedagogy

Narsai's title as head of the School of the Persians in Edessa, and then of the School of Nisibis, was *mpashqana*, "the exegete."[54] Scripture, therefore, had a central place in the School of Nisibis and in Narsai's theology. It is generally, almost vacuously, true that Narsai followed the "Antiochian" style of exegesis over the "Alexandrian," meaning that he, following Theodore and others, favored a close literal reading of the scriptures over an allegorical one.[55] Narsai was not, of course, opposed to seeing especially christological symbolism and typology in biblical narratives and characters, as the memre on Abraham and Jonah included in this volume both attest.[56]

More specific to Narsai's exegetical style is a sensitive, slow, and meditative reflection on a biblical passage verse by verse, seen in many of the memre included in this volume, such as that on the Thief and on Christ's Temptation. In many places, Narsai might be seen as simply repeating the biblical narrative, but it is particularly in those places that Narsai can often make his most penetrating and subtle commentaries. In the memra on Jonah, for example, Narsai takes the liberty of expanding God's command "Arise, go to Nineveh, that great city, and cry out against it" (Jonah 1:2):

43. Get up, go preach the sound of salvation among the drowning,
44. and wake those sleeping in sin with your own words.
45. Come, set out on the path of preaching among strangers,
46. and teach the new path of the adoration of my Majesty.
47. Come, go reconcile the wrathful who left my family,
48. and shepherd them to righteousness through grace.
49. Come, go and visit the sick who are tired out with the maladies of iniquity,
50. and through your words, chastise the fever of their consciences.[57]

By mixing metaphors, which he often does, Narsai is able to express poetically the manifold meaning of preaching, which is not a simple relaying of information, but rather a helping hand for the drowning, a wake-up call to the sleeping, a welcoming to the estranged, a reconciliation of family, a healing of the sick.

This is an important point in understanding the almost universal backdrop of Divine Pedagogy in the background of Narsai's memre. God is a Teacher and we and the angels are his students, which makes the created world a school. The memra on the Order of Creation, for example, begins with this idea:

5. And so, the Creator wished to make the working of his Power known to rational creatures.
6. In Moses he chose a disciple and inspired a spiritual book through him.
7. On Mount Sinai he showed him a marvelous vision,
8. and made a voice heard to him while drawing him to learn.[58]

Similarly, the memra on the Forming of Adam and Eve:

1. By means of his image, a faraway king is honored as if nearby.
2. The Creator wanted to instruct rational beings through his image, Adam.

3. In the world, the city of the kingdom, the Creator placed his image,
4. and through a visible image, he made known his hidden Power.[59]

In these and many other places, Narsai depicts not only the scriptures but the creation itself (or specific creatures, particularly the human being) as books through which God teaches his students. But again, God's school, like the School of Nisibis, is not simply a place to memorize information, but rather a place of formation, belonging, salvation, healing, and renewal.[60] This may be why Narsai preferred the backdrop of the "school" metaphor more than other metaphors, such as that of the Divine Economy/Family, or the Church Militant, or the Divine Artist, or Doctor. Narsai makes use of these and many other metaphors, but in some way all of them are included in his understanding of Divine Pedagogy: God being our Teacher also makes him our (re-)Fashioner, our King, and our Healer.

God's pedagogical style is, like that of any good teacher, based on the needs of his students. For one thing, his human students have a great capacity to learn, but also great limitations. This is seen, for example, in the Memra On the Order of Creation:

9. The Creator desired to show himself humanly to Moses,
10. and because of this Moses yearned to see his Nature.
11. "If, then, you have chosen me for yourself as a disciple, and if you love me,
12. show me the glory of your Nature, and let me contemplate your hidden Radiance."
13. "You have erred greatly, O Moses": the Lord said to him,
14. "no mortal can see me, for my Nature is above those who see."
15. "I called you unto myself in order to be taught, that you may learn that I am the Creator;
16. not that you may learn my Hiddenness, for that is incomprehensible to creatures."[61]

Indeed, the limitation of the human mind's capacity to understand God is an important and humbling theme throughout Narsai, and his "negative" or "apophatic" theology again stresses the expansive meaning of "teaching" beyond simply intellectual instruction.[62]

Again, because God's pedagogy is about the formation of character as much as it is about intellectual knowledge, God makes use of esotericism in his instruction. God not only reveals but also hides the truth from those who are not yet worthy or ready to receive it. The beginning of the memra on Jonah is the most explicit place this is seen:

1. The Creator placed great wealth within the Scriptures,
2. and hid it with a mystery until the determined time was fulfilled.
3. He covered the letters with parables like a garment,
4. lest the eyes of flesh look down on the treasure of the Spirit.
5. He hid his wealth from the ignorant youth
6. until it matured, and then he opened the door of mercies.
7. He cast fear upon those who know his Testaments,
8. that the power of his wisdom may increase before their eyes.
9. He did not give the immature access to his hidden things,
10. lest his valuables be disdained by weakness of soul.[63]

Thus not only is Narsai sober and humble about the human mind's limited inherent capacity to know the truth of God, but he is aware that the truth is misunderstood by those with bad intent and needs to be parceled out carefully to those who are able to receive it well. This is a reflection of Christ's own preaching, when he speaks in parables for the same reason.[64]

All of salvation history, then, becomes a classroom where God teaches the human race. Indeed, there is a first lesson that only the angels attend, when God speaks the physical world into being and reveals to them, since nobody else is there to hear, that he is the Creator:

107. In that ordering "in the beginning," he did not speak to be heard,
108. for there was nothing made who could hear and receive instruction.
109. But when he began to make it so that natures came to be, one by one,
110. through a whisper he desired to reveal his ordering to the angels.
111. The reason for the whisper, then, is this: that he may teach the angels

112. that the Lord of all, who upholds their assemblies, is the one who orders.[65]

Later, in creating the human being, God even hints at his Trinitarian Nature since there he speaks in the plural "let us."[66]

After the angels, Adam and Eve make up the first human class in God's school, and God uses even their sin as a teaching aid. Indeed, in Narsai's vision, God created Adam and Eve mortal from the beginning and, knowing beforehand that they would sin, takes the opportunity to teach them and their descendants about their mortality, the harmfulness of sin, and God's own mercifulness.[67] Through Enoch and Elijah, God shows the gifts he has prepared to those who are faithful to him, as well as the eventual destiny of the human race through Christ, which is the state of bodily immortality and glory.[68] Through Noah and the episode of the flood, God teaches us again that he is the source of life and that separating ourselves from him through sin equates to our own death.[69] After the flood, when humanity, mistrusting God's promise and attempting to subvert his ability to punish and teach, built a tower that would allow them to survive another storm, God reminded us of our vocation to fill the earth with life rather than isolate ourselves from nature through technology.[70]

Through Abraham, God chooses one man to establish a nation that belongs to him, and what that means is that "the people" (*'amma*, Narsai's term for the Jews) is meant to imitate God's teaching role among "the peoples" (*'amme*, Narsai's term for the Gentiles): "Through one people, he wished to instruct all the peoples" (Memra 3: 21). Abraham and Sarah themselves become symbols of God's blessings, since their fruitful sterility reveals that God can bring life even from the nations who are dead in sin (Memra 3: 65–66). This is ultimately accomplished through Christ, Son of the Virgin, whose birth and death are prefigured through Isaac (Memra 3: 244–249). Similarly, Joseph the son of Jacob prefigures Christ, who was rejected by his brethren, as the tabernacle built by Moses prefigures both the church and heaven, and the brazen serpent raised up by him prefigures the crucifixion.[71] Jonah, mentioned earlier, also becomes an unwilling symbol of both salvation and the Savior.[72]

Human Nature

Narsai begins his memra on the Forming of Adam and Eve by introducing one of his (and Theodore's) most important themes, the image of God:

1. By means of his image, a faraway king is honored as if nearby.
2. The Creator wanted to instruct rational beings through his image, Adam.
3. In the world, the city of the kingdom, the Creator placed his image,
4. and through a visible image, he made known his hidden Power.
5. The Creator bound up creation in his image when he fashioned it,
6. so that love toward Adam and love of him may resemble one another.
7. He made it akin to the angels, through a spiritual soul,
8. and united mute natures to it by molding its parts.
9. The Lord God fashioned Adam, dust from the earth,
10. and breathed the spirit of the living into him, making him living and rational.[73]

This passage contains several aspects of Narsai's teaching on human nature and deserves to be looked at closely.

Narsai interprets Genesis 1:26, which describes God making the human being, both male and female,[74] in his image and likeness, by comparing God to a king and the human being to a king's statue. Because the statue resembles the king, it represents him and can receive the honor due to him even if he is far away. But God is everywhere, and moreover, he is not visible in any way, which means it is impossible for a visible being to resemble him literally speaking.[75] The human being does not and cannot, therefore, resemble God in his own infinite nature. Something else must be happening. Narsai is never far from the theme of Divine Pedagogy, and the second verse of the passage interprets the "king" metaphor in terms of the "teacher" metaphor: God wishes to teach his creatures about himself through the human being. But again, he is invisible, and we, the creatures capable of learning about him, rely on our senses for learning,[76] so God makes use of a visible being to reveal his invisible nature. He uses our nature to teach us about himself: "through a visible image, he made known his hidden Power." But if we teach through our own nature, then we are images of God the Teacher. The human being, then, is God's image not only in soul, but in both body and soul.[77]

How does this work? The fifth and sixth verses give us two other important parts of this picture: that the human being is the "bond" that unites all creation, and that our operation as God's image in the world comes about through love. These are all intimately related notions: God's pedagogy is not merely intellectual instruction but formation of character, and so his teaching means teaching to love, and to love him. But he is invisible, and so we learn to love him by loving his image, which we see in human beings.[78] In one sense, this love is the bond through which creation is tied together, but in another sense, the human being is itself the bond, since in our nature all creatures are tied together: material natures in our body and spiritual natures in our soul.[79] A related analogy used frequently by Narsai is that of the human being as the temple of God, where creatures come to worship their Creator and be united to him.[80] Finally, even the Trinity is hinted at in the creation of the human being, since there, unlike when creating other creatures, God speaks in the plural.[81] This, in fact, is exactly what enflames the jealousy of Satan, who proceeds to mar God's image by leading them into sin and therefore into death.[82]

Through sin, however, the bond of love is broken, and through death (the consequence of sin, according to Genesis), the body and soul of the human being unbind. Sin and death, therefore, mar the image of God in the human being:[83] how can a selfish sinner reveal God's love, and how can a soul without a body, or a carcass without a soul, be a visible representation of God or the bond tying the universe together? Similarly, how can a human being who has rejected love be the visible dwelling place of God, who is love? How can a person who turns inward in selfishness be an image of the Trinity? This ruin results not in God being harmed, which is impossible, but in the suffering of the human being. This is not only the case for Adam; indeed, Adam reveals, to Narsai, a pattern that is there in the life of all human beings.[84] In our broken state, though our "discernment" (*paroshutha*) is awakened, our "inclination" (*yaṣra*) tends toward evil rather than toward good.[85]

Because sin and death undo the bond tying creation together in the human being, angels and physical creatures both turn away from us. Narsai compares the angels to the older brother in the Parable of the Prodigal Son, who remained with his father and was embittered at his brother's rebellion.[86] Physical nature also rebels, as God says in Genesis 3:17–19, and this fills human life with deep discomfort, both external and internal:

125. If the sun grows hot, his mind grows hot regarding his crops,
126. and if the rain stops, his thoughts dry up along with his plants.
127. If heat gains the upper hand, thirst has killed him;
128. and if cold increases, he is consumed by frost.
129. If he is impoverished, he conceives depression and begets complaining;
130. and if he is made rich, he puts on pride and arrogant spirit.
131. If he is justified, he derides and mocks sinners;
132. and if he sins, he despairs and decides there is no hope.
133. If he is made wise, he forgets the clay of his wretched nature;
134. and if he glorifies himself, he becomes a beast without understanding.[87]

And yet, Narsai is quite clear that the human being was created mortal by nature,[88] that God foreknew all that would happen and intended to use Adam and Eve's sin for pedagogical purposes.[89] Our sufferings, therefore, are not an unnatural punishment, as harsh as they are, but rather the discipline offered from a loving Father to his children.[90]

Soteriology

God's teaching after the marring of God's image due to sin now means restoring human nature and remaking us into what we were always meant to be. Doing this is impossible through merely human effort, however, because of the severity of our defeat by sin and death and the fallout of our weakness.[91] Narsai utilizes the legal-economic language of "debt" and "bond" familiar from the Gospels to help explain our situation. Satan tricked us into committing a crime against

God, the giver of life, and made us guilty and indebted (which come from the same root in Aramaic). The wage of sin is death, and so the legal bond written by Adam requires that payment.[92]

But again, God foreknew what would happen and planned it in his pedagogical providence. His image therefore never entirely left the human race but instead was passed down from generation to generation, and Narsai, in his close reading of scripture, notes which of the just were named "image" and recounts how this was passed down from Adam to Seth to Enoch to Lamech to Noah to Shem to Abraham, whose progeny are chosen to be a blessing for all nations.[93] Consistently, what it means to be God's image for Narsai is to resemble God in love, and the righteous who passed down this image did so by living in love by God's grace.[94] From Abraham, God's image passed through David to Mary:

185. From Abraham the promise went forth and dwelt in David,
186. and from the house of David, it arrived and came to Mary.
187. In Mary, the course of the path of the promise of life concluded,
188. and in her body, it entered, rested, and dwelt as in a harbor.
189. The daughter of man became a harbor of peace for human nature,
190. and the harsh waves of mortality did not crush her.
191. She carried our entire race in her womb like a ship,
192. and she went out and placed it on the shore of the kingdom above.[95]

Through Mary, the New Eve who brings life rather than death[96] and the New Earth from which the New Adam was fashioned,[97] God fulfills the plan he had from the beginning of time, to renew and perfect his Image through Christ, the Son of David.

Narsai's soteriology, therefore, is nothing more or less than a recounting of the life of Christ, who renewed the Image of God through all he did, thereby rebinding creation to its Creator in himself, the true Temple where Creator and creation are perfectly united.[98] Narsai's interpretive key to the life of Christ and its salvific power is Colossians 1:13–20:

> He has delivered us from the dominion of darkness and transferred us to the kingdom of his beloved Son, in whom we have redemption, the forgiveness of sins. He is the image of the invisible God, the first-born of all creation; for in him all things were created, in heaven and on earth, visible and invisible, whether thrones or dominions or principalities or authorities—all things were created through him and for him. He is before all things, and in him all things hold together. He is the head of the body, the church; he is the beginning, the first-born from the dead, that in everything he might be pre-eminent. For in him all the fullness of God was pleased to dwell, and through him to reconcile to himself all things, whether on earth or in heaven, making peace by the blood of his cross.

This passage is the source text for many aspects of Narsai's theology: image, bond, life and death, and temple. The subject of all of them is not Adam, however, but Christ, who for Narsai fulfills preeminently all that the first Adam failed to be, and much more. Christ is the true Image of God, who reveals Divinity itself through his Body; Christ is the ultimate Bond of the universe; he is the perfect Temple where God dwells and is worshipped. This is all revealed through the life of Christ. I will focus on three events that showcase this for Narsai: Christ's temptation, his crucifixion, and his ascension.

As Satan was enraged with envy at Adam's creation in God's image and likeness, he is confounded at Christ's baptism when he is named the Son of God by the Voice from the heavens.[99] In order to verify whether this is true, Satan tempts Christ as he did Adam. Memra 21, included in this volume, is an exposition of Christ's temptation and gives us Narsai's picture of how Christ defeated Adam's first foe, which was sin. Here, as in other places, Narsai describes Christ as an "Athlete" who vindicates the members of his human race through his victory.[100] He does this by resisting Satan's temptation for food by his obedience, by resisting the temptation for material wealth by recognizing the worthlessness of worldly goods, and by resisting the temptation to jump off the temple by affirming that he is himself the true Temple.[101] Sin, therefore, was defeated, Love was victorious, and through Christ, the human race became perfected as God's image.

Adam's second opponent to be defeated was death, and Christ's sacrifice and resurrection accomplished this defeat and revealed Christ's status as the Temple of God.[102] Again mixing metaphors, Narsai sees death as the debt owed due to sin. But Christ, who did not sin, accepted an unjust death and thereby reversed the lawsuit made against Adam. Satan therefore lost his claim on the human race, and Christ rose from the dead.[103] In doing so, he became the perfect Bond of the universe, uniting God and creation in himself. He is therefore the true Temple where God dwells, and the Visible Image that reveals God to all creatures in their worship:

507. There, all tongues will confess One Person,
508. and will repeat one hallowing there to the Word and the Body.
509. They will together adore the Hidden and Unveiled One in one equality,
510. and while it may seem they are two, they are preached as One.
511. Through their worship they will there see a great marvel,
512. that with the Maker, the One Made will receive the worship of all.

The themes of image, bond, and temple are finally united and fulfilled at the ascension, in the adoration of Christ, whose humanity reveals divinity:

533. A Man filled the place of Existence for man and watchers,
534. and in seeing his Body, their sight rests and their seeking is silenced.
535. This is the reason for the greatness of his station and authority:
536. that he may preach the Power of Hiddenness through his Unveiling.

Indeed, the Man Christ receives worship as God:

561. Look at the greatness of the heavenly who praise this,
562. and do not cease or be silent in glorifying how glorious it is.
563. Well was it fashioned that man may become Divine,
564. and no one is able to repay thanks to its Fashioner.[104]

This brings us to the topic of Narsai's Christology.

Christology

While Narsai is clear that human language will always fall short in describing Divine things, his theology is full of analogies that attempt to grasp at some aspect or another of the mysteries of God.[105] The central analogy employed by Narsai in his Christology is that of the Word of God dwelling in Christ the Man as a Temple. This is, again, taken from Colossians 1:19: "For in him all the fullness of God was pleased to dwell," as well as Christ's own words in John 2:21: "But he spoke of the temple of his body." It is worth noting, first, that Narsai often uses "body" (*paghra*) and even "flesh" (*bisra*) to refer to the fullness of humanity, rather than a body apart from a soul, which, indeed, would not be a living body at all but a corpse.[106] The Temple of the Word referred to in John's Gospel and in Colossians, then, is the Man Jesus Christ, body and soul.

Narsai makes use of this analogy in order to show a profound relation between the two natures in Christ:

259. For our comfort, he fashioned a Temple of Flesh and dwelt in it,
260. that we may adore the outer Holy Place and him who is hidden in the Holy of Holies.
261. We see the outer Holy Place of his Body through the eyes of flesh,
262. and the Holy of Holies of his Hiddenness through the spiritual powers of the soul.[107]

The Man Christ, then, corresponds to the Holy Place of the Temple, and the Word to the Holy of Holies. In other words, the only way to know or reach Divinity is through Christ, the way in which the inner Sanctuary of the Temple was only accessible through the outer one.[108] Christ's humanity is the way to his Divinity; the former reveals the latter, and the latter is only revealed, and worshipped, through the former.[109] Narsai's use of the Temple analogy is not a description of a static fact but a "functional"[110] or perhaps "dynamic" Christology.

Another analogy Narsai uses, more closely related to his larger theme of Divine Pedagogy, is that of the Word that is eternally with the Father but is written and expressed in the Ink that is the humanity of Christ:

43. A word that is from a soul is not visible openly,
44. and when it is written in ink, it is seen through letters.
45. And though indeed one confines it in letters, and limits it in garments of ink,
46. it is in letters in name, but entirely dwells in the soul.
47. The pupils see ink, when they look at the letters,
48. but the word does not give its nature over to be limited by pupils.
49. The Son was hidden with his Begetter, from the lofty and lowly,
50. and he was shown to us by his Will, in the ink of the Body of Adam.
51. While he truly was clothed with the garment of our nature in his Divinity,
52. his Will dwelt in our nature, and his Nature remained hidden.
53. The Body he wore was not a limit to his Nature, which is unlimited,
54. and the eye of flesh did not see his Hidden Divinity.[111]

Narsai expresses several ideas in this analogy. First, it is important that the Word of God did not cease to be with the Father, and therefore everywhere, after the Incarnation. The Word did not stop existing in other places when he became Flesh and was located in the womb of the Virgin—that would be blasphemy of the highest order. Rather (again taking the clue from John's Gospel), the way a word can be thought of in a human mind and then spoken or written down, but still remain in the mind, the Word of God remained with God, but was written on the earth "in the ink of the Body of Adam." But again, this Ink of Christ's humanity is the perfect expression and revelation of the eternal Word.[112]

Much of Narsai's christological writing comes in the form of polemics against those who deny or ignore the humanity of Christ. Memra 81, included in this volume and quoted above, is a running commentary on the Prologue of John's Gospel, and as such touches on verses that are at the heart of the controversy. Central among these is John 1:14: "And the Word became flesh and dwelt among us." What does "become" mean and how should it be understood? It is impossible, of course, for "become" to mean here "change into a different kind of being," for that would mean that the Word is no longer God, or never was, and would vindicate the Arian heresy.[113] The only possible orthodox way to interpret "become," for Narsai, is in terms of the immediately following words, "and dwelt among us." The terminology of dwelling, again related to the Temple imagery explicitly announced by Christ later in John's Gospel, is the interpretive key to understand the meaning of "become." The Word became flesh by dwelling in the Temple that is the Man Jesus Christ. In this way, the true distinction between Christ's Divinity and humanity is retained, as well as their dynamic relation that is so important for Narsai's understanding of soteriology and Divine Pedagogy. Denying this distinction is to destroy salvation itself, for if Christ is not man then he is not the Son of David, and humanity was not saved;[114] nor is humanity glorified and worshipped in heaven now.[115] Those who refuse to accept this distinction either reduce the Divinity of the Word or take away the glory of man.[116] Ink expresses the Word, but it must remain ink in order to be visible.

Narsai is therefore motivated to speak with great care, since even though our language is limited in speaking of Godly things, we can still easily fall into heresy and do damage to the faith. For this reason, Narsai does not make use of the "communication of idioms," wherein we posit things done or suffered by Christ directly and indiscriminately to God. While it is true, for Narsai, that Christ was born of Mary, learned, hungered, suffered, and died, he avoids phrases such as "mother of God," and "God died," seeing the latter as especially blasphemous, though he does manage to call Mary "mother of the Image in whom there is shown forth the image of the hidden [Divine Nature]" as well as "mother for the Lord of the universe."[117]

Narsai is absolutely clear that the Word was and is united perfectly to Christ from the first moment of his conception and could never be separated from him even for a moment, indeed, even from Christ's Body in the tomb.[118] When he is unconcerned with polemics against Miaphysites, he has no problem calling the Man Christ the Creator, Divine, the Lord and glorious Spring of Life, and God.[119] Indeed, it is the same grammatical subject who is spoken of in verses like this:

He is entirely a man because of the wholeness of (his)
body and soul,
but holier and more glorious than corporeal beings
because of his fashioning.
His nature is like that of his mother from whom he exists,
but he is more exalted than she because it is not from
seed (that he has acquired) his (bodily) structure.
He is entirely a man because of the wholeness of (his)
body and soul;
he is also God because he became the dwelling place for
the God of the universe.
He is the son of a woman because from her is the nature
of his (bodily) structure,
but he is the Son of the (Divine) Essence because he is
equal to this by the power of his Assumer.[120]

Nor is there any question in Narsai's mind regarding the unity of the Person of Christ. As important as it is for Narsai to affirm the distinction between Christ's Divinity and humanity, Christ is emphatically one Person and one Son of God.[121]

The Trinitarian God

Narsai's modest views on human language and intellect have been described above, and it is clear already that God's Nature is something utterly incomprehensible (*la mittdarkana*) to human minds. Even in the context of revelation, God's Nature is beyond human understanding:

[God] taught [Moses] the Name of his Existence to unveil
it before the Hebrews:
that he is, and he is without beginning and without end.
"Indeed, I am not named by a name by the bland,
But rather in the power and deed of Making.
I am the Being, and this is the Name of my
incomprehensible Existence,

> And no one may place a different name for me besides
> what I am."[122]

Respecting this, Narsai's common name for God is *ʽYthutha*, which is simply "Existence." Because names, for Narsai, follow natures, no other name can be given to God properly speaking, since he shares no nature with any other being, but rather is the source of all other natures.[123] Even besides proper names, descriptive adjectives fall far short of being able to approach God fully:

239. No one knows how to call you by a name that is fair to your Name,
240. for all names are small compared to the greatness of your Glory.
241. If we call you Good, the sound of your Justice thunders on earth;
242. but if Just, heaven and earth are filled with your mercies.
243. If we call you Hidden, your works are unveiled before the eyes of all creatures;
244. if we call you Unveiled, there is none among things made able to see you.
245. If we call you the Hearing One, our voice is heard by you before we call,
246. and the Gracious and Forgiving One, your Love precedes us and our malice.
247. We know neither how to pray nor how to glorify,
248. and we are afraid to speak words unfit for you.[124]

From two poles, then, theology is a tenuous and humbling activity: human language is hardly up to the task, and the Divine Nature is beyond all possibility of perfect description.

This again stresses the importance of God's pedagogy and our need for his instruction, which takes the form of revelation. In particular, the Trinitarian Nature of God is a mystery that needed to be revealed even to the angels, and required hints and suggestions such as the use of the plural "let us" in Genesis to prepare the minds who were eventually to receive it.[125] Narsai, of course, knows the trinitarian teaching of the Council of Nicaea and affirms the equality in Divine Nature (*Kyana*) of the Father, Son, and Holy Spirit, as well as their distinct Personhood. In his trinitarian teaching, he makes use of the term *Qnoma*, which is difficult to translate accurately because of the history of its use in later writers and documents of the Church of the East, and will be translated as "individual" in this volume.[126] Here, Narsai uses *Qnoma* as the term for each of the Persons of the Trinity, while in his christological teaching, he uses the term *Parṣopa* to refer to Christ's one Person. Later authors of the Church of the East will standardize the teaching that Christ has two natures or *Kyane*, two *Qnome* (plural for *qnoma*), and one *Parṣopa*, while the Trinity has one *Kyana* and three *Qnome*.[127] The best way to understand this is to read *kyana* to mean nature in the abstract and *qnoma* as a particular example of a nature—not independently existing as implied by the Greek *hypostasis*, but individual as opposed to universal or abstract. Thus, in the developed terminology of the Church of the East, Christ is both God and Man, but neither one generically. Rather, he is one *Qnoma* of the Divine Nature (namely, the Son) and one *Qnoma* of human nature (namely, the Man Jesus). To say only that the Word assumed human *kyana* is to say he assumed an abstract universal concept, not flesh.

In his trinitarian teaching, Narsai makes use of two analogies to illustrate the three divine *Qnome*: fire and the soul. The analogy of fire is used to illustrate how the Father and the Son cannot be without each other:

57. The Begotten of the Father resembles him, and is with him as Light:
58. for as is light with fire, so is the Begotten with his Father.
59. The light of fire is with it, and there is no fire without light;
60. for through its light it is seen, and through it is light shown.
61. With the Father is also his Begotten, and the Son is with him without beginning.
62. Neither is there Father without his Begotten, nor Son without his Begetter.[128]

The analogy of the soul is, for Narsai, more significant because it is humanity, rather than fire, which is God's image, and which therefore is more capable of revealing God. It is also the analogy he reserves to illustrate the entire Trinity:

71. A manifestation of the three Individuals of one Being is fastened, for us, in our soul:
72. for the Son and the Spirit are from the Father as reason and life are from the soul.
73. Along with the soul is born reason, and power, and vitality,
74. and along with the Father are the Son and Spirit without beginning.
75. Two powers accompany the soul: reason and vitality as well;
76. and two Powers with the Father: the Son and Spirit without beginning.
77. The Son, the Begotten without beginning and the Spirit who proceeds from the Father:
78. one Begotten and one Proceeding; one equality in Nature.[129]

Thus if the soul is the source of reason as well as of life, and these three elements exist together, the Father is the source of the Son and Spirit, existing together eternally.

Dramatically yet unsurprisingly, Narsai stops the analogies and his analysis here. While fire and the soul both illustrate multiplicity within unity, they fall short, since in neither case are the multiple terms truly distinct *qnome*. Yes, the soul brings about both reason and life, but reason and life are not persons, as are the Son and Spirit. Memra 62, which I have been quoting here, begins with an investigation into the Nature of God and the *Qnome* of the Trinity, but this investigation ends abruptly and Narsai shifts to the larger theme of the memra, which is a commentary on the two creation accounts of Genesis. He concludes his section on the Trinity, however, with a note on holy piety:

87. His very creatures are incomprehensible, and his deeds are too difficult for us.
88. How therefore can we presume to investigate his Existence that is without beginning?
89. What is made cannot investigate the Existence of the Maker;
90. and as much as he inquires "how did he begin?" he will find him without beginning.
91. As much as the mind wishes to investigate his Existence, one thing alone can it handle:

92. that it will not be comprehended by its nature.
93. This will suffice as regards our subject matter: that we may examine only his works,
94. but as for the issue of his Existence, let it be honored by us in silence.[130]

Christian Life and Spirituality

Because the Nature of God is mysterious, our sharing in his life is also a mystery (*raza*), a word that Narsai also uses to name sacraments and symbols. Sacraments are the cause of our sharing in God's life and the fulfillment of our call to be his image;[131] symbols are what we become when we live this out well. Both the beginning and the end of Christian life, therefore, are mysterious.

Some of the earliest English translations of Narsai's works were, in fact, of his works on the liturgy and sacraments.[132] While there is doubt whether Narsai wrote Memra 35, on the Eucharistic Liturgy, which is attributed to him, we can examine those on baptism and on the priesthood with some confidence.[133] One of the important points worth making is that Narsai sees the liturgical rituals of the church as theological sources, similar even to the scriptures themselves.[134] That is, Narsai sees the liturgy as something he needs to be instructed and formed by, rather than what seems to be more common in our time, something to form. His "Exposition" on Baptism is a commentary on the rite itself, similar to his running commentaries on biblical passages and can even be used to help reconstruct the liturgy as it was in his day.[135]

Our concern here, however, is theology. Narsai develops his from the rituals before him in a way rich and consistent with his overall doctrine. It is initially by baptism that we are reconstituted as images of God:

> Who suffices to repay (His) love to the Fashioner of all, who came in His love to beget men spiritually? Too little is the tongue of height and depth to give thanks with us to the power of the Creator who has renewed our image and

> blotted out our iniquity. As in a furnace He re-cast our image in Baptism; and instead of our clay He has made us spiritual gold. Spiritually, without colors, was He pleased to depict us; that the beauty of our image might not again be corrupted by death. O Painter, that paints an image upon the tablet of the waters, nor is His art hindered by opposition! O Artist, that breathes the Spirit (and works) without hands, and sows life immortal in mortality![136]

God the Artist, whose self-portrait was damaged by sin and death, refashions it through Christ; he applies this refashioning to each of us through baptism, in which we are washed clean of sin and freed of the bond of death by being united to the resurrected Christ.[137] We are, moreover, fed with the Eucharist, which is truly Christ's own Body and Blood and the very fire of Divinity on this earth, and become, like Christ, temples of the living God.[138]

The church, as well as church buildings, are also temples of God, and this comes about because of the priesthood of the church.[139] Priests are mediators and ministers of the Mysteries of God,[140] fathers to the children of the church,[141] and greater even than the angels.[142] They can bind and loose sins and are therefore physicians meant to heal the sick (an image prominent in Aphrahat[143]), and through their celebration of the Mysteries, especially that of the Eucharist, they imitate God in redepicting the image of Christ's sacrifice.[144] Because of this, however, priests have the highest responsibility to live a holy life, and yet, in Narsai's time and today, fail at it through their weakness and wickedness and await the harshest judgment.[145]

Though Narsai is far from ignorant of human failings and their consequences, his ethical teaching comes through in various ways. Most prominent is his use of various biblical figures as examples or paradigms for the faithful to follow.[146] Christ, of course, is primary, and Memra 21, on Christ's Temptation, illustrates how Narsai presents events for us to imitate. Similar, and also included in this volume, are the memre on Abraham and John the Baptist, the Thief crucified next to Christ, and even the anti-hero Jonah, who is presented to us as a counterexample to virtue. Negatively, Narsai is also known for a genre of memre called "chastisements," wherein he employs often harsh rhetoric in order to awaken his audience from their slumber of sin.[147]

Unsurprising considering his experience of empires, Narsai's view of human political communities can be quite negative, and this is related to an undeniably negative element in his anthropology.[148] But Narsai the theologian-poet inverts this negativity about humanity into a praise of God's glory, with a flourish:

327. In every age, the just ones prayed and you answered them;
328. in our age that is deprived of the righteous, may you persuade yourself.
329. The persuasion of your Kindness is greater than all the just,
330. and the treasury of your mercies is incomparable to that of things made.
331. Your Love provoked the will of the just to persuade you,
332. so if there are no just, send your Will without the just.
333. Yours are persuasion and the words of persuaders,
334. whom would you load with your own grace to the sons of your household?
335. May Goodness be entirely yours, as it is indeed,
336. and so grant us what you granted at the beginning of time.
337. Who convinced you to create creation when it did not exist?
338. And who advised you to bind up the world in the construction of man?
339. Who was it who advised you to call us your image?
340. And who showed you how to complete your work in our construction?
341. So if in our very existence, and all existence, you needed no help,
342. what help do you need regarding our wickedness—a miserable gnat?
343. Our wickedness is a gnat compared to the greatness of your Divinity,
344. and it is only a cup if compared to the sea of your mercies.[149]

Far from falling into discouragement or despair, Narsai turns the fact of human misery during his "evil times"[150] into a foundational element of his spirituality: that all goodness and glory belong to

God. This is the fruit also of meditating on future things, such as the eschaton or renewal of creation, the subject of Memra 44. Indeed, God being all in all is the eventual theme of Memra 13, the final one in this collection, and though it discusses themes such as fasting, prayer, and bearing misfortune during the voyage of our life, in comparison to God's glory, all else turns into nothing.

Style, Works, and Hymns

The *Ecclesiastical History* tells us that Narsai, in response to Jacob of Serug's eloquent but heretical writings, began writing memre of his own, in order to protect the orthodox faith by means of "sweet tones."[151] These were not Narsai's first memre, according to the same source, since it mentions that he wrote two memre during his exile from Nisibis due to the incident with Barṣawma and Mamai. These two are named by their first lines and extant (Memre 25 and 80), and their titles tell us that they were written in the typical "Narsaian" twelve-syllable meter.[152] If the *Ecclesiastical History* is to be trusted regarding Narsai's writing as a response to Jacob of Serug, it may be trusted regarding Narsai's two earlier memre, and it is therefore possible that Narsai, rather than Jacob, was the first to use this new meter.

Of Narsai's extant memre, seventy are in the Narsaian twelve-syllable meter, and twelve are in the older seven-syllable meter. The "sweet tones" mentioned by the *Ecclesiastical History*, as well as the immemorial practice of the Church of the East, suggests that their intention was to be sung.[153] Some helpful studies have been written about Narsai's poetic style, pointing out his use of couplets (pairs of lines that go together by comparison or contrast) and anaphoras (litanies of lines that begin with the same words but make subtle changes as they progress).[154] Curiously, very little has been written about Narsai's rhythm, and in fact there is perception among some Western scholars that Narsai, and in fact most authors writing in Syriac, do not utilize rhythm at all but only count syllables.[155] This is quite false, and a vocal reading of any of Narsai's memre will reveal a strong trochaic pattern on every line, in both the twelve-syllable and seven-syllable memre. Here, for example, are the first lines of Memra 5, with the stressed syllables in bold:

__Rabb__uth __ḥubb__eh __swa__ Ba__ro__ya __d-nig__li __b-na__sha
__W-ash__ma' __qa__la __la__-shmay__ya__ne __d-ni'__bidh __na__sha
__Bra__ kul __midd__im __min__ la __midd__im __w-la__ ith__mall__ak
__W-ṣedh__ bar__na__sha, __ta__ lam __ni'__badh __na__sha __b-ṣal__man

This rhythm is consistent in every extant memra of Narsai.[156]

Aside from memre, a few other works are attributed to Narsai. Included in manuscripts of his memre are also "dialogue poems," or *soghyatha*, which thematically accompany the preceding memra. For example, after Memra 4, on the Birth of our Lord, there is a dialogue poem between Mary and the Magi. There are nine such dialogue poems in the manuscripts, only one of which is in twelve-syllable meter. Basically all scholars doubt the authenticity of these dialogue poems, though none of the reasons seems conclusive.[157] Indeed, there are many dialogues within the memre themselves, and it is clear that Narsai has a flare for the dramatic. I have included one in this volume, accompanying Memra 5: the Dialogue between Mary and the Angel.

There are two important liturgical hymns attributed explicitly to Narsai in the *Ḥudhra*, the Liturgy of the Hours of the Church of the East, which I have translated to be sung according to their traditional melody. The first is also included in the memre manuscripts, falsely titled a *soghytha*, and accompanying Memra 33, on the Prodigal Son:

* All thanks to him who saved our race
  from slavery to sin and death!
* He reconciled us with the hosts
  above, who scorned us for our sin.
* Blessed is he who had mercy,
  who sought and found us, and rejoiced.
* He symbolized our straying and
  returning in his parable:
* He named our race the heir and son,
  who strayed, returned, who died and rose.

* He gladdened all the hosts above
through our return and our rising.
* The great love which the Lover of
our race showed cannot be described:
* For from our race, he took on flesh,
and reconciled us to himself.
* It is a thing too great for us;
it is a new thing he has done:
* he has made his temple our flesh,
in which he is worshipped by all.
* O Come, earthly and heavenly,
and marvel at our lofty place:
* our race has reached the greatest height
of infinite Divinity!
* Heaven and earth and all therein
give thanks to him who renewed us,
* For he has wiped our sins away,
named us his Name, and has crowned us.
* Worthy is he of praise and thanks
from every mouth, who raised us up.
* Let us proclaim our praise to him,
forever and ever, amen.[158]

The second is chanted during every Sunday morning prayer, following a similar hymn attributed to Ephrem:

* Error, like the darkest night, had been spread across the world,
but the Light of the Messiah dawned and gave the world clarity.
* History, from Adam on, had resembled darkest night,
and the day of Christ's unveiling was the daylight hours' running-course.
* Our Lord even compared morning to his preaching's start,
and the evening to the ending, when the world will rest from its work.

* Priests and kings and prophets had waited with this hope in mind,
and the Maker gave them comfort in the day that he was revealed.
* In his day all creatures rest, who had once been crushed in sin,
and the world begins to ponder the meaning of the world to come.
* The New Covenant he gave to all who accept his creed,
and with his own Blood he sealed it, that his promise might never fail.
* With his promised Paradise, he made fast the course of man,
and behold, on earth and heaven all await his coming again.
* The new coming of the King who rules from our race has neared:
come, let us prepare to meet him with the hosts of heaven above!
* Let us take the oil of love for that day filled with despair,
lest we hear the voice then saying, "begone, I know not of your works."
* While we live, then, let us work in the vineyard of the Word,
that we may then hear the voice which says: "Come and receive what was vowed!"
* Let us fix our mind's sojourn with the hope of life to come,
and arrive, through love and faith, then, at the harbor of all delights![159]

Both of these hymns are evidence of the enduring honor given to Narsai by all the living branches of the Church of the East.

There are several thematic collections of some of Narsai's memre that have been translated into English, which can be found in the Bibliography, and there is currently an important project attempting to publish English translations of all of Narsai's memre in several volumes forthcoming from Peeters. A volume of scholarly essays on Narsai edited by Aaron Butts, Kristian Heal, and Robert Kitchen was recently published,[160] as well as a "Clavis" detailing each of Narsai's memre, their manuscript attestation, current translations, and studies.[161] The numbering of the Memre in this volume follows that of the *Clavis*, and the translation for each chapter is based on the following editions:

Chapter 1. Memra 62: On the Order of Creation, and the *Qnome* of the Trinity
M.2: 180–193 [*Clavis* 60–61]
Chapter 2. Memra 49: On the Forming of Adam and Eve, and the Breaking of the Command
M.2: 100–114 [*Clavis* 48–49]
Chapter 3. Memra 3: On Abraham
M.1: 57–68 [*Clavis* 4–5]
Chapter 4. Memra 14: On Jonah
M.1: 134–149 [*Clavis* 15–16]
Chapter 5. Memra 5: On the Incarnation (with *Soghytha*)
P.1: 104–134 [*Clavis* 6–7]
Chapter 6. Memra 7: On John the Baptist
P.1: 163–185 [*Clavis* 8–9]
Chapter 7. Memra 21: On the Temptation of Christ
P.1: 312–334 [*Clavis* 21–22]
Chapter 8. Memra 37: On the Thief
M.1: 327–341 [*Clavis* 37]
Chapter 9. Memra 16: On Human Nature
M.1: 257–270 [*Clavis* 17–18]
Chapter 10. Memra 81: On Christology
P.2: 206–218 [*Clavis* 76–77]

TRANSLATION STYLE

There are as many translation styles as there are translators. The translation in this volume attempts, as do most translations, to remain as close as possible to Narsai's original words and style while being as readable as possible in English. The tension between these two poles is where the individual translator is forced to make a judgment call on practically every line, if not every word. I have erred on the side of faithfulness to Narsai, and chosen to translate harshly where he is harsh, simply where he is simple, and strangely where he is strange. If a word or phrase strikes the reader as unusual, it is hopefully because the original text is unusual, and perhaps because Narsai wanted to sound unusual. He is a writer that, I think, intends to be surprising, and rather than insulate his sharpness, I have attempted to transfer it into English as well as I could.

In particular, Narsai uses various names to refer to God, including "Existence," "the Being," "the Dawn," "the Power," and many others. I have in most cases translated these names quite literally, since in most cases they sound as strange in Aramaic as they do in English, and in all cases the single word is less clunky than its multiword explanatory alternative. The result of this is an English text with many capitalized words, which is still the clearest way to indicate a name referring to the Godhead. For similar reasons, I have capitalized *Man* when referring to Christ and generally used that gendered term rather than something like *human* in order to stay closer to the scriptures (e.g., Acts 2:22–23), which were Narsai's main theological source, and to avoid Nestorian-sounding ideas that, as discussed above, I do not believe should be attributed to Narsai. The memra introductions, titles, and subtitles are mine.

TERMINOLOGY

Below is a list of terms with their translation equivalents in this volume.

`ythutha—existence (capitalized when referring to God)
`ythya—being (capitalized when referring to God)
ʿwydha—a thing made, a creature
ʿamma—the people (the Jews)
ʿamme—the peoples (the Gentiles)
ʿawla—iniquity, wickedness
ʿyra—watcher
bisra—flesh
bysha—evil
dinḥa—dawn, epiphany (capitalized when referring to God)
ḥayla—power (capitalized when referring to God)
ḥtytha—sin
kyana—nature
nagged—drag
paghra—body (vs. carcass), but can also mean human nature itself
paroshutha—discernment
parṣopa—person
qala—voice, sound
qnoma—individual, individuality, self (one member of a natural kind as opposed to the universal nature; capitalized when referring to God)
raza—mystery, symbol, sacrament
rimza—signal[162] (capitalized when referring to God)
taqqen—fashion, construct
tuqana—fashioning, construction
tupsa—type, symbol
takhsa—order
zkha—vindicate
yaṣra—inclination

TRANSLITERATION

Consonants

Name	As in…	Transliteration	Consonant
Alap	air	ʾ	ܐ
Beth	boy	*b*	ܒ
Gamal	girl	*g*	ܓ
Dalath	dog	*d*	ܕ
Heh	hello	*h*	ܗ
Waw	wow	*w*	ܘ
Zayn	zip	*z*	ܙ
Ḥeth	(guttural h)	*ḥ*	ܚ
Ṭeth	(guttural t)	*ṭ*	ܛ
Yodh	you	*y*	ܝ
Kap	cat	*k*	ܟ
Lamadh	love	*l*	ܠ
Mym	mom	*m*	ܡ
Nun	name	*n*	ܢ
Simkath	sip	*s*	ܣ
ʿe	(guttural e)	ʿ	ܥ
Pe	pen	*p*	ܦ
Ṣade	(guttural s)	*ṣ*	ܨ
Qop	quilt	*q*	ܩ
Resh	red	*r*	ܪ
Shyn	sheep	*sh*	ܫ
Taw	tent	*t*	ܬ

Modified/Softened Consonants

Name	As in…	Transliteration	Letter
Weth	wow	*w*	ܒ݂
Ghamal	(softened g)	*gh*	ܓ݂

Dhalath	the	*dh*	ܕ݂
Khap	Bach	*kh*	ܟ݂
Phe	phone or wow	*ph* or *w*	ܦ݂
Thaw	thick	*th*	ܬ݂

Vowels

Name	**As in...**	**Transliteration**	**Vowel**
Zqapa	ball	*a*	ܵ
Zlama Kirya	bit	*i*	ܸ
Pthaḥa	balloon	*a*, followed by a doubled consonant	ܲ
Zlama Qishya	bear	*e*	ܹ
Waw Rwykhta	boat	*o*	ܘܿ
Waw ʿyqta	boot	*u*	ܘܼ
Ḥwaṣa	beet	*y*	ܼ

ABBREVIATIONS

Memra XX: YY—The memra of Narsai as numbered ("XX") in the *Clavis*; "YY" refers to the line numbers.

Editions

M.1 or **M.2**—Alphonse Mingana, *Narsai Homiliae et carmina* (2 vols. Mosul: Typis Fratrum praedicatorum, 1905).

P.1 or **P.2**—*Homilies of Mar Narsai* (2 vols.; San Francisco: Patriarchal Press, 1970).

English Translations

Connolly—R. H. Connolly, *The Liturgical Homilies of Narsai* (Cambridge: Cambridge University Press, 1909).

Frishman—Judith Frishman, "The Ways and Means of the Divine Economy: An Edition, Translation, and Study of Six Biblical Homilies by Narsai" (PhD diss., University of Leiden, 1992).

McLeod—Frederick G. McLeod, SJ, *Narsai's Metrical Homilies on the Nativity, Epiphany, Passion, Resurrection and Ascension* (Patrologia Orientalis 40, no. 1; Turnhout: Brepols, 1979).

Younan—This volume.

Other Sources

BHK—*Narsai*, ed. Aaron M. Butts, Kristian S. Heal, and Robert A. Kitchen (Tübingen: Mohr Siebeck, 2020).

Clavis—Aaron M. Butts, Kristian S. Heal, and Sebastian P. Brock, *Clavis to the Metrical Homilies of Narsai* (Louvain: Peeters, 2021).

Ḥudhra—*Ḥudhra* (Trichur, India: Mar Narsai Press, 1960).

Sources—Adam Becker, *Sources for the Study of the School of Nisibis* (Liverpool: Liverpool University Press, 2008).

Synodicon—*Synodicon Orientale*, ed. Jean-Baptiste Chabot (Paris: Imprimerie Nationale, 1902).

Vööbus—Arthur Vööbus, *History of the School of Nisibis* (Louvain: Peeters, 1965).

I

Creation, Nature, and Revelation

Chapter 1

MEMRA 62: ON THE ORDER OF CREATION, AND THE *QNOME*[1] OF THE TRINITY

INTRODUCTION

This Memra combines in a semiorganic way the Christian doctrine of the Trinity and a concise commentary on the two creation accounts of the Book of Genesis. The overall structure follows that of Genesis, but trinitarian doctrine appears in two places: in an exposition of the Divine Nature (following an account of Moses asking to see God in Exod 33), and in the context of the creation account, helping to explain the use of the plural in "let us create man in our image" (Gen 1:26).

A subtle but important theme in this Memra is that of humble piety when discussing the Divine Nature. This is first introduced in line 13 in God's response to the request of Moses to see him and applied in concluding the long section on the Trinity in line 94. Indeed, throughout the Memra, we find Narsai's humble piety expressed by his self-limitation to the text of Genesis with little speculation regarding what is not in the text itself. For example, in line 98 he warns us not to ask what is "before" the beginning and to have the intelligent sense to inquire only into what is appropriate to our minds. He does, however, allow himself to deduce certain conclusions from the biblical text, such as the implicit creation of fire, water, and angels "in the beginning" before light, along with the heavens and the earth (line 104). The argument seems to be that the first line of Genesis, "in the beginning God created the heavens and the earth," describes an initial act of creation *before* God's utterance "let there be light." This makes sense of the following verses, which mention and take for granted preexisting matter, and justifies Narsai's conviction that despite the second verse of Genesis, God created all out of nothing (lines 40, 106, 108, etc.).

Narsai's trinitarian teaching is essentially orthodox when one accepts the term *qnoma* (plural *qnome*) as a sufficient equivalent to "person" in reference to the Trinity, which is less controversial than in the context of Christology (the topic of Memra 81, chapter 10 of this book). Each of the divine *Qnome* (a term I will translate as "individual") is distinct and personal, defined by its relations to the others. Various metaphors attempt to relay some aspect of the Trinitarian Mystery, such as fire producing light, or the soul being the principle of reason and life (lines 59–76). Ultimately, however, all comparisons fall short, among other reasons, because the distinctions within natural things do not amount to a distinction of *qnome*, and a distinction of *qnome* in natural things amounts to a separation of beings. In the end, again, we are forced to accept the Mystery in humble piety.

Each day of the creation account is given its own short treatment, with "day" being defined, as it is both in Genesis and in the liturgical life of the Church of the East, as beginning in the evening (lines 135–137). The overall structure of the creation, however, is one of the establishment and then adornment of light, water, earth, and finally the human being (lines 333–344). The first day brings light, and the fourth the "adornment" of it by means of the heavenly bodies; the second day brings water, and the fifth day its adornment through water animals (and birds, which belong to the water above the firmament); the third day brings earth, and the sixth day the adornment of earth through land animals; finally, man is created, and he is adorned by his wife Eve (line 276).

While God is the ultimate cause of all that is, Narsai is no occasionalist, and he affirms that creatures are given true agency: even those as basic as light (line 126), and water (line 143), as well as earth (166). Indeed, each creature has a part to play in the overall ordering of the created world, but Narsai notes that only two are created *directly* from nothing according to the text of Genesis: light and the human soul (lines 217–218). There are, moreover, seemingly Augustinian themes in Narsai's commentary, such as the gradual increase of importance in creatures made as the days progress (for example, line 158), and the speaking of God being done for the sake of the knowledge of the angels (line 110). The blessings of the seventh day and the rest commanded on it, finally, are there to remind us that it is ultimately God who works (line 230).

The importance of the human being, which will be the theme of the next chapter, is broached here as well. While God speaks in the singular person in creating the rest of the world by his word, Adam is created by a conversation, with God speaking in the plural (lines 233, 252). The result of this is no ordinary creature, but one who reflects and images the very essence of God in his own nature—in some mysterious way, the very Trinity is revealed only in the human being (line 256), an honor denied even to the angels (line 262). In relation to creation, the human being is the image of God in the sense of a proxy through whom other creatures recognize and glorify God through their obedience (line 293).

TRANSLATION

I. Introduction: God and Moses

1. The son of Amram [Exod 6:20] opened a great treasure for us in his prophecy
2. regarding when the great Power of the Creator began to make.
3. These things were hidden from all: how he began creating,
4. and by what power heaven, earth, and all therein were fashioned.
5. And so, the Creator wished to make the working of his Power known to rational creatures.

6. In Moses he chose a disciple and inspired a spiritual book through him.
7. On Mount Sinai he showed him a marvelous vision,
8. and made a voice heard to him while drawing him to learn.
9. The Creator desired to show himself humanly to Moses,
10. and because of this Moses yearned to see his Nature.
11. "If, then, you have chosen me for yourself as a disciple, and if you love me,
12. show me the glory of your Nature, and let me contemplate your hidden Radiance" [Exod 33:18].
13. "You have erred greatly, O Moses": the Lord said to him,
14. "no mortal can see me, for my Nature is above those who see."
15. "I called you unto myself in order to be taught, that you may learn that I am the Creator;
16. not that you may learn my Hiddenness, for that is incomprehensible to creatures."
17. "I am the Lord and God, and this is my Name: I AM [Exod 3:14].
18. With my own power I uphold heaven, earth, and all therein."
19. "And because mortals are unaware that my Majesty has dominion over all,
20. I designate you a messenger and a mediator to instruct them."
21. "Through you I wish to reveal what regards my Existence and my works,
22. and in you I desire to instruct the whole race of rational creatures."
23. "See, O Moses, that I reveal to you the hidden mystery of my orderings:
24. descend and preach among mortals that I am Maker of all that is."
25. For forty days the Teacher perfected the new disciple,
26. and the mind of a mortal became able to comprehend the limit of all that is.
27. He made the Power of the Spirit dwell in him, in which he sang wondrous songs,
28. and heavenly and earthly creatures were dazzled at the sweetness of his melodies.
29. His word was like thunder, and both mute and rational heard it,
30. and his phrases were like trumpets that proclaimed the Power of the Maker.

II. The Creator

31. Thus, "in the beginning"[2] the Creator began and created everything that is,
32. and fixed the times, in his knowledge, of the beginning and the end.
33. And while not beginning in his Existence (for his Nature is without beginning),
34. he made creation in time, as he foreknew.
35. It was not a new thought that led him to make creatures,
36. for this was set from eternity in his Knowledge and Existence.
37. Nor was it for his own satisfaction that he formed heaven, earth, and all therein,
38. but rather in love and mercy that he revealed his will to his creatures.
39. He is indeed Good in his Nature, and his Nature is full of blessings,
40. and in his grace he wished to bring everything from nothing.
41. For this is fitting in the Maker, that in his works he may proclaim his Power,
42. and that through the ordering of his creatures, they may gain knowledge.
43. His Existence is without beginning; his Lordship is without end.
44. For his creatures, however, there is a beginning, temporality, and composition.
45. His Existence is incomprehensible by the minds of creatures;
46. nor can it be contained by sight, for his Nature is greater than this.
47. His Existence is immeasurable: for what is before the beginning?
48. Nor is there any time when he was not, for he existed before all.

III. The Trinity

49. There was the Nature, perfect in being, without beginning:
50. Father, Son, and Holy Spirit, three Individuals, one Power.
51. The Father, perfect, without beginning, who begat the Son without alteration;
52. the Son is from him and like him, and there is no interval of time between him and his Father.

53. The Spirit, who is of the same Nature, is an existing and true Individual,
54. the equality of whose Nature witnesses that he existed with the Father.
55. The Begotten of the Father resembles him, for he is with his Father from eternity,
56. and because he is with his Father [John 1:18], the ages do not confine the Begotten.
57. The Begotten of the Father resembles him, and is with him as Light [John 1:4]:
58. for as is light with fire, so is the Begotten with his Father.
59. The light of fire is with it, and there is no fire without light;
60. for through its light it is seen, and through it is light shown.
61. With the Father is also his Begotten, and the Son is with him without beginning.
62. Neither is there Father without his Begotten, nor Son without his Begetter.
63. The Son, however, is not constituted without an Individual, like light.
64. Rather he is a true Individual and an Image [Col 1:15] that resembles his Begetter.
65. The Son does not form the Father, nor is the Son named "father";
66. for the difference in their Names proclaims the truth of the Individuals.
67. The Spirit is an Individual from the Father who is equal with him in everything.
68. As the Son is equal to the Father, the Spirit is equal to the Father and Son.
69. The difference of their Names does not injure the equality.
70. The Names are to be taken in order, but the Individuals are equal in Essence.
71. A manifestation of the three Individuals of one Being is fastened, for us, in our soul:
72. for the Son and the Spirit are from the Father as reason and life are from the soul.
73. Along with the soul is born reason, and power, and vitality,

74. and along with the Father are the Son and Spirit without beginning.
75. Two powers accompany the soul: reason and vitality as well;
76. and two Powers with the Father: the Son and Spirit without beginning.
77. The Son, the Begotten without beginning and the Spirit who proceeds from the Father [John 14:26]:
78. one Begotten and one Proceeding; one equality in Nature.
79. The Spirit is from the Father and is not named "Begotten,"
80. nor is this strange to nature or to the order of language.
81. Eve was fashioned out of Adam, and she is neither his daughter nor his sister,
82. and, while from him in nature, she was called simply his wife.[3]
83. Thus he fastened an image of his Being within our nature as in a mystery,[4]
84. and so whoever wonders about the Son will see him explained in what is our own.

IV. Piety Regarding the Mystery of God

85. He has instructed us to examine his Greatness through our own nature:
86. for if what belongs to us is not clear to us, how mysterious it is to inquire about him!
87. His very creatures are incomprehensible, and his deeds are too difficult for us.
88. How therefore can we presume to investigate his Existence that is without beginning?
89. What is made cannot investigate the Existence of the Maker;
90. and as much as he inquires "how did he begin?" he will find him without beginning.
91. As much as the mind wishes to investigate his Existence, one thing alone can it handle:
92. that it will not be comprehended by its nature.
93. This will suffice as regards our subject matter: that we may examine only his works,

94. but as for the issue of his Existence, let it be honored by us in silence.

V. First Creation Account

95. Let us heed, then, to his orderings, and praise his handiwork,
96. for it is the duty of a creature to give thanks to the Creator for everything he created.
97. For he began "in the beginning" in creation, thus we heard from Moses [Gen 1:1],
98. and what is before "in the beginning," its manner and quality, we are not to inquire.
99. Let us inquire, therefore, as intelligent men, in a search appropriate for creatures:
100. what was the reason that he spoke of his orderings in a voice [Gen 1:3]?
101. "In the beginning," then, he began and created heaven and earth first,
102. and five other natures that he did not call by name.
103. By this word, then, in the ordering "in the beginning,"
104. fire, water, darkness, and rational and mute angels were implied.
105. In this word, "in the beginning," was the ordering of angels,
106. and that the Creator of everything made them out of nothing.
107. In that ordering "in the beginning," he did not speak to be heard,
108. for there was nothing made who could hear and receive instruction.
109. But when he began to make it so that natures came to be, one by one,
110. through a whisper he desired to reveal his ordering to the angels.
111. The reason for the whisper, then, is this: that he may teach the angels
112. that the Lord of all, who upholds their assemblies, is the one who orders.
113. O Whisper mightier than all, which was spoken "in the beginning,"
114. and that drew all intellectual natures toward him in love!
115. Darkness was covering height and depth together,
116. and the earth was covered with water before it received order.

117. The earth, in the beginning, was without visibility or order [Gen 1:2],
118. and he calls it "formless," since it was not yet decorated with trees.

VI. The First Day

119. The Spirit, as related, was above the water of the abysses
120. when he called the wind of the air to blow upon the ethereal wind.
121. The Word of the Maker, then, was like the order of teaching,
122. and he made the voice heard to angels, that there may "be light" to enlighten all.
123. O Voice from out of nothing that brought light into being!
124. O Light that, along with the sound, formed a nature that was not!
125. Light pursued darkness, which had covered creatures,
126. and spiritual beings marveled at the power that gave it authority.
127. Regarding the Word that created light another sound was heard
128. that praised his ordering, that he may fashion something even better.
129. O wise Craftsman who is so secure in his fashioning,
130. who placed a limit for the light, regarding how much it may rightly rule.
131. He distinguished between light and darkness, that one may not assail the other,
132. and he established a law for their courses in the hours of night and day.
133. He called the light "daytime," and the darkness he called "night,"
134. and in their names he named them according to the realities of their hours.
135. There was an evening and a daytime, then, "one day," as it is written,
136. and he called it the first day, for there was yet none other like it.
137. He established, then, a beginning: a night for the first day,
138. that he may guard the order of his creation since darkness existed first.

VII. The Second Day

139. The first day, then, is completed: night and daytime—one day.
140. Then another voice cried out "let there be a firmament from the waters" [Gen 1:6].
141. O Voice having such authority—with the word, the deed!
142. O Power that bound and made the firm out of the liquid!
143. From the water he created the firmament to bear the waters above it,
144. and he who was first in the beginning named it "heaven."
145. He made the firmament in the middle like a nearby ceiling,
146. that it may be close in visibility and still divide water from water.
147. What an unshaking measure, which divided the waters equally:
148. half for the earth for its use, and half for the ridge of the firmament!
149. What a Craftsman who fashions all, whose knowledge is incomprehensible,
150. who knew what was useful for something before it was made!
151. He was prepared to hang the lights, the nature of fire, in the firmament,
152. and he gathered water above it, that may not be burned away by the fire.
153. The Creator also knew, before he made all that is,
154. that another dwelling was useful for rational beings at the end of time.
155. For this purpose he created the firmament like a rooftop in the middle,
156. that at the end it may become a spot of land for our rest.
157. There was, then, a morning like an evening, and the second day was completed,
158. and he turned and praised his fashioning, that he may fashion something even better.

VIII. The Third Day

159. The third evening came so that it may not differ from the first,
160. for there was One Power that commanded that something should be, and it was.

161. “Let the waters be gathered,” he said, “let there be seas in one place,
162. and let the surfaces of the earth be revealed, so that it may be suitable for living” [Gen 1:9].
153. O unwearied command, O unhindered Word!
164. For once his will was commanded, the waters were gathered into the seas.
165. The earth was brought to light and gladdened, and a command came out to it:
166. “let the earth burst forth and sprout herbs, plants, and trees.”
167. The command became the deed, and the earth was adorned with fruits,
168. and there came to be plants and trees, and the Good One praised his ordering.

IX. The Fourth Day

169. There was, then, an evening and a morning, and a completed third day,
170. and another command issued forth, commanding there to be lights [Gen 1:14].
171. There then came to be lights in the firmament above the earth,
172. so that ages, months, and years may be known by their courses.
173. The Word set out to act, and immediately there were lights,
174. and he established a law that does not pass for the courses of night and day.
175. O Craftsman who adorns all, whose will has authority over all,
176. for whom, from something or from nothing, it is easy to make everything.
177. Out of light he created the lights, from that first light,
178. when he divided it into portions for the moon, the stars, and the sun.
179. He did not fasten them in the firmament, lest their courses entangle,
180. but rather he hung them like candles, and arranged the course of their hours.

X. The Fifth Day

181. The fourth day was thus concluded, in the limiting of the evening and morning,
182. and another command came forth: that there may be moving things from the waters [Gen 1:20].
183. And so the waters gave birth to animals of innumerable kinds:
184. creeping things, fishes and dragons, and deadly animals.
185. O Power to whom difficult things are easy, according to his will,
186. who from water constructed and made innumerable species.
187. From water he created birds, the nature that swims upon the air,
188. and while it is from the water like a creeping thing, the air carries it and it moves.
189. O Good One, how great is his love, who keeps his command for his possessions,
190. who, at the end of their formation, supplies them with blessings:
191. "Give birth and multiply on the earth—on the sea and dry land together."
192. And meanwhile their species were kept in succession, one after another.

XI. The Sixth Day

193. On the fifth day was completed the creation of creeping things and birds,
194. and on the sixth day he began to create beast and cattle [Gen 1:24].
195. The earth put forth and brought out the living soul of every species:
196. beasts, roaming and grazing, and moving things born from the earth.
197. O mute nature that budded with living things from within it!
198. For while soil is miserable to look at, it gives birth to the beauty of all species.
199. Not that it gave birth of its own nature, but rather the power of its Maker:
200. he who solidified earth in the beginning commanded, and it gave birth to living things.
201. On the sixth day cattle and beast were created with Adam,

202. such that those who were useful for his work may receive their forming with him.
203. On the sixth day was completed the ordering of all that is,
204. and the Creator showed his power in his works that he spoke and made to be.

XII. The Seventh Day

205. On the seventh day the Maker rested from his fashioning [Gen 2:2],
206. and he blessed the seventh day, and called it a holy day.
207. Not because that Power was wearied, and not because his will could be hindered:
208. he created something from nothing—in six days, everything.
209. It would not have been difficult for his will to make everything in a moment,
210. but rather in one day and in many it was appropriate for him to make everything.
211. He made his creation an ordering, just as he had foreknown,
212. and for the sake of teaching rational beings he completed all in six days.
213. For the angels saw his ordering and examined it,
214. and whenever the word he spoke came to be, the spiritual cried out his praise.
215. The Knower who knows all accomplished all in knowledge:
216. from something or from nothing, he brought creatures into being.
217. He created light from nothing, to show his greatness,
218. and our soul also from nothing to show he has authority over all.
219. He created the lights out of light, the lamps of the sun and moon,
220. and the assemblies of angels exulted in praise to the Power who orders all.
221. To these methods did the Creator look when he fashioned all,
222. and he tarried for the sake of his works, in order to teach his power to the rational.
223. With holy blessings he supplied the seventh day,
224. that it may not be a stranger to him, since he did not wish to create anything on it.

225. That day also became a day like the first days,
226. and to retain his order he called it "holy" [Gen 2:3], that we may not reject it.
227. It is the knowledge of its holiness that gives rest from labor,
228. for when we hear the word "labor," we learn who the Creator is.
229. This day was destined to be a lesson for the seed of Abram:
230. for when they guard it from labor, they learn the Cause of what is.
231. Now, to each thing that came to be from him, he made a voice heard when it came to be,
232. and he himself praised his ordering, that he may fashion something even better.

XIII. Second Creation Account

233. Up till now there has been a singular voice about all things together,
234. but at the end of his ordering, another voice spoke:
235. "Let us make rational man, in our image and likeness,
236. and let him have authority over all that is, for it was fashioned for his sake" [Gen 1:26].
237. O Craftsman so wise, O Good One so overflowing in his love,
238. who created and adorned everything, and then formed an heir!
239. He built him an earthy abode, and provided and filled it with good things,
240. and he gave him mute and rational beings alike for his service.
241. In all these things he honored the mortal, in his fashioning and authority,
242. in that he called him his image and subdued all existing things to him.
243. For all other things that came to be and were fashioned, he sounded only one voice,
244. but here, in the fashioning of Adam, there was a new counsel and thought.
245. "Let us make man in our likeness, and let him have authority like us,"
246. so that through his manifest image, he may proclaim his power to creatures.
247. "In him I will reveal my Hiddenness to intellectual natures,

248. and in him I will manifest my Lordship to mute and rational alike."
249. "I place him as a statue for things made to observe,
250. so that through love toward him, everyone may recognize me."
251. The fashioning of Adam is a marvel, and different from that of things made,
252. since he made all that is with his word, but for [Adam] he spoke a conversation to make him.

XIV. The Trinity in Adam's Forming

253. Glorious is the forming of the earthly one, and there are hidden mysteries buried within it,
254. for he did not say "let him be like me," but rather "in our image and likeness."
255. O mortal in whose forming are hidden mysteries!
256. O earthly one who manifests three Individuals to us in his fashioning!
257. In the fashioning of the image of Adam, he taught us as through a mystery;
258. in [saying] "in our image and likeness," he made three Individuals known to us.
259. The Being without beginning of the Father, Son, and Holy Spirit
260. is honored in the image of Adam as a mystery by all that is.
261. Otherwise, to whom did he call, in equality with his Greatness,
262. "in our image come, let us make?" He did not say so to angels [Heb 2:16]!
263. In saying "our image" he taught us about the distinction of Individuals,
264. and in "our very likeness" about the equality of the Nature.

XV. Formation and Authority of Adam and Eve

265. "Come, then, let us make man, and bind all existing things within him,
266. so that in kinship toward him, all their needs will be fulfilled in love."

267. And so God made Adam in his image out of dirt from the earth,
268. and breathed into him a living soul [Gen 2:7], a living and rational nature.
269. O the love toward our race! O the honor of our fashioning!
270. He chose in his love to breathe into us, the very life that is in us!
271. O uncomposed Nature, O immeasurable Essence!
272. When he fashioned our nature, he made us with hands and a mouth.
273. He did not make us like the beasts, who were males and females,
274. for Adam was first in his creation, and then Eve from his rib.
275. He fashioned Adam first and then the woman from Adam,
276. to teach the power of the Maker—that he himself adorns his creation.
277. And so the Lord God formed Adam, earth from the ground,
278. and placed him in the paradise of Eden, that he may be an heir within it.
279. In a beautiful and desirable dwelling he placed Adam as his image,
280. that creatures may call upon the Maker in love through one close to them.

XVI. Adam as the Imperfect Image

281. The image resembles the Creator in name, but not in nature,
282. for he gave him as much authority over all he fashioned as the Creator has over him.
283. He becomes a father when he begets, and he begets a son who resembles him,
284. as the Father who begot the Son in his Nature without beginning.
285. He becomes a father in time, and in time begets a son,
286. but Existence begets without time, and there is no delay between him and his Son.
287. He makes something from something, and while it is not,
288. he fashions it, like the Maker who brought all into being out of nothing.
289. He makes something from something, and resembles the Creator.
290. He looks upon all that is on earth and his own vision is in heaven.

291. For by the symbol of his looking, he seeks his place above;
292. in this an earthly being resembles, as a mystery, the Creator.
293. And when he commands natures, by word and life,
294. in the name of image by proxy, he names him the First Adam.

XVII. Christ and Paradise

295. He becomes an Image in actuality in Christ, the Second Adam [1 Cor 15:46];
296. here "come, let us make in our image" receives fulfillment.
297. Because the Creator took on his image and made it the dwelling of his Honor,
298. the promises to Adam became actual in Christ.
299. Because he called him his image and he was ruined,
300. he returned and renewed him in Christ.
301. By reason of Adam's image, the greatness of paradise was related:
302. for Adam knew his honor because he placed him in such a glorious land.
303. The Lord God thus made paradise in Eden first [Gen 2:10–17],
304. and he made trees grow within it, suitable for food.
305. One of the trees he set in the middle of paradise,
306. and he called it the Tree of Life, that Adam may acquire life by it.
307. Then he planted another tree, and called it "the knowledge of duties,"
308. since the knowledge of what was hidden was to be revealed in its fruit through Adam.
309. It is related that there was a spring from Paradise that sprung forth,
310. from whose greatness four springs were distributed to every corner.
311. The first river was Pishon, which encircled the land of Huyla,
312. where there is gold, beryl, gems, and shiny pearls.
313. The second river was Gihon, which waters the land of the Cushites,
314. and through its overflowing it reaches the Egyptians and the Medians.

315. The third river is the Tigris, that was made an ambassador to Assyria,
316. and the peoples around it were pleased by its sweetness.
317. The fourth river is the Euphrates, which passes through the middle of the earth,
318. and it gives itself to the workers who irrigate lands by it.
319. The prophet [Moses] did not relate these things to glorify paradise,
320. nor to praise the greatness of the rivers in it.
321. He honored the Power of the Creator [in showing] that difficult things are easy for him,
322. For how can paradise's spring cross the sea to us?
323. The water passes through waters, and water does not mix with water,
324. and this witnesses to the greatness of the Power that fashioned all.
325. O command protecting water within water as in a jar!
326. The water of Eden does not mingle with the troubled waters of the firmament!
327. Thus mute and silent works cry out at every hour about his Power,
328. teaching rationality that the Maker is in his works.
329. The story of paradise reveals life-filled teaching to us,
330. and the history of the tree brings us near rationality.
331. Through [many] causes the Creator wished to instruct our rationality,
332. and with the stories of the rebuke, he made known the freedom within us.

XVIII. Summary of Creation

333. Through his ordering, he taught spiritual beings that he is Existence and Maker,
334. while through nature he instructed us that he may reveal his Hiddenness through us.
335. In the beginning, he fashioned earth and heaven when they did not exist,

336. and along with the power of the beginning, the intellectual powers came to be.
337. He created lights while making the sound heard to the spiritual assemblies,
338. and by the existence of light he taught that he had adorned them.
339. He made the firmament out of water, and loaded water upon it,
340. and adorned it with brilliant marks in an adornment fit for rational beings.
341. He gathered waters away from earth in the pool of seas and abysses,
342. and he adorned [earth] with plants and trees for the life of man and beast.
343. The waters made living things move, and the earth gave birth to every species,
344. and through silent orderings, he greatly instructed rational beings.
345. He made our nature from the earth, and breathed into us a living spirit,
346. and in the love toward our race, he tied together the mute and the rational.

XIX. Pre-knowledge of God

347. All of these orderings were hidden from of old in his Intellect,
348. and he brought them to manifestation and showed his love to his possessions.
349. His Will, then, was before his orderings, along with his Existence,
350. and he knew how many natures he would make before he created.
351. He was able to make two orders suffice for [all] rationality:
352. the dwelling of earth for mortals, and heaven for immortals.
353. He knew the thoughts of rational beings before they were,
354. and hidden things that would happen after a time were already manifest to him.
355. He had examined all that is before it came into being,

356. and the works that came to be from him waited within his Mind.

XX. Reason for Creation

357. It was not to fulfill his own need that he brought creation into being.
358. Rather, he showed his hidden Will, and how much he loves his possessions.
359. He is the Spring filled with Life who possesses Life in his Nature,
360. and he fashioned everything out of nothing, and gave vitality in rational beings.
361. His richness is his Will, and his great treasure is his Mind,
362. and while the recipients did not request it, he opened up his treasuries and enriched all.
363. His Love is extended upon all his creatures, and he visits his possessions every day.
364. He keeps his command toward natures, rational and irrational together.
365. He established a law for mortals, and they will live if they keep it,
366. and he set a spiritual power for the service of their needs.
367. These things were established from of old to happen according to his will,
368. and so through the incomprehensible Mind, he limited the time of his works.
369. Every day he proclaims his Hiddenness through the manifest works of his hands [Rom 1:19],
370. while the sun and moon in their courses relate his Greatness.

XXI. Reason for Thanksgiving

371. His orderings have a duty to give thanks to him for his gift,
372. for he adorned them in mercies and so they should give thanks to his Existence in love.
373. Nor is it to fulfill his need that there is thanksgiving from his works;

374. thanksgiving is to our advantage and is not desirable to God in himself.
375. Who could have praised his Nature when he existed eternally?
376. And who could have offered him glory before he created creatures?
377. His glory is in his own Nature, and his exaltation is with his Existence;
378. and he does not increase or decrease, since his Nature is above these things.
379. He makes us great when he calls us and brings us near to his Knowledge,
380. for when we know him he gives us the kingdom in exchange for thanksgiving.
381. In the love of the soul, let us give thanks to the Maker for his orderings,
382. since it was for our sake that he fashioned all—to him be thanksgiving from what is his!

Chapter 2

MEMRA 49: ON THE FORMING OF ADAM AND EVE, AND THE BREAKING OF THE COMMAND

INTRODUCTION

The subject matter of this memra is the story of Adam and Eve, from their creation until their expulsion from Paradise, as well as the birth of Cain and Abel, their sacrifices, and their tragic end. Thematically, however, the memra is tied together as an explication of divine pedagogy—and, if Narsai is to be believed, the biblical account of Adam and Eve is about this as well. Adam and Eve's formation and sin, as well as that of their son, is itself about God and the peculiar way he teaches human beings. The theme of God's teaching style or pedagogy is introduced as early as the second line but recurs explicitly throughout the memra, with an entire section dedicated to it as a theme (beginning with line 291). Indeed, the Narsaian theme of humanity as God's image in the sense of a king's statue is itself only an example of God's teaching. Through Adam, who represents God to the physical creation, all creatures come to learn about God. But God teaches not only for the sake of theoretical knowledge, but also for edification, and so when creatures obey Adam, they are obeying God himself (line 94).

Narsai shows himself again a highly sensitive reader of the scriptures, noting small details such as God needing to tell Adam how Eve was formed, since he had been asleep at the time (line 20), or the tempter (never named "Satan" in this memra, though certainly identified with the fallen angel in line 104) needing to ask about the command about the Tree since he was not there at the time it was given (line 134). He also affirms, in several places, the natural equality of the sexes (lines 18, 25, and 39), while maintaining the typical patriarchal authority one would expect from his time. It is relevant that the authority of Adam over Eve is not, as such, a punishment for sin, since, according to Narsai, none of the supposed "curses" were a departure from the natural order, but rather simply a return to it (line 217). Today we would term this a removal of the preternatural gifts.

The "fall" of Adam and Eve was therefore not a failure on the part of the Creator who somehow did not know what would happen (which is absurd, according to the section beginning on line 41), but rather always part of his instructional plan. Humanity was always meant to be mortal (line 57), and the result of the disobedience and the eating of the fruit was not a suddenly concocted punishment, but an establishment of the always intended natural order. What was gained in the meantime, through the whole episode of the Tree of Knowledge, was the awakening of the human conscience (line 241 and the section following 291). What is true for Adam and Eve, is, of course, true for us, and the hardships we face when God leaves us to our own devices are our opportunity to learn to trust his commands all the more.

Narsai also mentions (in line 170) a standard teaching in the literature of the Church of the East, that the fruit of the Tree of Knowledge was a fig (not an apple or any other fruit). The prooftext for this is the fig leaves with which Adam and Eve clothed themselves (Gen 3:7), since they realized they were naked and felt shame and would naturally have reached for the leaves of the tree they had just eaten from. While little is made of this idea in this memra, it is an important point in making sense of Christ's various curses on fig trees in the Gospels. Especially poignant are Christ's words in Mark 11:14: "May no one ever eat fruit from you again." Similarly popular among Church of the East writers such as Aphrahat is the supposed fire that consumed the sacrifice of Abel and therefore showed him God's acceptance (line 331).

The serpent (or "snake," as rendered here) is interpreted as a jealous angel, one who refuses to accept that a being of dust could be honored so much (line 106) and be created by a word (which the angels were not, line 114), and this causes him to be angry with God and seek vengeance against him by harming his image (line 116). The fallen angel, who is called "deceiver," "rebel," and "backbiter" throughout the Memra, is responsible not only for tempting Eve but also for introducing polytheism when he promises her, "you will become gods" (line 145). He also becomes the teacher of Cain, his first and faithful student in both envy and deception (line 330 speaks of Cain being insincere in offering his sacrifice and therefore a liar). Cain is envious of Abel and seeks revenge against God because of it (line 356), and even when he is caught red-handed, he rejects the opportunity to repent and instead impudently lies to God's face (line 377). Because of this, Cain is punished with being a vagabond but also (following the text of the *Pshyṭta*) with bodily tremors (line 397). This punishment is so severe that (contrary to the typical reading) Cain asks God for death, even one by murder, which God denies him by placing his mark upon him (line 409). The "mark of Cain" is therefore not an act of mercy on the part of God, but one of justice (that his punishment may be completed to the full) as well as pedagogy (that others may learn from Cain: line 412).

The general principle expressed in this memra is that much of what God does (and allows) in the scriptures is for us and our instruction, not for God. This is certainly the case for creation itself, but it applies even to small details such as God "making noise" in the garden or "talking to himself" regarding the Tree of Life (lines 176, 179, 233). But the whole story, from the creation of Adam until the birth of Seth (alluded to in line 413), is a story of God who teaches us (often harshly, according to our need). The disobedience of eating the fruit is a lesson about conscience; the expulsion from Paradise is a lesson about obedience; the punishment of Cain is a lesson about violence; finally, the birth of Seth is a lesson about God's loving kindness after our trial is over. We begin as innocent children, requiring milk (line 423), but after we sin, repent, and grow, we are better off even than before we lost our innocence.

TRANSLATION

I. Introduction: The King's Image, the Formation of Adam and Eve

1. By means of his image, a faraway king is honored as if nearby.
2. The Creator wanted to instruct rational beings through his image, Adam.
3. In the world, the city of the kingdom, the Creator placed his image,
4. and through a visible image, he made known his hidden Power.
5. The Creator bound up creation in his image when he fashioned it,
6. so that love toward Adam and love of him may resemble one another.
7. He made it akin to the angels, through a spiritual soul,
8. and united mute natures to it by molding its parts.
9. The Lord God fashioned Adam, dust from the earth,
10. and breathed the spirit of the living into him, making him living and rational [Gen 2:7].
11. The Lord God then saw that all he had made was completed;
12. Eve alone was missing, who would be a helper to Adam.
13. The Lord God threw a silence upon Adam and he slept,
14. and he took a rib from his ribs, and fashioned a woman like him [Gen 2:21–22].
15. He took a part from Adam, and he made a human like Adam,
16. and he filled up the part for Adam, that he may not be incomplete.
17. Adam saw a new marvel: a human that had come to be from a human,
18. who was perfect in everything, in body and soul, like he was.
19. The Maker then suggested a revelation, as he could do,
20. and made Adam know the formation of Eve, the portion from his flesh.

21. Adam prophesied and said of her who was constituted a temporal dwelling:
22. "Eve is bone of my bones, she will be called woman" [Gen 2:23].
23. In his forming, God showed Adam he had placed him as head,
24. and Eve, who fulfills the man's service, second in order.
25. Eve is equal to Adam in nature and in forming,
26. but she is less than him in authority, for Adam is the head and she the legs.

II. Eden and the Command

27. The Creator fashioned them outside the dwelling of Paradise
28. and placed them in the land of Eden, where the lights dawn [Gen 2:15].
29. The Lord God took Adam, the image of his honor,
30. and placed him in the Paradise of Eden to be his heir within it.
31. He also established a command that was fit for him at the time,
32. that he may know the power of his nature, and learn the authority of the Maker.
33. The Lord commanded Adam, and placed a limit for him regarding the tree,
34. that the discerning power of his nature be made known through this.
35. "I have given all the fruits of Paradise for your enjoyment;
36. from one [tree] only you may not eat, for death is born of its fruits [Gen 2:16–17].
37. If, then, you keep my commands, and do not presume upon the tree,
38. I will give you the fruit of life once I have tested your freedom."
39. He placed this law for both of them equally,
40. lest they blame each other when they break the commandment.

III. Theological Problems and Solutions

41. O Spring of all wisdom, who knows all before it is,
42. who, while knowing his own construction, presented things as if he did not.
43. This conversation has provoked me to speak regarding the tree,
44. how a mute thing is able to become a knower of wise things.

45. And if [God] knew that [Adam] would not keep the law he had placed for him,
46. why did he make the mortal a mortal against his will?
47. And if he did not create Adam, the head of our race, mortal,
48. why did the Knower who knows all not stop him from this?
49. Hearing the word of the reading [in Genesis] greatly troubles the simple,
50. that the disobedience of Adam made our race mortal.
51. "If the ignorance of Adam condemned Adam and his sons,
52. why did the Knower who knows all ignore this?
53. Why did he fashion creatures that are so appropriate for mortals?
54. And why males and females in nature for posterity?"
55. God forbid! It is wrong to say about the will of the Creator,
56. that he did not know that we sin, and that anger changes his will.
57. He knew when he fashioned us that he would make us mortals,
58. and his creation witnesses to his knowledge, that it was created for mortals.
59. He made us rational and discerning, and filled us with his wise things,
60. and wished to bring our discernment to the open through a trial.
61. Adam was fashioned and adorned in body and soul together,
62. but his discernment was hidden until the breaking of the commandment.
63. The commandment was like a furnace, and [God] brought Adam to it for a test.
64. His discernment was revealed, and the fact that he was not lacking in his nature.
65. He called it the Tree of Knowledge, though it was mute in its nature,
66. because the knowledge hidden in Adam was revealed through its fruit.
67. Adam was pure gold before eating of the Tree,
68. and after he ate the fruit, he showed the beauty of his features.
69. The fruit was like a furnace, and Adam like gold within it;
70. the power of eating blew into it, and he accepted the taste of knowledge.
71. The fashioning of the world to come was revealed to us through the Tree of Life;

72. [God] placed it in a place of reward, for the enrichment of his will.
73. The desire for the fruit of the Tree excited the childishness of Adam,
74. that when his soul ate of it, the Fruit of Life would renew him.
75. In announcing the two trees, [God] he told us the story of both worlds,
76. and like to children, he wished to reveal his Hiddenness through a symbol.
77. He tied earthly wealth to the Tree of Knowledge,
78. and through the Tree of Life he revealed heavenly wealth.
79. Adam was unable to learn this story at that time,
80. because it was through his enticement with the Tree that he became capable of knowledge.
81. He who created Adam and all else knew all,
82. and in the fashioning of the mortal, he wished to reveal his wisdom.
83. He forbade him from one Tree, and enticed him to the enticement of the other,
84. and [the question whether] to eat or not eat was placed in the will of Adam.

IV. Adam and Other Creatures

85. He placed the simple in the dwelling of Eden and honored them,
86. and he subjected all that was from him to the authority of his image, Adam.
87. The Lord God created cattle and wild animals,
88. and he passed them before Adam, that he may name his possessions [Gen 2:19–20].
89. His Maker gave him power to give names as much as was needed,
90. teaching him through this that he established him as master of all.
91. Marvelous how much the Creator honored his image,
92. for his lordship extends over all, and he subjugated all to it.
93. To it the living, the irrational and the rational were tied,
94. and in their relation to him, they extolled him as a king.
95. Height and depth for his dwelling; sea and land for his sustenance;

96. winds and breezes for his vitality; summer and winter for his comfort.
97. Creatures were pleased in him, and heeded him as master;
98. the angels were stirred to his service while rejoicing.
99. Mute and rational natures assembled in love for him,
100. and the nature of all of them rejoiced to share in honoring him.

V. The Evil One

101. One alone did not bind himself to the lordship of the love of Adam:
102. and harmony did not please him, for he had swallowed the arrow of envy.
103. He was not tied to others: he insisted on being an opposer,
104. he who was created good in his nature, like his fellow angels.
105. There was no cause for his envy, nor place for his bitterness,
106. besides the greatness of Adam, for he saw he was honored by all.
107. The envier's bitterness disturbed him, and he completely became an opponent,
108. and he was enraged against the Creator, because he had honored the image of Adam.
109. He burned in his thoughts with the evil wrath that ignited in him,
110. and he schemed with every chance to bring his schemes to the open.
111. His hateful anger said: "Why is Adam honored,
112. and why are mute and rational natures bound to love him?
113. I am the chief of the air and all the spiritual legions;
114. but [God] did not honor us with a word when he formed our nature!
115. But in the forming of this wretch, worthless dust of earth,
116. [he said]: 'let us make man in our image, and let him be honored like us.'
117. He made him like a master upon earth, and called him the image of his Hiddenness,
118. and he is honored by all that is like the Creator in his creation.
119. He even subjected the heavenly and the earthly to honor him!

120. He is a mortal molded from earth, wretched in his nature like dirt,
121. yet the authority of his word reigns over the lofty and the lowly!"
122. The fire of his envy brimmed, and the wrath of his jealousy blazed,
123. and he desired to go to them and bring his thoughts to the open.
124. He did not show them his schemes as he is accustomed to do now,
125. for he was not able, at that time, to resemble the form of man.
126. He made a snake his garment, and he wore it and hid his hatred,
127. lest they fear the surprise of a sight they were unused to.

VI. The Sin of the Fruit

128. The innocent ones were shocked and silenced, and kept the order of the Maker.
129. Their sight was proper to one another, in the modesty of their minds [Gen 2:25].
130. The deceiver began to speak in a voice through a harp of flesh,
131. "What has prevented you from eating every fruit?"
132. He asked them first, as if to learn truly,
133. for it was impossible to him by nature to be able to know hidden things.
134. The command that the Creator placed for Adam's house had not been heard by him,
135. and for this he asked them to learn the word and then to cause the error.
136. The snake, crafty against the clear-minded, said to Eve:
137. "Did the Creator forbid you from all the desirable fruits of Eden [Gen 3:1]?"
138. She told the story to the deceiver: "He did not forbid from the trees,
139. but from one tree there, for death is hidden in eating it" [Gen 3:2–3].
140. The deceiver found an opportunity, and began sowing his weeds [Matt 13:28],
141. and the fruit of his will bore fruit, a lie from the beginning.
142. "No, indeed, you will not die," the snake lied to Eve,
143. "you will become like gods, knowers of secret things" [Gen 3:5].

144. Woe to the hater of humanity, who troubled the peace of creation,
145. to whom it was not enough to lead astray, but even introduced polytheism!
146. Here his malice had dawned, and by his words he condemned himself:
147. he so envied Adam and his children, that he introduced many Existences.
148. "Indeed, you will become gods, and not one God only,
149. and because of this he forbade you from the Tree and called it 'death.'
150. Approach and enjoy its fruits, and your eyes will be opened,
151. for life is hidden in eating them, to make humans into gods."
152. The woman then saw the Tree, whose sight was entirely desirable,
153. and she took and ate of its fruits, and give to her partner, who was with her.
154. It says that she ate first, to pick for herself the name of gods,
155. for she was led by the promise "you will become like gods."
156. Then she who would first become a god gave some to her husband,
157. for the promise of the backbiter had misled her into a false hope.

VII. Immediate Consequences of Sin

158. Their eyes were then opened with the eating of the fruit, and they saw,
159. and they blamed themselves for the vile vision.
160. They did not know shame before eating of the tree,
161. but when they broke the commandment, they saw they were naked and undressed.
162. They adhered fig leaves out of shame from one another,
163. for the sin had made them suddenly naked and despicable.
164. Discernment had been hidden in the minds of the simple ones,
165. but when they ate of the tree, they became discerners of lamentations.
166. This is why the Tree they ate from was called "of Knowledge":

167. the knowledge of their own consciences dawned by eating of it.
168. Not that it gave knowledge (for this was not in its nature),
169. but that by means of it, they learned about disobedience.
170. They made a covering for their bodies with the leaves of that very tree;[1]
171. through the cause that gave them knowledge, by its leaves they covered their flesh.
172. He who knows hidden things did not neglect what he had made,
173. for even though he had placed the command, he knew that it causes sin [cf. Rom 7:7].
174. At the turn of the day, the sound of the feet of the Creator was heard [Gen 3:8],
175. as he came to demand of them an answer for their disobedience.
176. O uncomposed Nature, which is not limited in its works,
177. which had a sound for his walking when he came to rebuke Adam!
178. O Spring of all Wisdom, who bears the limit of all things,
179. who asks, as if not knowing, where the son of his own house is!
180. He made the sound of his walking heard in order to embarrass those who had sinned;
181. he asked, "where are you, Adam," in order to show that he knew where he was.
182. "Where are you, Adam," the Maker said to the image he had fashioned,
183. "where are you, heir of Paradise? Why have you hidden your misdeeds?"
184. O Good One, how much he loves the image, Adam the earthly one,
185. for he seeks after his lostness through mournful melodies!
186. "Where are you, O honored Adam, whom I made master on earth?
187. What has made you naked, O embarrassed one who has taken off his splendor?"
188. Adam responded to his Maker: "I heard your sound and hid myself;
189. I am ashamed to see your face, for I am naked and unclothed" [Gen 3:10].

190. The Lord said to his servant: "What has made you naked?
191. Who has taken off your covering, O honored one who has disgraced himself?
192. Has the sight of the Tree enticed you to eat,
193. and the limit I set made you naked, without garments?"
194. Adam the young man said: "The woman gave me and I ate" [Gen 3:12],
195. thinking he would show he was distant from the crime.
196. God said to Eve: "What is this you have done?"
197. She passed the cause to another: "the snake misled me and I ate" [Gen 3:13].
198. [God] did not then ask the deceiver the way he had asked Adam,
199. for he has no cause for his envy, to say "another misled me."

VIII. God's Judgments

200. The Creator who had fashioned them then began passing judgment,
201. and he began with the snake, for it had been the cause of the evils.
202. He cursed the snake, cursing the backbiter,
203. commanding the fall of the one who would deign to take away his authority.
204. He was the prince of the air, and the general of his companions,
205. but because he led Adam and Eve into error, he fell to the earth and became feeble.
206. God said to the snake: "Because you have done this and made them err,
207. you are cursed among all crawling things, and your movements are bound up in you.
208. Dirt will be your food, and upon the dirt your turning,
209. and because you banished the heir from his glory, your punishment will be upon dirt.
210. You will henceforth be an enemy to Adam and all his sons,
211. and he will press your head into dirt, and you will strike him when he sins" [Gen 3:14–15].
212. After the snake, [he spoke] to Eve, judged after him,

213. for she had accepted his advice first, and extended her hand to the fruit.
214. He cursed her with pains and lamentation, and bound her with the chords of childbirth,
215. and gave her to be subjected to the man, to fulfill his neediness [Gen 3:16].
216. O what wise devices the Creator has for what he has made,
217. for he placed things fastened to nature as if they were rebukes.
218. Finally, the Creator cursed Adam, the image of his Honor,
219. for the harshness of the judgment of the snake and of Eve had become bland.
220. So the Lord said to Adam, the Maker to the image he had fashioned:
221. "Because of you, I curse fruits, seeds, and trees.
222. Because you listened to the voice of your wife, and ate the fruit of Knowledge,
223. you will become a laborer on earth, and only then will it give you fruits.
224. You are dirt, O Adam, from earth, and to the earth you will return, because you sinned.
225. Because you despised the command that I had placed for you,
226. the rational and the mute will despise you.
227. Lo, you are henceforth a god, according to the deception of the evil one;
228. command, then, the natures to obey you, if his prophecy is true."[2]

IX. Adam and Eve Cast Out of Paradise, Lesson Learned

229. The Creator made these sounds heard while he derided him:
230. "Lo, Adam is like one of us now; he has now become a god.
231. Let us cast him out of Paradise, this heir who did not discern his dignity,
232. lest he also extend his hand and take of the Tree of Life" [Gen 3:22].
233. The Creator made these sounds heard in order to teach,

234. that [Adam's] ignorance may grow in his own eyes, and that he may hate sin more.
235. If he breaks the command, God will make him a stranger to his dwelling;
236. how much, then, should he honor his Creator, and sin no more.
237. As lovely as Paradise was, and as much delight as he found in it,
238. so much he complained of sin when he became weak and was expelled.
239. He broke the command as if he were a teacher, and [God] instructed the simpleton;
240. and the passing of judgment and punishment made him hate sin.
241. Through the Tree, the covering over his mind was uncovered,
242. and through the longing of its fruit, the freedom in him was made known.
243. Adam began to prophesy, through the power the Creator gave him,
244. and he spoke openly of the things to come in his nature.
245. Adam called the name of his wife Eve, the Bearer of Life,[3]
246. for she was destined to become a mother, and bear man in posterity.
247. The Lord God then made garments for Adam's family,
248. since their minds were moved to cover their bodies [Gen 3:21].
249. The Creator clothed them with garments of skin,
250. because he had let knowledge dwell in them, and so their needs were filled.
251. Everything of the judgment and rebuke had occurred for their instruction,
252. and to comfort them, he fulfilled the needs of their bodies.
253. He commanded them to leave the beautiful dwelling of Eden,
254. lest they enjoy the fruits of the Tree that gives life.
255. Lest Adam turn and take from the Tree of Life,
256. he went out to the place he had been fashioned, to work the land of curses.
257. One day, the earthly ones were heirs of the dwelling of Paradise,
258. and by the turn of the day, they had moved out, sojourners in a different land.

259. In the morning, they had accepted their forming, and after nine hours rebuke;
260. on the same day they were formed, they ate, sinned, and went out.
261. The prophet writes for us in the Spirit, that it was day in the land of Eden,
262. and he said, "at the turn of the day," so it was not a different day [cf. Gen 2:4].
263. Adam went out from Paradise and dwelt in the land around it,
264. and it saddened the earthly one to become a stranger to his dwelling.

X. Outside Paradise

265. [God] closed off Paradise in his face with a spear, a weapon of war,
266. and set up a guardian, a fearful cherub, to protect it [Gen 3:24].
267. O wise Creator, how he loves his fashionings,
268. for he keeps miserable things from him, that they may honor him with glorifications.
269. He greatly honored Paradise, by setting up a guardian for it,
270. so that Adam might know his stupidity and return to seek its honor.
271. [God] made [Adam] aware of his sin, that he may honor the command of his Lord,
272. for when he worked the earth with his strength, he might know what he had lost.
273. Adam left Paradise, and his sadness was yoked to him,
274. and the hater began to brag, "Adam has become my slave!"
275. The spiritual assemblies mourned, for they saw the misery of the honored one,
276. and they all wore sadness, for the freeborn now labored in slavery.
277. They had rejoiced in his forming, and were joyful in seeing him,
278. for they had seen that their nature was akin to his.
279. They put on the suffering of love, for death had come to rule over Adam,
280. and they ached as they saw that his soul would divide from his body.

281. The whole creation mourned over the beautiful image of Adam,
282. for it had been joined to him in love, and sin had detached their binding.
283. The spiritual beings turned their faces away from him like strangers,
284. and they no longer wished to move the elements in aid of his life.
285. The beasts also rebelled against him, and creeping things ran and hid in the earth,
286. and all his possessions despised him, for he had despised the word of his Lord.
287. Through his will, he had become a stranger to the lordship given to him,
288. and the lowly things that had become rebels deeply despised his honor.
289. The mute and rational natures put on mourning due to his leaving,
290. and only one rejoiced: he who had ached at his honor.

XI. Divine Pedagogy

291. [God] gave the mortal a dwelling in the neighborhood of Paradise,
292. that he may always be reminded of both his inheritance and his stupidity.
293. The Creator schemed, with these devices, to lead Adam,
294. and he dragged him to knowledge through the harshness of his punishments.
295. These things were always hidden in the knowledge of the Creator of all,
296. and he brought them into the open through the breaking of the command.
297. He had created Adam a mortal, and had formed an appropriate dwelling for him,
298. and he placed the cause of mortality as the sin of the breaking of the command.
299. He instructed all of nature by means of Adam's kin,

300. for if sin made death, we should therefore hate what has killed us.
301. The judgment was great, and greatly led the simple one,
302. for if sin threw death into the mix, he should learn who it is who gives life.
303. The command instructed him as well and made him know his own nature,
304. lest the earthly one become inflated and forget his feeble nature.
305. The Maker piled up wise lessons for what he had made,
306. and made him the master of his freedom, who is led according to his own will.

XII. Cain and Abel

307. He established pleasant powers within him, natural love and desire,
308. so that the sustaining of his whole species may be from the source of his body.
309. And so Adam knew his partner, and Eve conceived life;
310. she gave birth to a child and called him "A possession from God."[4]
311. Lo, the wisdom of our nature, which the Maker moves within it:
312. the gift that he first gave he considered his own possession.[5]
313. Eve rejoiced in the possession of Cain, the first firstborn,
314. and after him she gave birth to another and called him by the name "emptiness."[6]
315. She named Abel "emptiness," for his life would vanish like emptiness,
316. hiding in her prophecy that his brother would destroy his life.
317. Eve and Adam saw that they had gained rational fruits,
318. and those who through sin had become mortals gained life through their children.
319. Abel became a keeper of sheep, and Cain a worker of the earth,
320. and the first fruits of their work they offered to the God of all.
321. Abel offered a lamb, and along with his offering, his will;
322. Cain an herb from the earth, but did not mix his will with it [Gen 4:2–4].
323. In their offerings, the choices of their minds were revealed,

324. and it was exposed and confuted to the deceiving one[7] that his offering was rejected.
325. The Maker who had confuted Eve and Adam when they erred
326. wished to bring to light the will of Abel and his brother.
327. His Knowledge became a balance to weigh them both,
328. and the love of the innocent one outweighed the will of the deceptive one.
329. With love, he accepted the offering of Abel who was pure of heart,
330. and he despised and rejected that of Cain, whose intention was not pure.
331. The Creator showed through fire whose offering was accepted,
332. for it overcame and consumed that of Abel, but did not go near that of Cain.[8]
333. Cain put on great mourning, and his face was greatly downcast;
334. he murmured against his Maker, asking why his offering was rejected.
335. The Lord then said to Cain, openly in a calm voice,
336. "If your will becomes noble, I will accept your gift,
337. but if the bitterness of your mind does not transform into sweetness,
338. your sin lays down at the door and will not leave your body.
339. Look, O envier, your offering I give back to you—why are you sad?
340. You are in charge of what is yours; go manage it yourself."

XIII. The Murder of Abel

341. Cain's will did not change after his rebuke,
342. and he did not accept correction despite the admonition offered him.
343. He complained in pride, like the backbiter,
344. and he added wrath to wrath, and his mind conceived murder.
345. The rebel thought that, when he killed the innocent one,
346. he would upset the Creator since he had rejected his offering.
347. Through Abel he would have revenge against the Maker,
348. like his teacher Satan, who reviled his Fashioner through Adam.
349. So Cain said to his brother, the envier to the innocent:

350. "Let us go to the field and see the beauty of the earth" [Gen 4:8].
351. He who was hot with envy constructed a covenant,
352. that through the guise of love, he may go and fulfill his wrath upon the simple one.
353. The simple believed the crafty, like Eve [believed] the deceiver,
354. and he went out with him to the field, innocent, not knowing.
355. Cain the killer assaulted, and he betrayed natural love;
356. he killed his brother in envy, in order to upset God.
357. O heart that gave birth to murder, new deed upon the earth;
358. O rebellious will, which tread the path to the house of the dead!
359. Through Abel, the path was tread, and death began to walk it;
360. and Adam learned, through this, that he is also mortal.
361. The backbiter, through Cain, fulfilled the wrath of his envy,
362. and he was comforted in the fullness of time, for he saw that death had been given authority.
363. The teacher taught his student deception and disparagement,
364. and he hid the murdered one in the earth, lest he confess when questioned.[9]
365. The killer thought that the blood of Abel was hidden,
366. and he did not know that the One who rejected his offering saw him.
367. Cain hid the murdered one, and hid his will along with him;
368. he wished to hide his deed from the One who knows hidden things.

XIV. The Judgment of Cain

369. The Maker spoke out of the silence, and called loudly to the murderer:
370. "O envier and deceiver, how did the innocent one offend you?
371. Where is Abel your brother?" the Lord said to Cain [Gen 4:9].
372. He answered him impudently, knowing why he called him.
373. O Knower of all, who asks as if he does not know;
374. as he asked in Paradise, thus he asks the murderer.
375. In Eden, he asked Adam "where are you, Adam?" while he saw him;
376. here he asked Cain "where is your brother?" about Abel, while seeing him.

377. He asked as if he did not know, that perhaps the rebel might repent,
378. so that if he confessed his offense, he may extend forgiveness to him.
379. Cain was the first and best-prepared student of the tactics of his teacher,
380. and the teacher and his student lied, so justice ensnared them.
381. "Where is your brother Abel?" He did not wish to confess his crime,
382. but rather answered maliciously, "Am I my brother's keeper [Gen 4:9]?"
383. He spoke impudently, and the murderer did not feel shame:
384. "If I were to destroy your beloved, what would I owe to you?"
385. Justice bound Cain's voice with terrible cords,
386. he who did not want to confess his will, and it revealed, made known, and laid him bare.
387. "What is this that you have done?" the Lord said to Cain.
388. "The blood of your brother cries out to me," as he judged the murderer [Gen 4:10].
389. "You are henceforth cursed on the earth, and the earth will not be formed under you;
390. because it has received innocent blood, you will accept curses along with it.
391. Your body will suffer in trembling,[10] in place of the body your hands have destroyed,
392. and you will be a terror to those who see you, for your heart did not fear murder.
393. Because you have spilled first blood, and have offered first fruits to Death,
394. I will exact revenge for the innocent blood on your hands for seven generations [Gen 4:24].
395. Because you have trodden the path to the house of the dead, on which many men will journey,
396. I will make a lesson of you, that I may avenge blood with blood."
397. The threats became reality, and clothed the murderer with trembling;
398. his flesh shook with the earth, shaking shattered him entirely.
399. He besought the Creator with unwilling repentance,

400. and requested death for himself, that he may be saved from punishments.
401. Cain said to God: "You have cast me out from the earth,
402. and clothed me with quaking and trembling, which are terrible to see.
403. I request one thing, if I can, for you to grant me in your mercies:
404. that your curses may be taken from my body through death."
405. The Lord said to Cain: "Not thus, murderer,
406. not thus is your error avenged by death.
407. I have measured out the harsh tortures of your evil for seven generations,
408. and the punishment of your murder will be spoken of in the whole world."
409. The Lord placed a sign upon Cain, that he may not die through the hand of man [Gen 4:15],
410. placing this sign, that his command may protect him.
411. He protected the murderer for the terror of the generations to come,
412. that when they inquire after the punishment, they may flee from murder.

XV. Seth and Divine Pedagogy

413. The time was fulfilled, and Eve and Adam were comforted as they procreated [Gen 4:25];
414. the grief over their children doubled their own error.
415. They wept over Abel who was killed, and whose image death had ruined,
416. and they mourned over Cain, who had brought quaking into creation.
417. The Creator bound them in love of natural affections,
418. for the pleasure of nature dulls the pain of difficulties.
419. The Maker taught us, through this covenant,
420. that we may gain love for him through the wounds and pains of death.
421. He occupied us with earthly things, through earthly fashioning,
422. that when we become aware of our weariness, we may ask for life without labor.

423. He brought up our childishness with milk [cf. 1 Cor 3:2], with weak things according to our strength,
424. that when we grow to completion, we may be in knowledge of life.
425. He did not give us authority over our treasure when we were children in our knowledge,
426. for as long as an heir is childish, he cannot take care of his possessions [Gal 4:1].
427. Through the life of the soul, he granted temporal life to sustain us;
428. and when we become immortal, he will protect us by the power of the Spirit.
429. The Creator of our nature has persuaded us through everything in our nature,
430. and has led us wisely, from meagre things to great things.
431. So that when we learn in knowledge who has brought us these things,
432. we may confess the Power that formed all, who loves our nature so much.

Chapter 3

MEMRA 3: ON ABRAHAM

INTRODUCTION

This memra follows the events of Abraham's life from his calling to leave Ur of the Chaldeans up to the sacrifice of Isaac (Gen 17—22). The latter event is the memra's focus and culmination, and Narsai takes time to present a christological exposition of the Akedah (Isaac's sacrifice), illustrating how Christ's sacrifice on the cross (and in a more subtle way, in the eucharistic liturgy) fulfills the symbol shown in Isaac.

This style of memra, similar to many of Narsai's, has a perhaps unfamiliar style of spirituality. On the surface, it may appear that much of this memra is simply a recounting of events. But Narsai is not simply restating a narrative. In the midst of his exposition he takes the time to reflect, verse by verse, on the meaning of the events within the big picture of God's providential care for the human race. This is an invitation for us to a similar kind of slow, reflective, beat-by-beat reading of scripture that is distinct from both a bare textual reading and an exegetical analysis. There is movement through events, but the movement is methodical and slow-paced; there is analysis, but the analysis comes in the midst of, and never at the expense of, the narrative itself. The primary thing to Narsai (at least in memre such as this) is the story of God's work in the world. Theological speculation comes second, and within this context.

The overall theme of the memra is announced in the first lines: God chose Abraham and the people that are his offspring to teach the other nations about himself. The events of Abraham's life, therefore, are meant to be known by both Jews and non-Jews, in order to lead all to a unified faith (line 64). Indeed, Abraham's leaving of his own people is depicted as a kind of rejection of nationalism itself (lines 47–48), not only of polytheism and sorcery (lines 49–52). Thus God's goal is to make all the nations into his own people, with himself as their king (line 18). Abraham's election, therefore, is not a rejection of other nations, but rather their ultimate salvation (lines 19–20).

The "Voice" (*qala*) personified through much of the memra, as well as the "revelations" (*gilyane* or *galyatha*) through which Abraham understands God's requests, are true supernatural events and cannot be otherwise for Narsai, since human power is helpless to accomplish the love and unity God wills for the human race. Indeed, the human power sought by the nations is symbolized by Abraham and Sarah's sterility: it bears no fruit without God's blessing (line 66). Similarly, the birth of Isaac represents hope for the hopeless and life for those who are lifeless (line 240). This is all fulfilled in Christ (himself Son of the Virgin), who was sacrificed for the salvation of the nations (lines 244–249). It is in Christ that the nations who are dead in sin finally bear living fruit.

The narrative of the Theophany to Abraham reveals the Persons of the Trinity as well as their single Divine Nature, since the three men who visit Abraham in Genesis 18 are addressed by him in the singular "my lord" (lines 180–186). Both Abraham and Sarah's trust in the promise, despite their sterility, is a sign of faith and hope, again to be instructive for the nations. Sodom and Gomorrah are destroyed, in contrast, because of their disobedience and rebellion (line 196), but even their destruction is instructive of God's justice (line 222), as Lot's survival is of God's mercy (line 224).

The sacrifice of Isaac depicts Abraham as a man of virtue whose mind is able to overcome his affections (lines 274–276), as well as a priest of a new order (line 277). But Isaac is the prefigurement of Christ, the true Lamb of God who is God (line 266). Thus through Abraham, God revealed not only his will for the human race, nor only his Triune Personhood, but most significantly he revealed the Cross of Christ. Narsai's exposition of the narrative shows God discussing this explicitly with Abraham (lines 292–308). Christ's death on the cross is prefigured by the wood; his resurrection is prefigured (loosely) by Isaac not actually dying; the nails in his hands by Isaac's binding. Thus Narsai takes quite seriously (and quite literally) Christ's statement in John 8:56 that Abraham saw his day. This is central to this memra's theme: Abraham is the father of faith and the instructor of all the nations because he believed in Christ's sacrifice symbolically through the sacrifice of Isaac. Thus he is an example to all the nations because his faith in Christ prefigures the faith of all.

There are typical "Nestorian" christological terms in this memra, such as the Word of God putting on humanity like a "garment" (line 319) and the Pauline terminology of an indwelling of goodwill (line 321), but as usual Narsai dodges charges of heresy, affirming (for example) that all will worship the Godhead through the Body of Christ (line 322). Narsai's Christology will be discussed in greater detail in later chapters.

The memra concludes with a group of exhortations to the weary to take solace in Abraham's journey (line 349), to the rich to imitate Abraham's generosity (lines 351–352), and to those who are childless to trust in God's power rather than resorting to sinful means of procuring offspring (lines 362–364). God intends Abraham and Sarah to be an example to all nations, not only through the sacrifice of Isaac, but also through the lives that they lived.

TRANSLATION

I. Introduction: The Chosen People

1. The Lord of creation chose one people to be his own,
2. and through it he taught of his great power to all the nations.
3. He left all the peoples in the hands of the freedom he had placed in nature,
4. and through his revelations he united one inheritance to himself.
5. He cast the seal of his Name upon them and signed them,
6. that they may not mingle with the nations and forget his Name.
7. He enclosed them with the Law of his words like a rampart,
8. and bound them with observances as with cords.
9. He chose a dwelling in the people he chose, that it may be his,

10. to teach them how much he loves the sons of his house.
11. He obliged them with sacrifices of flesh and blood,
12. that they may offer him sacrifices of love as to a Hidden One.
13. He honored them before the eyes of the nations by the power of his aid,
14. and exalted them above the peoples through the victory of his power.
15. He showed that he is just, who continued with them though they had sinned,
16. and preached his power through the victory that he granted in battles.
17. For all the peoples, he ordered and raised up rulers,
18. but in the people he chose, he led them through his own Name [cf. 1 Sam 8:4–9].
19. He did not reject the peoples and choose the people[1] out of malice,
20. because that which would happen, he foreshadowed and showed in the people he chose.
21. Through one people, he wished to instruct all the peoples,
22. that his signal had made all things and upholds all things.
23. He placed the people as a foundation for the beginning of a house,
24. and he completed the building of the peoples upon it, as it pleased him.

II. Abraham's Election

25. He planted Abraham among the peoples as a root,
26. and brought up his soul through divine revelations.
27. He cut off a shoot from a bitter-souled tree,
28. he turned and planted it, and its branches bore fruits of glory.
29. From paganism, deprived of spiritual fruits,
30. the love of Abraham flowered with pleasant fruits.
31. He bore, of himself, and gave a voice of religion,
32. and he offered a groan of faith like his first fruits.
33. The signal of the power of the Creator dragged him from Babylon,[2]
34. to leave his land and go live in a strange land.
35. He who knows all revealed this to him mysteriously,[3]

36. that he may leave error and come to be enlightened by the light of his knowledge:
37. "Unbind your will from the chains of mute idols,
38. and I will give you freedom of soul regarding your worship.
39. Leave behind the inheritance of the thorny house of your fathers,
40. and I will give you the inheritance of love to my Lordship."
41. He did not mourn when he left his country and deserted his people,
42. nor was he indignant by asking why another country.
43. The name of a vexing foreign land did not upset him,
44. and the deprivation of love among strangers did not sadden him.
45. He left his land by a road full of pain and suffering,
46. and along with his body, he girt his thoughts for the sake of his Lord.
47. He became a stranger to the fellowship of the sons of his people,
48. and he loved and held dear being in the household of his Lord.
49. He left Babylon, a fountain pouring out Chaldeanness,[4]
50. and he came to Haran, a mother giving birth to sorcery.
51. The clarity of his soul was not troubled by the fortune-telling of Babylon,
52. nor was his faith shaken by the idols of Haran [Gen 11:31].
53. His will's love was not changed in changing lands,
54. nor was it weakened through the pretensions of idolatry.
55. The country could not weaken his righteousness,
56. for his will's love strengthened his faith.

III. Abraham and Sarah's Sterility and God's Promise

57. His body was deprived of bodily reproduction [Gen 15:2],
58. and so he bore the fruits of praise in his mind at every hour.
59. Sterility of the flesh had accompanied him and Sarah,
60. but their thoughts begot the sound of thanksgiving at every hour.
61. His Lord had tested him through sterility as through a fire,
62. and he showed his beauty through an undivided thanksgiving.
63. He did not teach him who knew him before his fashioning;
64. rather, he revealed the firmness of his faith to the ages to come.
65. He moved in a pilgrimage among strangers,

66. to sow love and faith in a sterile land.
67. He left Haran to go to the land that was promised to him,
68. and there he cast the fire of love and burned up the thorns.
69. He went out rejoicing in the promise of his Lord who cannot lie,
70. and without hope, he believed in the hope that he would inherit the earth.
71. The righteous man went out with the covenant of the land that was promised to him,
72. and he firmly believed that his seed contained nations.
73. He was a sojourner in the land he would accept through the promise,
74. and like a stranger he dwelt in the country that was promised him.
75. He increased and worked the land of Canaan through his revelations,
76. and he returned the fruits of hope, love, and faith.
77. Every day, he heard the Voice: "Your seed shall inherit the earth,"
78. but there was no heir or confirmation of a sound without deeds.
79. "Lift your eyes and look at the flames of fire in the sky,
80. and measure out the sand on the seashore as much as you can:
81. thus will the child of your loins multiply" [Gen 15:5], the Voice cried out to him,
82. "and your seed will be uncountable, as much as I have spoken.
83. Stretch out your thoughts to the four corners and see the lands
84. that your seed is destined to tread through tribute.
85. I have vowed to myself, and I do not lie in my hidden Nature:
86. in you the peoples of earth will be blessed through faith [Gen 12:3; Gen 15:6; Rom 4:3].
87. In exchange for the ugly garment of paganism you have taken off,
88. I will cover the shame of the peoples with your faith.
89. Because you have trodden the path through the confession of one Creator,
90. I will drag all toward faith in me through the path of your love.
91. Because you have opened the door to my hidden Majesty through your will,
92. through you I will open the door of life to those dead in sin.
93. Lest you doubt my promises while they are far off,
94. I make you the head of life in the kingdom above.

95. Because my hidden Majesty has dawned within your conscience,
96. from you will dawn the One who will gather the peoples into one.
97. In place of exile in countries filled with vexation,
98. I will make you a harbor of peace for all who are wearied.
99. Upon you I will build a building of love and faith,
100. and in you I will fasten the hope of life for all the peoples."
101. He who knows all proved the upright man through his promises,
102. and he believed in the distant things as if they were nearby.

IV. The Flight to Egypt

103. While [God] knew that [Abram] would not doubt in his promises,
104. he revealed the truth of his faith through a test.
105. He knew before he tested that his love was true,
106. and he had proved him before he called him not to doubt.
107. He wished to exhort the sons of his species through his works,
108. and he wrote them in the Scripture of his words, that they may imitate him.
109. He engraved the beauty of his faith like a statue,
110. that each may fasten his own endurance upon his conscience.
111. His body had dried up in sterility like a drought,
112. but his soul was watered by the stream of the Spirit, and he bore fruits.
113. He had said that he would give the land of Canaan to his seed,
114. but he drove him out of it to the land of Egypt like a captive [Gen 12:10].
115. He raised a shoot but struck the earth with a terrible famine,
116. that he may run from it to another country because of the famine.
117. He intensified his test by the changing of countries,
118. that all may hear that he did not weaken because of his troubles.
119. He ran from famine, to save himself in the land of Egypt,
120. and he divided his loins and plundered them for the part that was with him.
121. He did not complain that evil men had taken the land of his seed,

122. nor did he doubt because they had taken from him the vine of his fruits.
123. It was certain to him that the Voice that called him could not lie,
124. that another society would reach the land of his society.
125. He became rich in the land, and he increased greatly in his abundance [cf. Gen 13:6],
126. and the richness of his faith surpassed that of his earthly things.
127. He lived in a corner that demons had farmed with idolatry,
128. and the fruits of his faith blossomed among the weeds.
129. O tree that raised itself among the thorns,
130. and subdued the fruits of the evil by the branches of his love!
131. O sojourner who entered among strangers in exile,
132. whom kings and freemen knelt before unwillingly!
133. O refugee who came to fulfill the needs of his life,
134. and who lifted a staff and struck the country's citizens!
135. The Lord struck Pharaoh and the sons of his house,
136. because of Sarah, the wife of Abram, whom he had seized from him [Gen 12:17].
137. While in the world, [Abram] was tortured regarding the perseverance of his portion,
138. his riches surpassed and grew through the command of his Lord.
139. His honor increased by means of Sarah whom the king had taken,
140. and he confessed his Lord who had given him wealth through these pretexts.
141. The wise man became rich in a country that was poor in knowledge,
142. and he took his wealth and went to the land that was promised to him.

V. The Theophany to Abraham

143. He returned and settled in the land of Canaan, as in his own land,
144. gazing at the promise that his Lord had given him [Gen 13:14].
145. The years of his life had completed ninety-nine,

146. and [God] spoke to him through a revelation, that he should circumcise his flesh [Gen 17:11].
147. The servant fell upon his face, and worshipped before his Maker,
148. and he made a covenant with him to sign his seed in his Name.
149. He changed his name, which had been given in the name of one people,
150. and he changed his name to one that translates to "Father of the Peoples."
151. Along with changing his name and calling him "Father of the Peoples" [Gen 17:5],
152. he cried out and said he would henceforth receive the promised child [Gen 17:19].
153. "Lo, my promise to you is fulfilled in deed,
154. and I give you a son of grace, outside the natural order.
155. Lo, I whet your dead body, and give it seed,
156. and I germinate the shoot from the sterile one who had aged and worn out.
157. I will console Sarah the sterile from her sterility,
158. and I will gladden her from her bereavement with a fruit from her.
159. I will remove the taunt of her flesh, the name of sterility,
160. and I will give her a reward, a child, for her perseverance."
161. The promises were fulfilled, the pledges confirmed, toward the sterile ones,
162. and the Hidden One came openly to give a reward to the just.
163. The Lord revealed himself to Abram in the land of Mamre,
164. and he sat at the door of his house when the day became hot.
165. O fervent one who is not weakened by the bitter heat,
166. and who despises comforts, that we may not be impoverished by accepting him.
167. He lifted his eyes as he looked at the crossroads,
168. that he may fulfill his love through providing for the poor.
169. Abraham saw a new and amazing sight:
170. three angels wearing the form of man [Gen 18:2].
171. He ran rejoicing and fell and worshipped before the spirits,
172. and he convinced them to fulfill his love in comforting them.
173. He called to them by the Name of the Creator through a revelation:

174. "Do not, O Lord, pass by from the house of your servant who awaits you."
175. O Being Hidden from all and Invisible,
176. who reveals himself to Abraham through the form of man!
177. O just man who was worthy to see mysteriously
178. the Word of the Father who was destined to come and wear the body of man!
179. Three men entered the house of Abraham in this form,
180. and Abram spoke with one alone as if to God.[5]
181. The Word of the Father wore this form mysteriously,
182. and Abram rejoiced, for he saw the Hidden One revealed in the flesh.
183. He had a reception for a lord and servants (according to what he saw),
184. and he comforted them with bread and water (according to what he thought).
185. The spirits themselves showed him as he was prepared to see,
186. for they showed that they ate (while they did not eat) for the sake of his love.
187. The nature of spirits cannot take food,
188. and spiritual beings are not nourished with earthly things.
189. Out of love for Abram they took comfort in food and showed that they ate,
190. and they remained without nourishment as they always were.
191. The "lord and servants" accepted the love of the good servant,
192. and they rewarded him with conception and birth beyond nature.
193. He said to him, "At this time [next year], I will return to you,
194. and Sarah the sterile will have a fruit while she is alive" [Gen 18:10].

VI. Sodom and Gomorrah

195. He accepted his love and gave the reward of hope in conception,
196. and he revealed and showed the condemnation of the evil who trample his commands.
197. "The shouting of Sodom and Gomorrah has entered before me,

198. and I will come down and see if the deed is as bad as the sound" [Gen 18:20].
199. O Knower of all whose love bears the difficulty of our species,
200. who while knowing our evil inclination, delays his anger.
201. He revealed to Abram that he would rain down fire upon the rebellious,
202. and he showed that he would hold back if there are any righteous ones, and still his wrath.
203. Abraham saw that the will of his Lord wanted to forgive,
204. and he begged and pled that, if possible, he would cease his anger.
205. He humbled himself before the Maker through his begging,
206. for he saw his nature was too small to plead for forgiveness.
207. [God] accepted the begging of his love, as much as he pled:
208. "if there are any righteous, I will not destroy the country in my wrath."
209. Abram asked, "if there are fifty, would you have pity on the place [Gen 18:24]?"
210. and the Sweet One went down with him to ten.
211. "If there are ten just men in Sodom, I will forgive it";
212. while knowing there was not even one, he said "if there are."
213. The spirits left Abram and came to Sodom,
214. and the kinsmen of Abram accepted them like Abram.
215. Fleshy ones lusted with the desire of the flesh for the spirits,
216. for they saw them as if wearing a furnace.
217. He who knows all sent them with this agreement,
218. that they may be witnesses to the evil of man who destroyed order.
219. And because the wretched nature assaulted and ruined its path,
220. the Good One did not mingle mercies with his wrath when he judged them.
221. With fire, he trampled the fervor of the desire of the rabid,
222. and made an example of the place to wickedness to rebellious men.
223. He saved the righteous one from destruction with the wicked [Gen 19:15],
224. and showed his mercies through one who was rescued, for he is the Friend of man.

225. Abraham rejoiced at seeing the Hidden One through his revelations,
226. and while he is earthly, he was worthy to speak with Existence.
227. His Lord accepted the pleading of his love through Lot who was saved,
228. and he consoled him and gave him the reward of conception and a child.

VII. The Birth and Sacrifice of Isaac

229. The promises were fulfilled, the pledges confirmed, and Sarah conceived,
230. and gave birth to a child beyond the order imposed upon nature [Gen 21:3].
231. The righteous ones who awaited the reward of payment accepted their pay,
232. and they gave thanks to the Voice that had whetted their flesh.
233. The sterile righteous ones accepted what was promised through Isaac,
234. and they rejoiced to see the Distant One through him who was near.
235. He who knows all comforted them with a parable,
236. and showed them what was to come through a mystery.
237. In place of what they had distinctly willed, they knew the Lord,
238. and he made them worthy to see the mystery of the expectation of the peoples.
239. He gave a reward to the wills of the bereaved,
240. that hope to the hopeless may dawn from them and increase.
241. They rejoiced and were comforted at seeing a hope that could not lie,
242. for the One who promised sealed and gave them through vows.
243. Even the Principle of the fulfillment of the mysteries to the just,
244. verified and spoke, "Abraham saw my day and rejoiced in my expectation" [John 8:56].
245. Through the birth of Isaac, he comforted them in their sterility,
246. and brought them as in a furnace to the mystery of his Sacrifice.
247. The Lord called through revelations, "Abram, Abram!

248. Bring your only-begotten and take him up for me to the top of the mountain [Gen 2:22].
249. I ask you to offer me a new sacrifice,
250. for I know your love to me, which does not lie."
251. The good servant did not delay in the command of his Lord,
252. and did not murmur to turn and take what his words had promised.
253. Abram began a day after he was commanded,
254. and he prepared wood for the fire and took it with a pure heart [Gen 22:3].
255. The Voice that led him on the path dragged him for three days,
256. and the love of the just man did not divide from his readiness.
257. The One who called him revealed and showed him the place of sacrifice,
258. and he left his servants and took his son as he willed.
259. He took a knife, and fire, and wood, to prepare the sacrifice,
260. and did not reveal the mystery of the killing of Isaac to his household [Gen 22:5–6].
261. The servants remained in this agreement in the foothills of the mountain:
262. that he would go up and worship, he and the young man, and return to them.
263. The sacrifice spoke to the sacrificer, the son to his father,
264. "Lo, here is the fire, and wood for the sacrifice—where is the lamb [Gen 22:7]?"
265. The father answered his child with a hopeful voice,
266. "My God will find and prepare for himself[6] a lamb for the sacrifice."
267. He comforted his son with the expectation of his Lord, to not sadden him,
268. and he accepted that the word of his father would not deceive.
269. He built an altar, and placed wood around it, and bound the sacrifice,
270. and with his will he drew his knife to destroy his son [Gen 22:9–10].
271. O mind who bound up his love with a body,
272. the love of whose binding is untied by the love of his Lord.
273. O mortal, clothed with the sadness of the sufferings of the flesh,

274. who controlled himself when the whips of love beat upon him.
275. O athlete who held a match against himself,
276. and conquered the passions of the body by the power of his mind.
277. The exalted ones were amazed at the endurance of soul of the new priest,
278. who held back his mercies to bind up his love with love of his Lord.
279. He held the knife to destroy his son, undividedly,
280. and the Voice stopped him: "I do not desire the sacrifice of man."
281. The Lord called to him: "Abram, Abram," speaking to him [Gen 22:12],
282. "stop your hand from your inheritance, and do not destroy him.
283. Your sacrifice is accepted along with your will, as that which is sacrificed,
284. and you have made known your love to me before the spirits.
285. In exchange for the fact that you obeyed me and did not delay to obey my command,
286. your seed will be like the sand of the seashore.
287. Because you did not hold back your son from being a sacrifice to a knife,
288. by my Nature I vow to pour out my blessings upon your children.
289. In place of the offering your hands offered with a full heart,
290. in you I bind up the peace that disobedience had torn apart.

VIII. Isaac and Christ

291. I do not desire that the sacrifice of a man be offered to me;
292. I wish to reveal to you what is to come by what has occurred.
293. By the sacrifice of a Man, I will someday bind up the peace of all,
294. and I have prefigured and depicted, in the sacrifice of your son, the death of my Beloved.
295. If your son dies, he does not repay the debt of his species;
296. but my Son, from your seed, will unravel the authority of Death by his death.
297. I will take One from among your seed in the fullness of time,[7]
298. and I will make him the perfect Sacrifice that forgives all.

299. Through the death of Isaac, I have signified the death of Him who dies without dying,
300. for he will die, but his body will not decay in Sheol [Ps 16:10].
301. By the binding of the hands of Isaac, I depict the nails in his hands,
302. here in mystery, and there in truth and in deed.
303. Love and mercies toward his Lord had bound Isaac,
304. and love and mercies for his species will bind [Christ].
305. In Isaac, you fulfilled love toward my Lordship,
306. and in [Christ] I will show my richness and love toward all.
307. In Isaac I have depicted [Christ's] death and the resurrection of his life,
308. for I will raise him after his death and he will not decay.
309. A male beast saved Isaac through a command,
310. and [Christ] will be saved from death through the hidden Power that dwells in him.
311. I have made you the head of life, O Abram, here and there,
312. through the mystery of the truth, I complete my promise to you.
313. I have shown you the mystery of salvation through the sacrifice of your son,
314. for I will sacrifice One in the fullness of time for the salvation of all.
315. I have given you a mute sacrifice—complete your will;
316. untie the rational one and destroy the silent one, and complete your sacrifice.
317. See, O Abraham, that I have rewarded your love toward me,
318. for the mystery I hid from the exalted ones I have revealed and shown you.
319. I am going to put on your Seed like a garment,
320. that through his revelation he may make known the power of my Only Begotten Son.
321. Through goodwill I will dwell in the Headship of your seed [Col 1:19],
322. and at the door of his Body, every man will worship my Nature.
323. Lo, I have accepted the sacrifice of your hands along with your will;

324. go down rejoicing in the fulfillment of your sacrifice, which is the salvation of the peoples."
325. Abram lifted his eyes and saw a ram on the mountain,
326. which connects to the symbol upon the tree,[8] for the redemption of his son.
327. He fulfilled his will and completed the sacrifice with a mute ram,
328. and he rejoiced to see the truth in the Mystery that his hands had served.[9]

IX. Concluding Exhortations

329. With this expectation, the Good One gladdened the just,
330. and made them the head of the formation of the Kingdom above.
331. In their remembrance he promised to all who are invited,
332. that he would give rest to those who are weary as in a harbor.
333. He honored them with promises of things to come,
334. and he signed the image of their actions for the generations to come.
335. He invited the peoples of the four corners to their banquet,
336. to come and rejoice spiritually in their feast.
337. Abraham was worthy to become the beginning of the Kingdom above,
338. and he trod the path of the conversion of the peoples through his faith.
339. His confession became like the foundation of a house,
340. and upon it, love, hope, and faith were crowned.
341. Because the righteous one considered his sterility and did not doubt,
342. [God] placed him as a father to the peoples, that they may imitate his faith.
343. Abram became an example through his works,
344. and our soul should behold it, lest it become ugly through secret sin.
345. Let us sow hope and love upon the soil of his faith,
346. and harvest the fruits that are spiritual and unending.
347. In him, the sterile who are deprived of the promise are tested;
348. may they gain a child without delay, like him.

349. May the weary among us journey in the company of his love,
350. that he may be a restful harbor for them in their struggles.
351. May the rich gain wealth in the type of his wealth,
352. that they may be sons of the inheritance of the riches above, along with him.
353. May those who have earthly treasures imitate him,
354. and gain with him heavenly things that are unending.
355. May his beauty be a vision for all who see,
356. and let them give love and timely provision to those in need.
357. May rich women who possess much look upon Sarah,
358. for when she had possessions, she served the spirits with her hands.
359. May humility of soul humble rich women,
360. for the love of Abram did not change through the riches of Egypt.
361. Let us denounce, through the constancy of her faith,
362. those bland women who ask for a child from impure demons.
363. May the duration of her peacefulness chastise adulteresses,
364. she who received a child without expectation after a hundred years.
365. May Sarah be an example to the daughters of Eve,
366. and may they look upon her and not doubt the Creator.
367. Through Abraham, may those who love wealth see themselves,
368. for he distributed his wealth and humbled himself like a poor man.
369. May the just be unveiled images in their works,
370. and may everyone paint the image of their beauty within his conscience.
371. With love of our soul, let us bind our love unto the Creator,
372. that he may give us the reward for our faith, with his true ones.

Chapter 4

MEMRA 14: ON JONAH

INTRODUCTION

This is another reflective memra following the events recounted in the Book of Jonah. It begins with an explicit discussion on the esoteric nature of God's teaching (lines 1–14). God's pedagogy, his teaching style, understands human weakness. Because of this, he is careful not to speak too openly to those who are not ready for the fullness of truth, but rather hides the truth through symbols. That way, those who are spiritually ignorant do not have the opportunity to look down on the scriptures. In particular, while creation is open to the eyes of all, the mystery of salvation remains mysterious until we are ready to receive it (lines 13–14). The Book of Jonah is a symbol of just that mystery.

The mystery of salvation begins, as we saw in the previous chapter, with Abraham, who is called to be a blessing for all nations. This fact is forgotten by Jonah, the son of Mattai (named "the signal" in line 131), who symbolizes the element tending toward isolationism not only in the Jewish people, but even in the Law itself (line 27). Jonah's resistance to preach to Nineveh is Israel's resistance to union with other nations, and Nineveh is a symbol of "the nations" or "the peoples," terms referring specifically to uncircumcised Gentiles, whom God also wishes to save through Jonah. Despite his best efforts, Jonah causes the Gentiles to repent even while he runs to Tarshish. During the miraculous storm (which, according to Narsai, affected only Jonah's boat—line 117 and following), the dumb elements become instructors of God's will, and the Gentile sailors become preachers to Jonah, whose prayers cannot be heard because of his rebellion (lines 123, 148).

The fish that swallows Jonah also becomes a symbol, and it is here that the fulfillment of Jonah's story (called a *raza*, which means either "mystery" or "symbol") points directly to Christ and his death and resurrection. Jonah is at once alive and dead (line 213), while Christ died but did not decay (line 241). The fish becomes Jonah's tomb, which holds him for exactly three days (line 244). Narsai notes the oddities of the story of Jonah and asks (in the style of a "chastisement") why the Jews do not allow themselves to see the christological symbolism in it (section VIII).

Jonah repents while in the fish and prays for salvation while promising to obey God's will (lines 287–290). The fish vomits him out, and he makes his way to Nineveh, in the land of Assyria (line 332). The symbol expands, as Jonah's resurrection from Sheol represents the city's resurrection from the death of sin (lines 337–340). The city repents, and the king decrees penitence for all (section XII), hoping that God may spare them, which is exactly what happens.

The repentance of Nineveh causes Jonah's second rebellion against God, and he leaves Nineveh in hopes that it still might be overturned in the end (line 425). Here the memra reaches its apex. The story of the gourd plant illustrates not only Jonah's selfishness and shallowness (lines 433–436), but the plant, a speechless thing like the storm at sea, also becomes a teacher (line 453). This is a thematic bookend with the beginning of the memra, since God's esoteric pedagogy works exactly by means of such symbols, which are sometimes silent (like the sea and the gourd) and often unwilling (like Jonah) agents revealing God's truth.

The memra ends with a beautiful exposition, spoken in God's voice, about his will to save all nations. Jonah's bitterness over the withered plant is not merely selfish, but absurd. The plant came to be rapidly and went away just as rapidly; Nineveh (and, by extension, the whole human race) has existed and been guided by God for centuries (lines 353–354). Most poignantly, the gourd is a nonhuman thing that Jonah cares for; how much more does God (and should Jonah) love the Ninevites, who are his own (as well as Jonah's—line 463), and made in God's image (line 470)?

TRANSLATION

I. Introduction: God's Esoteric Teaching

1. The Creator placed great wealth within the Scriptures,
2. and hid it with a mystery[1] until the determined time was fulfilled.
3. He covered the letters with parables like a garment,
4. lest the eyes of flesh look down on the treasure of the Spirit.
5. He hid his wealth from the ignorant youth
6. until it matured, and then he opened the door of mercies.
7. He cast fear upon those who know his Testaments,
8. that the power of his wisdom may increase before their eyes.
9. He did not give the immature access to his hidden things,
10. lest his valuables be disdained by weakness of soul.
11. The heir was young, and unable to handle his wealth,
12. and in grace, he gave of his riches to us as to strangers.
13. Although he had revealed his hidden things through what he had formed,
14. he had hidden the salvation of our lives through a mystery until the end.

II. The Chosen People

15. He chose one people and called it by his Name like an heir,
16. that through it he may open the treasure of his mercies to all the peoples.[2]
17. But the son who had seen that he was called by the Name and set apart from all
18. stole the scepter without understanding and looked down upon all.
19. The young-minded one looked at the letters with the eyes of flesh,
20. and did not consider the power of hidden things with the faculties of the soul.
21. The youth thought that the wealth was his alone,
22. and he despised and insulted his kinsmen with foolish pride.
23. He did not know that he was honored among all for the sake of all things,

24. for that which was[3] hidden within him would reconcile all with the Lord of all.
25. Even the righteous went along this path of the election of the people,[4]
26. and considered the course toward the nations unprofitable.
27. Even the Law strengthened them toward what was written,
28. and agitated them toward love of the people and hatred of the nations.
29. They did not want the uncircumcised to become their family,
30. lest the chosen people be cast out from its inheritance.

III. Jonah as a Representative of Israel, His Calling

31. They were not pleased with their ambassadorship toward the nations,
32. and Jonah bears witness, for when he was sent, he fled and hid himself.
33. The Hebrew heard the sound of resurrection, which is the revival of the dead,
34. and he mourned greatly, lest [the peoples] live and the people die.
35. A new gospel fell upon the ears of the son of the Hebrews,
36. and terror seized him at the new news of the conversion of the nations.
37. He put on inconsolable sadness because of what he had heard,
38. and he decided to run rather than be sent on the path to the pagans.
39. One circumcised in the flesh heard about the uncircumcised being saved for free,
40. and in place of a garment, he tore his mind with doubts.
41. A revelation called him and spoke to him mysteriously [Jonah 1:2],
42. "Go out and gather for me the rational sheep to the sheepfold of life.
43. Get up, go preach the sound of salvation among the drowning,
44. and wake those sleeping in sin with your own words.
45. Come, set out on the path of preaching among strangers,
46. and teach the new path of the adoration of my Majesty.

47. Come, go reconcile the wrathful who left my family,
48. and shepherd them to righteousness through grace.
49. Come, go and visit the sick who are tired out with the maladies of iniquity,
50. and through your words, chastise the fever of their consciences.
51. Take medicine from the treasury of my hidden Majesty,
52. and bandage them with repentance for the sake of forgiveness.
53. Prepare and pour out pity and mercies upon their consciences,
54. and wash away the filth of sin with the salve of sweetness.
55. Take the lamp of the light of the knowledge of me and place it before their eyes,
56. and chase away the darkness of error that has blinded them.
57. Season those who are without intelligence with the salt of my knowledge,
58. that through you they may gain the sweet flavor of [knowing] one Creator.
59. First, show them harsh words before deeds,
60. and if they suffer, comfort them with the sound of forgiveness.
61. Arm yourself with the power of divine aid,
62. and go down to the contest and crush sin that has killed humankind.
63. Take the sword of the word of the Spirit upon the tip of your tongue [Eph 6:17],
64. and destroy iniquity, the tyrant that has rebelled against justice.
65. Tear down the building of polytheism that error built,
66. and place the confession of one God in the human mind.
67. Get up, go to Assyria, to the city of kings that rebelled against me,
68. and instead of arrows, shoot words of rebuke at it.
69. Call out and shake that place filled with pride with the sound of your words;
70. drop in its ears a bitter overturning, and it will be shocked.
71. Go and tell it that I will shake the ground beneath it,
72. and the news of the day of your fall will trouble all the nations."

IV. Jonah's Fleeing

73. The son of Mattai heard the Voice preaching this bitter overturning,

74. and he found it grievous to walk the path to the nations.
75. He saw the pity of the One who sent him overcoming his wrath,
76. and he wondered whether he should speak words that would not be believed.
77. "I know that you are merciful and have pity on iniquity,[5]
78. and that your great love transforms the harshness of wrath.
79. And I know that if I go preach fearful words to the Assyrians,
80. I will be shown a liar, for you do not act according to your threats."
81. Two sources of hesitation closed off the path in the face of Jonah:
82. that he might not be shown as a liar and that the chosen people might not be exiled.
83. The one who was sent considered the end of his path:
84. the condemnation of his people, and the doubt of his own words, terrified him.
85. He chose an escape, that he might not be sent on the path to the nations,
86. lest he undo the barrier of the Law by means of his going.[6]
87. Jonah got up to flee and hide from the Knower of all [Jonah 1:3],
88. and dwell in a land in which the voice of revelations had not been heard.
89. Not that the preacher indeed fled from God;
90. he changed countries with the intention that he might not be sent.
91. For he knew that the power of the Creator was in all,
92. and that the work of his hands cannot hide from God.
93. He changed countries according to the interpretation of the prophecy,
94. thinking that revelations dwelt in Judah alone.
95. The son of Mattai thought that if he distanced himself, [God] would disregard him,
96. and he would not again hear the Voice of revelations saying to go to Assyria.
97. He chose a path over the wet sea to the land of Tarshish,
98. [thinking that] as far as he goes, so distant would the Voice of the Creator be from him.
99. He hired a boat, that he might not be hired for the salvation of the nations,

100. and he left his country, that the nations might not become kinsmen to the people.
101. He ran from the dry land, lest the heart of the uncircumcised become softened,
102. and he journeyed on the sea, lest the sound of his words be made a lie.
103. The one who fled went down to the boat, and slept out of sadness,
104. and the signal went out like an ambassador and shook the sea.

V. The Storm at Sea

105. The storm became like a fisherman, and it cast its nets,
106. and Jonah fell with the sailors into nets of water.
107. The signal thrashed the sea with a staff of spirit [Jonah 1:4],
108. [asking]: "why are you hiding, O servant who has fled from the Knower of all?"
109. It struck the silent, and shook the rational,
110. and the mute taught the rational about the Creator.
111. Wind and water crushed each other because of Jonah,
112. to capture the preaching for the nations.
113. The sea was shaken unnaturally because of the son of Mattai,
114. as the awesome waves asked where he was hiding.
115. That storm was unlike those of all other days,
116. and its course was different from its ordinary one.
117. The thrashing did not extend over the whole surface of the sea;
118. it thrashed around the boat of Jonah alone.
119. A great marvel was shown among the waves,
120. for while the sea was restful, it shook upon Jonah and was quiet otherwise.
121. O command that gave understanding to insensible things,
122. and shook them for the sake of a rational being who wished to stay silent.
123. O silent things, deprived of mind, how wise they became,
124. for part were silent and part were shaking, beyond the natural order.
125. The sea was silent for the sailors journeying,
126. but it became embittered with severe waves in Jonah's area.

127. The air was restful, and the waves were quiet, and everyone journeyed,
128. but the boat of Jonah was being crushed by a storm.
129. The limit of the signal divided the sea for the sailors,
130. and they saw the wonder: while the whole thing was quiet, it was shaken for Jonah.
131. A portion of the sea was being lashed by the reins of the signal,
132. and while he passed through, the lashing of the wind was the border for the signal.
133. It lowered the boat to the depths, but it was not broken,
134. and it raised it to the face of the sea, but it was not overturned.
135. The signal was clear in it, and it dragged it along with a staff of spirit,
136. and it ascended above, and went down to the depths, and it did not destroy it.
137. The sailors were swallowed in severe thrashings in the thrashing of the boat,
138. and they gave up hope that they would ever be saved from the storms.

VI. The Sailors and Jonah

139. They advised each other to cry out, each to his own god [Jonah 1:5],
140. that they might be saved from the storms and see life.
141. The head of the sailors woke Jonah up, "Rise up and beg:
142. pray and plead from your God, that perhaps we may find peace" [Jonah 1:6].
143. Jonah was sunken in heavy sleep in the bottom of the boat,
144. and did not wake during the thrashing of the sea that occurred because of him.
145. The fleeing one arose and saw the sea was shaken up with waves,
146. and his thoughts judged that the storm was happening because of him.
147. He did not pray with the sailors that the sea might be calmed,
148. for he knew that he had been foolish, and if he begged it would not be accepted.

149. He was silent, not praying like one who understood he had despised a command,
150. for even if he had called, that One he had despised would not answer him.
151. The sailors saw that begging was superfluous,
152. and they were advised to examine the evil of their deeds.
153. They thought that sin was the source of the crushing of the sea around them,
154. for they saw it was calm, but for them it flowed devastatingly.
155. Through the thrashing of the sea, they gained clarity, and distinguished, and knew,
156. that the storm raged in that portion of the sea because of sin.
157. The blowing of the wind was great and it made them wise;
158. They thought among themselves that whoever has been foolish should reveal his sin.
159. Through the furnace of lots they tested each other like prudent men [Jonah 1:7],
160. that the deception hidden within the mind may come to the open.
161. They threw lots that might reveal who it was who sinned,
162. and he might pronounce judgment upon his own ignorance that shook the sea.
163. The command came down within the lots, and it tested them,
164. and the lot of the son of the Hebrews came up before the sailors.
165. The uncircumcised asked the one circumcised in flesh: "What is it that you have done?
166. Unveil your deeds and tell us your people, and show your country" [Jonah 1:8].
167. Jonah answered the sailors: "I am a Hebrew [Jonah 1:9],
168. and I am a servant of the God of all, who formed all.
169. From the God who knows all things I ran and hid,
170. and his signal has caught me in the stiff net of loose waters."
171. O preacher who wished to hide his preaching,
172. and revealed and unveiled, against his will, the fear of his Lord!
173. He was sent among strangers with this pretext,
174. to go and preach the one God for the annulling of error.
175. He ran from the people, and the nations caught the one who hates the nations,

176. and while unwilling, he became a preacher to the nations he hated.
177. "I fear only one Lord, almighty over all,
178. and it is he who guides the sea and dry land according to his will" [Jonah 1:9].
179. The uncircumcised learned from the Hebrew, who was a good servant,
180. that he had run and hidden himself from God who knows all.
181. The sailors feared, for they saw the marvel that occurred because of Jonah,
182. and they sought to return to the shore, but the sea would not allow them.
183. The boat without a movement was tied to the sea,
184. and when they directed it to the seashore, a command prevented it.
185. The blowing of the wind was shaking it from every side,
186. and the waves were armored against it like cavalry.
187. The storm attacked and surrounded it like an army,
188. and the blowing of the wind encompassed it like a wall.
189. The sailors fell between two thoughts regarding Jonah:
190. they considered which was worse, his death or his life.
191. They said, fearfully: "What are we to do with Jonah?
192. Saving you is hard, and your death is difficult—do not blame us."
193. Jonah answered the sailors like a prudent man:
194. "Take and throw me among the waves, and the sea will calm [Jonah 1:12].
195. For the mouth of the water, a raging lion, seeks me;
196. Give him his prey and he will not be provoked against your lives.
197. The great abyss cries out to me with the sound of its currents,
198. and the whirlwind has come out after me and shaken the sea.
199. The wall of wind has walled you in because of my foolishness;
200. it looks to bring me down, and behold, it breaks up the fence of its billows."
201. The sailors cried out to God in great terror:
202. "O Creator, may we not be guilty of the blood of the just man [Jonah 1:14].
203. You are the Lord, almighty over all in the sea and land,

204. and you will that this may be; complete your will!"
205. The sailors took Jonah and threw him among the waves,
206. and the storms calmed, and the men marveled at the Creator's power.
207. They then vowed vows and fulfilled them after a time,
208. and with this covenant, they became servants of the God of all [Jonah 1:16].

VII. Jonah and the Fish

209. The one who was fleeing fell into the net of water, and the waves ensnared him,
210. while the mute things judged his discernment in silence.
211. The Judge gave a sentence after his punishment,
212. and it was determined that he would go down to Sheol.
213. The living dead man's tomb was carved within a living body,
214. that the life of the fleshly one might be kept within living flesh.
215. A command went down after the fish, and pulled it up [Jonah 1:17],
216. and the living thing ascended and received the living one, and entombed him in itself.
217. The son of Mattai entered and dwelt in the fish, a tomb in a tomb,
218. and the signal shut the door in the face of the living dead man.
219. The fleeing one went down to the prison filled with darkness,
220. and his legs were tied up in moist stocks, the guts of the fish.
221. He fled the land, and the sea ensnared him and gave him to the fish,
222. and a tomb in a tomb encased and imprisoned him—the abyss and the fish.
223. O marvel accomplished in the son of Mattai,
224. who descended, while living, to two tombs, and did not decay!
225. O deceased one who was conducted to Sheol while alive,
226. O earthly one, who was enfolded in a corporeal garment!
227. O mortal who was entirely buried, and alive while dead,
228. O prisoner, entirely imprisoned, while traveling in a tomb!
229. The mortal did not live through the power of the power of life;
230. a signal protected him the way infants are within wombs.
231. The living among men cannot stand without the air,

232. and without air a fleshly one has not ever lived like the spirits.
233. It was not his to run or hide and not to not be sent,
234. for a great symbol of things to come was depicted by him in advance.
235. It was not that the Knower of all entombed him in a fish that he might die;
236. through his descent, he wrote the parables of future things.
237. Through a man, he would one day accomplish life[7] for all;
238. and through a man, he would free all from slavery.
239. Through the death of a man, he would one day unbind death's authority,
240. and he entombed Jonah as by a symbol before the deed [Matt 12:39–40].
241. The Body of our Lord did not see corruption in Sheol [Ps 16:10],
242. and [God] kept Jonah without corruption in the symbol of our Savior.
243. He entombed Jonah for three days in the bowels of the fish [Jonah 1:17],
244. that he may be a symbol for the hidden truth when it is revealed.
245. A living fish became a tomb for the one who depicts symbols,
246. and the Body of the One who fulfilled the symbol received a new tomb [John 19:41].
247. A new symbol was accomplished for the son of Mattai,
248. when the fish swallowed his body it kept him alive.
249. New also was the fulfillment of the symbol of Jonah,
250. for the Body that greedy death swallowed did not decay.

VIII. Scriptural Symbolism, and a Chastisement

251. The symbols of the things to come are new and marvelous,
252. for a body was entombed in a tomb of a body, and it lived and walked.
253. The son of Mattai trod a new path before actual deeds,
254. that when they are fulfilled they might not be rejected by those who see them.
255. Parables came about for the sake of the truth of the salvation of the nations,

256. that when they are saved, man by man, they may not be divided.
257. Otherwise, explain, O circumcised in the flesh but uncircumcised in the heart [cf. Jer 9:26],
258. what is the power hidden in the symbol that Jonah ministered?[8]
259. What was the need for him to be in the fish for three days,
260. and live a life that was alien to human life?
261. And [why] did he act stupidly and break the command of the word of his Lord?
262. Why did [God] not punish him with anything besides a fish?
263. When has he punished the sons of his house as he punished Jonah?
264. Who is it who has been imprisoned in Sheol while alive like the son of Mattai?
265. At what other time did he send his preacher to strangers,
266. and when did he send a prophet to the nations outside the people?
267. Why did [Jonah] not prophesy in the land of Judah,
268. for the Voice set him apart from the people to go to Assyria?
269. Remove the veil placed over your face, O son of Abraham [2 Cor 3:15],
270. and behold the truth hidden in the mystery Jonah ministered.
271. Take off the veil that Moses spread out, and end the fear;
272. And see unveiledly how the image of the King is.
273. Read and understand discerningly the Scriptures of the Spirit,
274. And you will learn that the mysteries have been fulfilled in the expectation of the nations.
275. Fix your mind upon the new mystery that the son of Mattai depicted,
276. and see that all the mysteries have been fulfilled in the One you crucified.
277. Extend your conscience to the great height of his preaching,
278. and compare his way to that of the nations, to the nations that have repented.
279. Nineveh should be like a mirror for the eyes of your heart,
280. so see that the sound of salvation has gone out to the four corners.
281. Go with Jonah, and descend to the abyss, and ascend in his company,
282. And you will arrive at the height above at the end of your path.

IX. Jonah's Prayer in the Fish

283. The son of Mattai descended and dwelt in Sheol [Jonah 2:2] in a symbol of our Savior,
284. and the signal protected him from the feeding of the insects in the bowels of the fish.
285. The buried one prayed in the temple of the fish prudently [Jonah 2:1],
286. and his thoughts judged and begged and pled that he may return to life.
287. "Hear the sound of my pleading, O God of all, and attend to my words,
288. and bring my life up from destruction to life.
289. I knew that I sinned in not serving you in the path of the nations,
290. and lo, you have taught me, in my life that you preserved, that you love mankind.
291. You called me to go for the salvation of man, but I did not like it;
292. save me from my binding, that I may go out and convert the dead to life.
293. I did not know that your love overflows toward strangers;
294. I thought you only had one inheritance, and loved it alone.
295. I thought that if the uncircumcised nations entered your inheritance,
296. perhaps the heir that you chose might be cast out of your house.
297. I judged this way according to the will of the Law,
298. for it has rendered the impure nations as strangers to its fellowship.
299. Now that I have heard from [the Law's] Author that he calls the nations,
300. I will not shut the door of my mercy in the face of the evil.
301. May my supplication enter before you, my God, and may I live by your word,
302. and may my life be a sign of life to those dead in sin.
303. I said in the sadness of my life that there is no salvation;
304. if you wish, I will again increase to see your Face.
305. Make me worthy to pay the vow of my lips in the land of the living,
306. for if I ascend, I will not be silent in preaching life."
307. O prayer of one enclosed in tomb within tomb,

308. and that broke the wall of the fish and water and the face of the sky!
309. O bound one, an exile of the depths of water,
310. who extended his will, in place of his steps, toward him who bound him!
311. O entombed one who conversed with his Entomber,
312. and tore open his tomb with the sound of his words, and returned to life!
313. The scribe of the Spirit wrote a letter in the depths of the water,
314. and gave it to a mind[9] to enter and read it before the Knower of all.
315. Spiritual powers carried it and gave it to the Hidden One,
316. and returned to [Jonah] with the hopeful sound that he would return to life.

X. Jonah's Return to Land and Second Calling

317. A signal dragged the tomb carrying a living dead man,
318. to bring up the body of the one buried in its bowels to the land of the living.
319. The fish was troubled as it ascended to the surface of the land,
320. for the signal that commanded it to swallow [Jonah] forced it to return him.
321. The cords of the signal forced it to repay what it had received,
322. lest the symbol be delayed in the tomb beyond the truth.[10]
323. The boat carrying the symbol of the salvation of the nations went up,
324. and placed its treasure on the seashore, and returned to its place.
325. The place it carried him when it went out to go to the deep,
326. there it came up when the Power's signal dragged it.
327. It rested in the same port from which it had gone out,
328. for the captain that stood in it dragged it there.
329. The fish placed Jonah in the same country it had swallowed him in,
330. for there he heard the same Voice he had fled from.

331. The son of Mattai went out and saw the light and heard the Voice,
332. which entirely resembled the first one, "Go to Assyria [Jonah 3:2].
333. Come now! Go and preach a new gospel to the uncircumcised nations,
334. for you have become a symbol—complete your symbol with deeds.
335. I buried you while alive and opened [the fish] for you for this reason:
336. that you may open the door to strangers to enter before me.
337. Through your resurrection, I sought to resurrect the buried living;
338. lo, I have taught you the salvation of your life—so save the lost.
339. Come now! Go and preach the salvation of life to those dead for so long,
340. and resurrect them through the living hope of repentance.
341. Work the land of the hearing of their consciences' ear,
342. and sow within it the good seed of the fear of the truth.
343. Pull up the weeds of idolatry that the evil one planted [Matt 13:28],
344. and plant the sound of one Creator, almighty over all."
345. Thus he taught him the path to the nations that he did not want,
346. and he taught him also that it was right for him to have mercy on the nations.
347. The son of Abraham gained the understanding of discernment,
348. for he called the nations to kinship with the house of Abraham.

XI. Jonah Goes to Nineveh

349. The one distinct from the nations began to go among strangers,
350. and he went on the path, as he was commanded, to Assyria.
351. The Voice taught him how large the city of Assyria was,
352. for he went three days within Assyria as he preached in it [Jonah 3:3].
353. He also revealed and showed him that its greatness is from God,
354. for through him it arrived at an abundance of wealth and population.

355. He began to enter, after the journey of a day, the midst of its markets,
356. and as he journeyed, he began with a voice filled with rebuke.
357. He preached and spoke, in the ears of all, a sound of wrath:
358. "The city of Nineveh will be overturned upon her citizens" [Jonah 3:4].
359. He limited its end to forty days, to confirm his words,
360. that either they repent, or it would happen as he had decreed.
361. The son of the Hebrews did not preach only the overturning,
362. for, behold, he also mingled mercy with the overturning, the end he determined.
363. He terrified the hard of heart with fearful sounds,
364. to take them down from arrogance to humility.
365. He cut into the wound of their deeds with hard iron,
366. that iniquity may not remain in the powers of their soul like an ulcer.
367. He placed an intense medicine upon the scab in their consciences,
368. to pull out from them the sign of iniquity that had killed them.
369. The preacher cried out like a trumpet in the city of Nineveh,
370. and the waves of the sound of his words shook the place filled with pride.
371. He blew upon her with the intense winds of the speech of his mouth,
372. and the whole [city] shook, for it was near its fall.
373. His voice terrified both kings and paupers, and all classes [Jonah 3:5],
374. and gathered them to hear his new preaching.
375. He did not revere the authority of leadership,
376. nor did he show favor to wealth or the crown honored over all.
377. The people and the king heard his words, and they were shaken and terrified,
378. for although he was worthless and insignificant, his voice terrified the kings of Assyria.
379. Assembly upon assembly was prepared to hear his word,
380. and he cast the net of his preaching and captured them.
381. His word cast a net for both young and old,
382. and in its quickness it ensnared the course of all classes together.

XII. The King of Nineveh's Decree

383. The sound of his preaching reached the king of Assyria,
384. and he left off his crown and despised his authority, and honored [Jonah's] word.
385. He preached a painful sound to all the nation,
386. that each one should turn from his deeds toward supplication [Jonah 3:7].
387. "Let us hate the iniquity belonging to the ugliness of our soul, which has made us impure,
388. and let us love the truth, beautiful in its name and its deeds.
389. Let us curse sin, which has cast its darkness upon our mind,
390. and let us see with the intellect the light of the word of the son of the Hebrews.
391. Let us focus ourselves on the work of fasting from enticements,
392. and stop the violence of licentiousness through modesty.
393. Let us restrain our mouth from food, bodily sustenance,
394. and stop our soul from the work of avarice.
395. Let even the beasts fast with us from sustenance,
396. and let the mute natures weep with us over our wrath.
397. Who knows; perhaps the God of all will pity us,
398. and let the anger of his wrath pass over us, and not destroy us" [Jonah 3:9].
399. The Good One saw that they were seen by him before they came into being,
400. for the iniquitous had repented, and changed his wrath into reconciliation.
401. He had made them hate iniquity although they were unwilling,
402. and his mercy repaid the prudence of remorse.
403. He had dragged them with a hidden signal toward knowledge of him,
404. and he gave the reward of his kindness to repentance.
405. It was not that the Ninevites tread the path of repentance;
406. the Hidden One revealed his Hiddenness in love to the sons of his house.
407. Through them, Jonah composed parables of things to come,
408. for [God] pities the Gentiles in the fullness of time through the Second Adam [cf. 1 Cor 15:45].

XIII. Jonah's Bitterness

409. The preacher saw that the Good One mingled mercies with his wrath,
410. and he mourned greatly that the verdict of his words was not fulfilled.
411. He turned to walk the path of his own inclination like before,
412. and he said that "This is what caused me to flee.
413. Indeed, O Lord, was this not what I said when I was still in my land [Jonah 4:2]?
414. For this I fled in advance, lest I be sent.
415. Indeed I knew that you are a most merciful God,
416. and when people repent, your love tends toward forgiveness.
417. Thus I have become like a liar before strangers,
418. and it is better for me to die and not be called a prophet of deception."
419. "Is it good that you are sad?" [Jonah 4:4]. Thus called a revelation and spoke to him.
420. He answered his Lord that his sadness had reached even death [Jonah 4:8].
421. The Hebrew saw that the uncircumcised repented and he accepted death,
422. rather than be pleased that the dead of the impure nations became alive.
423. The pain of sadness crushed him disorderedly,
424. and he chose death over life, that he might not be called a liar.
425. He left the city and went out to live in solitude [Jonah 4:5],
426. while he watched that, perhaps, the verdict [God] had decided might come to pass.
427. He made himself a booth in which temporarily to dwell,
428. with the excuse that perhaps the verdict would take place.
429. The Knower of all saw that his thoughts wished this,
430. and his Lord dragged him to expiation by means of temptation.
431. A signal swiftly sprouted a stalk of gourd,
432. and it extended its leaves above Jonah, and he rejoiced nearby it [Jonah 4:6].
433. The son of Mattai rejoiced over the leaves and fruits of a worthless gourd,
434. for he saw a marvel that it sprouted and bore fruit immediately.

435. He forgot his sadness in the pleasure of the love of fruits,
436. and he did not understand why it had blossomed immediately.
437. The signal bound him with love of the gourd that he might again be instructed,
438. that whenever he took it, he would suffer greatly, and learn its cause.
439. The command that gave it from nothing and bound him in love for it
440. turned and chastised him, and it dried up immediately, and he mourned nearby it.
441. A command signaled a harsh heat, and it blew immediately,
442. and the gourd dried up, and its leaves withered, and its fruits fell [Jonah 4:7].
443. The sun struck Jonah's head intensely,
444. and his lamentations doubled, his soul was saddened, and he asked for death.
445. The heat that came upon the preacher was not usual;
446. a signal enflamed it with heat outside the natural order.
447. The same command that shook the sea unusually
448. enflamed the glow of the sun outside the natural order.
449. It taught him by the sea not to resist the path to the nations,
450. and he corrected him by the gourd, so that he might not be sad about human salvation.
451. The shoot of the gourd became a teacher to him, and instructed his soul,
452. and bound him in love toward sinners though he was unwilling.
453. He became a rational student of the mute prophet—the gourd,
454. and the scribe possessing understanding learned from a silent thing.
455. The sultry heat upon his limbs fastened suffering in his heart,
456. and through this temptation he began to aim at expiation.
457. The symbol that was in the silent thing taught him love and mercy,
458. and interpreted them through a revelation so that he would not be sad.

XIV. God's Love for Nineveh and Mankind

459. The signal spoke to him through a sound according to his language:
460. "why are you saddened over a silent thing that blossomed immediately?
461. Why are you bound up in complete love to weak things,
462. and do not approach the glories that people can acquire?
463. Why do you love what is not yours and hate what is yours?
464. And why do you envy human life like a nonhuman?
465. Why do you not enter into a just judgment against your own thoughts?
466. Judge your own conscience regarding these affairs of yours.
467. Where has the wakeful inclination of your discernment drowned?
468. For you do not sense your own kinsmen as you do what belongs to you.
469. You are saddened over the ruin of a mute gourd,
470. how much should rational creatures engraved with my Image sadden me [Jonah 4:10–11]?
471. A manifest heat has bothered your outer body;
472. However, the hidden iniquity of human corruption has shattered me.
473. You have gained pity and great suffering over a worthless thing;
474. But how much should I forgive the honored who turn to me?
475. See twelve legions of young soldiers,
476. and extend your mind to the number of the whole people.[11]
477. Forgive, son of Mattai, so that the great city not be destroyed;
478. be like me in forgiving your neighbors [cf. Matt 6:14–15].
479. What will you gain in the destruction of a country that wrath ruins?
480. Nobody confesses the Name of my Existence within the dust.
481. Direct your will at the target of my mercies, and aim at it,
482. for because of this I called you to me, that you may imitate me.
483. I have made you a scout, to return the erring nations to me;
484. spread out your words like traps to hunt people.
485. I am going to spread a net of love upon all the nations,

486. and I have written, through you, the salvation of all, by means of the Ninevites.
487. I extend the adoration of my Majesty to the four corners,
488. And, behold, through deeds I have shown it to Nineveh who repented.
489. I am going to establish one of your species as a General,
490. And, behold, I have revealed my victory regarding him through your victory.
491. Through a man, I will convert all to my faith,
492. and in his type, I have invited the Ninevites to your preaching.
493. I will gather the nations and the people together through love of me,
494. and I have trodden the path before his coming through the path of Assyria.
495. In it I have undone the barrier of the Law for the sake of the nations,
496. with this intent I called and sent you among strangers."
497. The Hidden One comforted the son of the Hebrews mysteriously,
498. that he might not be saddened at the conversion of the nations who found salvation by him.
499. He taught him by his own to love his own, like a prudent man,
500. and he revealed through him the salvation of the nations hidden in the people.
501. By his path, he showed the new path of preaching,
502. and tread, through him, the peaceful route toward life.
503. With this condition, he extended the course of prophecy,
504. and concluded it with the people, and sent it out to the nations, through the son of Mattai.
505. Each was looking toward the fulfillment of his preaching,
506. and [God] showed through him the splendid image hidden in the symbol.
507. Blessed is he who signified the conversion of our life through the son of Mattai,
508. Thanksgiving to the Hidden One who revealed his Hiddenness through what is ours.

II

Christian Salvation History

Chapter 5

MEMRA 5: ON THE INCARNATION

INTRODUCTION

This memra is given the title "Of the Memorial of St. Mary" in manuscripts, but is more properly titled "On the Incarnation," since the section discussing Mary is a small part (lines 187–246) of a fairly long work. Mary's role in the incarnation, of course, is of the highest importance, and her section in this memra is one of its high points.

The memra begins, however, at the creation, as do many of Narsai's works. Here it is pointed out that while God made the world alone (that is, in the singular verbal case), when making humanity God said "let us," switching to the plural (lines 7–10). Narsai teases that this was not because God needed help or advice; nor was it a total revelation of the Trinitarian *Qnome* (line 39). For Narsai, this Divine use of the plural was, like many of the details of the creation account, for the sake of the instruction of the angels (an interesting thesis found also in Augustine). That is, God spoke in the plural here as an initial suggestion of the plurality of his Personhood, in order to make the full revelation of the Trinity more palatable when it happened at the baptism of Christ (line 42). In making humanity, therefore, God begins to reveal who he is, and thus the human being is the visible image of God that creatures look upon, and through which God is to be honored and loved as king (lines 51–52).

Adam, however, fails in his calling, and God's image is corrupted through his sin and eventual death (line 86). The failure of the mortal does not stop God's purposes, and God's image is passed on through Adam's progeny (line 95–96) in preparation for Christ who will be the true and ultimate Image of God (lines 107–108). This passing on of God's image is tradition and jubilee and passes from Adam to Seth, Enoch to Lamech, Noah, Shem, and Abraham, who is chosen from among all nations to retain God's image in his line (lines 143–154). Abraham is a special steward and protector of God's image, but the treasury entrusted to him is not only for him but for all nations, since all of humanity was created in God's image (line 157). If it were only for Abraham's offspring, this would indicate injustice and hypocrisy in God (line 168).

The conclusion and end goal of the passing down of God's image is Mary, in whom Life rested and dwelt like a boat in harbor at the end of its journey (lines 187–188). She thus carried the entire human race within her as mother and is the vessel that takes us to heaven within itself (lines 191–192). She accepted the strange birth described by Gabriel because she understood that the same Spirit that hovered over the waters at creation would work a new creation in her (line 200). Just as Adam came from the earth, Christ would come from Mary, the new earth (line 202).

The historical lineage is the foundation of the building of which Christ is the Capstone, and Christ himself, whose Body is the fruit of this lineage, is the Temple of God. Whereas Adam was meant to be the statue of the King honored by all creatures and failed at this, Christ is where all creatures and God dwell together as one. All physical creatures are present in his Body, human rationality in his soul, and the Word of God in him through will—thus in Christ, God and creation are united at last (lines 216–222). Christ renewed the image of Adam that had been destroyed in sin and death, because Christ is the Life that gives life, the Physician and Medicine (lines 211–213).

Narsai's christological terminology can be jarring to modern readers, especially in English. He refers to Christ the man as "he," rather than using the christologically "safer" phrasing of referring to "the human nature of Christ" as "it." Yet he is clear that there was never a moment of separation of any kind between the Divine Word and the man Christ (lines 235, 283), only a distinction between

Divinity and humanity (line 247). The fact is, the Word did not assume a generic or universal human nature but the man Christ, conceived in the womb of Mary. Is it not more proper, linguistically and theologically, to refer to this being as "he" rather than "it?"

Similarly jarring is Narsai's refusal to use the *communication of idioms*, wherein things properly said of Christ in his humanity are spoken of with God as subject, such as "God died on the cross." This, for Narsai, is either imprecise speech or utter blasphemy, implying that God can change (lines 247, 245–260). Rather, there is One Person (line 302) in Christ with two natures that are distinct and do not mingle (lines 288–290); God the Word remains unchanging eternally; Christ the man is a creature subject to change (lines 293–294). Because the Word cannot have or change location, he dwells in Christ "in will," since there is no other possibility (lines 247, 285). Narsai is defensive against the charge of heresy and insists on Christ's unity of Person (lines 354–355) and Sonship (line 358), demanding that his accuser spend the time to actually examine his teaching (line 364). He goes on the offensive, claiming blasphemy in the words of those who say that God suffers and dies, and calling those who want to kill God murderers (lines 370–379). Indeed, they are like Satan himself in wanting God to suffer—otherwise, why do they insist on saying that he does (line 401)? His obvious hyperbole here is probably a reaction to the unfair accusations of dividing Christ made against him.

The unity of Christ is not simply a static theological issue for Narsai, but rather an expression of dynamic soteriology and pedagogy. Speaking of Christ the man is important because it is a body *like ours* that is exalted in Christ, for he saved *us* (line 385). Christ's visible life on earth, from start to finish, reveals the invisible Word (line 309). Christ's miraculous birth reveals the Father's eternal begetting of the Son (line 227). His circumcision, fasting, hunger, thirst, suffering, and death are in virtue of his humanity, but the Word was united to him perfectly at every moment (lines 315–350; 417). The forty days between Christ's resurrection and ascension are particularly important in establishing Christ's humanity, since even in his risen state he ate and drank and had the marks of the nails and spear in his body (lines 439–442).

The ascension marks an especially important moment, since there Christ went to his proper place in heaven as the Son of God, and as the Word never left the man from the moment of his conception, the man will never leave the Word for all eternity and will reign forever (lines 444–456). In heaven, Christ fulfills Adam's destiny supremely and in a greater way. As Adam was meant to be honored on earth as God's image, Christ is worshipped in heaven as God (line 512). This worship of Christ the man is the final stamp of Narsai's orthodox Christology. Either Christ is truly God, man divinized (line 563), or the worship offered by all creatures to Christ is idolatry.

In the appended *soghytha* or dialogue poem, the author (traditionally considered to be by Narsai, though this is doubtful) focuses on the "annunciation" passage of Luke 1:26–38. Mary is depicted as full of questions, both before and after her acceptance of the words of the angel (who is here called a "watcher"[1]). This focus brings Mary into contrast with Eve, who accepted the proposal of the serpent without question. Mary's questions are therefore an expression of her virtue, since she refuses to accept something outside the natural order unless she guarantees it is from God (which occurs in verse *Mym*, the center of the dialogue).

TRANSLATION

I. God's Revelation at Creation

1. The Creator wished to reveal his great love in man,
2. and made the sound heard to the heavenly: "Let us make man" [Gen 1:26].
3. He created everything from nothing and was not advised;
4. but regarding man, "Come, let us make man in our image."
5. He made the spirits and did not wish to reveal the image of his Existence,
6. but in his fashioning of miserable dirt, he revealed his Hiddenness.
7. In fashioning everything, he did not want an assistant or an advisor,
8. but in the miserable thing, more wretched than all, he wanted both.

9. He brought forth creation, all that it was, and did not call it his image,
10. but he took a small hidden part of it, and called it his image.
11. He did everything he did wisely, in wisdom,
12. that through it he may instruct the work of his hands to know his Name.
13. He wanted to reveal the Name of his Existence in the image of man,
14. that while he is indeed One, there are equal Individuals in him.
15. He revealed his hidden Power mysteriously to his works,
16. and, what is impossible, he showed them through an unveiled image.
17. He taught the world that he is only One through his fashionings,
18. but he did not want to reveal the manner of his Existence until man.
19. He kept the mystery of revealing his Individuals until the end of his work,
20. and he taught everything the Power of his Existence and the Powers in him.
21. He made the sound heard before all: "Let us make man,"
22. and the powers above wondered at this, what it was, and whom it was about.
23. The spirits stood in great wonder as they attended and heard,
24. and they marveled at his novelty insatiably.
25. "What is this new thing that the Hidden Nature has announced,
26. and whom does he call an assistant with him in fashioning his image?
27. Who is advising him, and how can he make the image of Existence,
28. and how is it possible for the work of his hands to resemble him?
29. Who is with him who has the power of making,
30. whom he invites to the fashioning of the image of his image?
31. Perhaps he is with his Existence in another world?
32. Otherwise, what does it mean that he said 'Come, let us make'?
33. If he had said 'Come' as to one in what he said,
34. but because he said 'Come' [plural], it is understood that there are Two."
35. The spirits did not openly learn what I have spoken;

36. meditating, they meditated on what power is hidden in what they heard.
37. They only heard the sound mysteriously in the mind,
38. but they were unable to understand the meaning exactly.
39. The Creator wanted only to make this known to them:
40. that there is something hidden within his Hiddenness.
41. He revealed the mystery to them, not the interpretation of the mystery,
42. that when it is revealed, it may not seem strange to their eyes.
43. For their sake he made the sound that was not a sound heard,
44. and in teaching them, his labor was delayed to six days.
45. In six days he finished his fashioning and completed his words,
46. and on the seventh he rested, while he neither rested nor tired.

II. The Creation and Fall of Man

47. On the sixth day he made heard the sound "Come, let us make,"
48. and he made an image and bound up within it all the rational and mute.
49. He made and constructed him skillfully in body and soul,
50. that he may resemble the heavenly and the earthly.
51. He placed him as an image in the world, the city of the King,
52. that the rational and mute may look upon him lovingly.
53. He built the simple one like a furnace for the testing of all,
54. that by his heat he may test the discernment placed in the rational.
55. He brought and placed him in a beautiful place, that he may stir all to zeal,[2]
56. to see who rejoices in his love and who grieves in his station.
57. He proved the assemblies above by his honor of the earthly one,
58. and found that the gold of some of their minds was fake.
59. He placed a limit for him, knowing he would not keep it,
60. that through this he may reveal his inclination, and the will of the evil one.
61. He stopped him from approaching one fruit of a tree [Gen 2:17],
62. and because the evil one sensed it, he envied him and led him astray, and made him a joke.
63. Envy blinded the prudence of the prince of the air,
64. and he did not want to see the lovely beauty in the image of man.

65. The envier, enflamed with envy, did not envy man,
66. but rather the Being who named man in the image of his Image.
67. The rebel insolently envied the Hidden Being,
68. and because he could not rebuke the Being, he rebuked his image.
69. Like a spy, the deceiver entered before the innocent one,
70. and he plundered his wealth, and stripped and left him naked [Gen 3:7].
71. In shaming him, he thought the Name of the Creator would be shamed,
72. but the one blind with envy did not know that he harmed himself.
73. He stoned him like the image of the King of Kings,
74. but instead of rocks, he cast words of shame at him.
75. "The Creator stopped you from the tree in envy,
76. lest you become an inheritor of his Divinity.
77. The tree he stopped you from gives Divinity,
78. and if you eat, you will become a god like the gods" [Gen 3:5].
79. The evil one cast these words at the image of the Good One,
80. and he cast and threw him down, and mocked and laughed at his fall.
81. The Good One filled with grace looked at this mockery,
82. and he forgave his image, that he may not be mocked by the insolent.
83. He considered how he had fallen astray, and he turned and pitied him mercifully,
84. lest the hater be proud that he had cast him down insolently.
85. He determined a deadly punishment for his stupidity,
86. but made his body a fountain gushing forth life for his species.
87. Streams of man came forth from his body to the four corners,
88. and filled the earth with rational fruits from his members.
89. Fruits of life went out from him who had been killed by eating,
90. and the hater saw, and terror seized him over his transformation.
91. He thought that if he ate from the tree he would die forever,
92. but the Good One did not want his desire to come to fulfillment.

III. The Image of Life in Adam's Progeny

93. He placed the medicine of life, which is from life, in his body,
94. that he may run with his posterity without end.

95. He kept and continued the name he had given him through the seed from him,
96. that his great Name may not fail through his children.
97. He engraved his great Name upon the tablet of his fashioning,
98. but the evil one erased it, so he returned and engraved it again in Seth.
99. He said of Seth that in everything he resembles Adam,
100. in that in his body the mystery of the continuation of his species was hidden.
101. He did not call Cain or Abel the image of Adam,
102. for one of them died and the other was lost through condemnation.
103. Life dwelt in the third one that Adam brought forth,
104. and the son of Amram[3] did well to call him the image of Adam [Gen 5:3].
105. The Lord of Adam was destined to take on the image of Adam,
106. and he prepared and placed it in Adam and his sons from the beginning.
107. He placed his Name as a foundation in the building of man,
108. that each may build, one upon his friend, the image of the One to come.
109. With this intention he was advised "Let us make man,"
110. and in this order he called him the image of his Existence.
111. He was going to make One among man the Dwelling of his Love,
112. and he prepared and called the fashioning of man the image of his Hiddenness.
113. He placed the Name of his Existence upon man from the beginning,
114. that what he would complete through his deeds would not be doubted.
115. What he accomplished was kept for the fullness of time,
116. but he prepared and did it mysteriously until he completed it.

IV. How Can Man Be God's Image?

117. But lest one say something against my words,
118. "In what does the image of man resemble Divinity?

119. How can it be that the Hidden, Uncomposed Nature
120. can resemble an extended nature with composition?
121. How can a thing made be like its Maker,
122. and how can a finite thing suffice for the Infinite One?
123. How could one assert that man is an image of Divinity,
124. for Divinity has no limit or composition?
125. How can he be the image of Hiddenness as it is written,
126. for he rots and returns to his earth?
127. Lo, in every age death destroys and men are destroyed,
128. so how can he be an image—there is nothing like this among men?
129. And if someone says that he is destined to be, when he is renewed,
130. lo even there he cannot resemble Existence."
131. No, man, Existence does not have an unveiled image,
132. and there is nothing among things made that resembles that which cannot be resembled.
133. In love alone can man resemble the Hidden One,
134. and the Maker makes his own resemble his own in love.
135. In love he named the image of man the image of his Existence,
136. and in grace he called him names greater than he is.
137. In grace he gave him the name of his Existence at the beginning of time,
138. to depict the mystery that was to come at the fullness of time.
139. In the fullness of time, he verified the name "image,"
140. and for this he prepared and depicted parables of things to come.
141. In this naming he was proven right from the beginning,
142. and in this hope, he exalted what he had made.

V. The Image of God through the Generations

143. For this reason he chose the people, one of the peoples,
144. and separated it from all, that the leaven of life may be kept in it.
145. For this reason he honored the just, one after another,
146. that they may keep the mystery hidden in their members.
147. The righteous as well greeted one another for this purpose,
148. and passed and handed on the leaven in them from one to another.
149. Adam gave it to Seth, who was named by the name "image,"

150. and from Seth to Enoch, and to Lamech, and to Noah, given rest by God.[4]
151. Noah prophesied and gave it to his son through blessings:
152. blessed is the Lord, the God of Shem, who made peace with him.
153. From Shem it moved through tradition to Abraham,
154. and Abram kept it diligently, more than anyone.
155. Indeed, the Creator who saw his diligence in keeping his image
156. chose and established him a steward of the treasure of his Name.
157. In him he wished to reveal the great treasure he placed in his fathers,
158. and in him he promised to bless all through seed from him.
159. For his seed, he established a great covenant that cannot deceive,
160. and he sealed and gave it through vows that cannot be undone.
161. This was the cause of the election of Abram and his children:
162. that he may keep the treasury of life until it is revealed.
163. Otherwise let the son of Abraham, hater of the peoples, say
164. what was the reason the Creator chose him above all.
165. Why to him alone did he give the Law that gives life,
166. and estrange the peoples from the delight hidden within it?
167. If the entire Adamic race was his,
168. why did he choose one and reject the other in hypocrisy?
169. It is hypocrisy to raise up one and lower another;
170. it is injustice, when they are one, for them not to be one.
171. If he is the Creator, and the people and the peoples are his,
172. why is his creation not equal as he is equal?
173. Inequality is shown in the election of the people,
174. if the peoples are unable to delight in the blessings.
175. No, O son of Abram, do not divide the equality of our species,
176. and do not start a dispute between us and our Maker.
177. Your election is a cause in which is placed a treasury of life;
178. let our mortality be raised to life through the life that is from you [John 4:22].
179. The Creator chose you and placed life in you for the life of man;
180. why are you saddened that man lives life like you do?
181. The election of Abram and his sons was for all,
182. and like leaders they may show the path of life to man.
183. Life was hidden in the providing of the Law,
184. and one passed it to another mysteriously.

185. From Abraham the promise went forth and dwelt in David,
186. and from the house of David, it arrived and came to Mary.

VI. Mary and Christ's Conception

187. In Mary, the course of the path of the promise of life concluded,
188. and in her body, it entered, rested, and dwelt as in a harbor.
189. The daughter of man became a harbor of peace for human nature,
190. and the harsh waves of mortality did not crush her.
191. She carried our entire race in her womb like a ship,
192. and she went out and placed it on the shore of the kingdom above.
193. One spirit descended from above, from before the Hidden One,
194. and he directed her to tread quickly to the promise of heaven.
195. He brought a new gospel to the ears of the daughter of mortals,
196. and I am greatly astonished at the new sound he spoke to her [Luke 1:29].
197. The watcher preached a new conception without copulation,
198. and she accepted him without doubt, in faith.
199. Mary consented to the heavenly one in faith,
200. as the earth was completed in the beginning by the voice of the Creator.[5]
201. The same command that signaled to the earth that conceived Adam
202. also opened the earth of her flesh's womb for the second Adam.
203. The same Craftsman who took earth, but not with hands,
204. also fashioned in her a Body that resembles that first one.
205. The same Existence that breathed the spirit of life into Adam
206. also created a Soul that is akin to the one at the beginning.
207. In a new manner, resembling Adam, he fashioned Adam,
208. that Adam may resemble Adam in all that belongs to Adam.
209. His will took from the Adamic clay,
210. and fashioned and made him skillfully in Body and Soul.
211. Through him he renewed the image of that image that death had destroyed,
212. and engraved him in the same likeness in a bodily tablet.
213. His command mixed the medicine of life among his features,

214. that he may be able to give life to dead bodies.
215. He built him as a Temple for the dwelling of his Divinity,
216. in order to accept the adoration of all creatures through him.
217. He mixed something of all creatures in the clay of his fashioning,
218. to bind all into him in the peace that was unbound at the breaking of the command.
219. He enclosed the rational and the mute in the fence of his Body and Soul,
220. that they may look upon him as an Image that has every likeness.
221. He made him as a Dwelling-place of love, for himself and for all,
222. that the rational may inhabit him in love, and he in Will.
223. He revealed his Divinity in what he did,
224. that they may aim at the correct target of the revealing of the Individuals.
225. Through him, he revealed the Individuals hidden in him,
226. and he pointed them out through his fashioning as with a finger.
227. He preached his hidden Begetting on earth through the newness of his begetting,
228. and taught that he has a Son who is equal to his Existence.
229. In the name of his Begetting, he named his Son the Second Adam,
230. that he may tread the path to Fathering and Sonship.
231. The watcher also called him Son of the Most High as it was revealed [Luke 1:32],
232. that through his Name he may reveal the Son who is incomprehensible.
233. He was destined to ascend to the great station of the Word of the Father,
234. and he prepared and depicted him in his station through his name before the deeds.
235. He was to be one with the Son who is without beginning,
236. and he placed upon his head the Name of his Existence like a crown.
237. In grace he gave a crown and station to the Son of mortals,
238. and divinely exalted his conception and his birth.
239. For the sake of all, he chose him from all as a Firstfruit,
240. to reconcile all with his Being, and him with all.
241. For the sake of peace, he called and established him between himself and man,

242. that he may reconcile the division of peace through the peace of his Name.
243. Gabriel also gave a "peace" to his mother at his conception,
244. and called and invited the Power of the Most High to descend to her [Luke 1:28–35].
245. Spirit and Power dwelt together with his mother,
246. and perfected his great Name with the Son of the Hidden One.

VII. Distinction of Natures in Christ

247. It is not the Son of the Hidden One who came to a bodily birth,
248. but rather the Son of the daughter of man to whom the Will of the Hidden One descended.
249. The Will of the Hidden One descended from above, not Hiddenness [itself],
250. and dwelt in a womb not in Nature but rather in Love.
251. His Will descended to engrave a bodily Image,
252. not to engrave his own Individuality that is eternal.
253. He dwelt in another to sow life among mortality,
254. not to lose the Spring of Life through fashioning.
255. If not, how can he be what he is,
256. without being impoverished from that which he is; how could that be?
257. A new existence is entirely the undoing of the first one:
258. it cannot remain what it was when it is fashioned.
259. The Being is the Son of the Father, without time,
260. and if he came to a second birth, he has ceased being what he is.
261. He is without composition and without limit, like his Begetter,
262. and if he is limited in a womb of flesh, he becomes like everyone else.
263. All that the Father has, he has also, without beginning,
264. but if he is fashioned by the Holy Spirit, he is entirely made.
265. He said the Spirit would fashion the One in the womb,
266. so if this is so, he is made and not the Maker.
267. No, man, there is no man who makes himself,
268. and there is no one equal to him who can depict him like the rest.
269. The Nature that is eternal cannot change,

270. and the Limitless One cannot gain limit to his Limitlessness.
271. It cannot be for me to say that Existence accepted becoming,
272. and far be it from me to affirm that the Almighty was limited by flesh.
273. I do not accept the thing impossible to accept,
274. and I do not concede the thing impossible to concede: the fashioning of the Hidden One.
275. I do not believe that the One without beginning had a beginning,
276. nor that the Fashioner of all fashioned himself in flesh.
277. His Command fashioned Flesh in a womb of flesh,
278. in order to renew in him the flesh that was worn out in mortality.
279. He constructed Flesh in a new manner, without copulation,
280. and filled him with the Spirit, to beget man spiritually.
281. He completed his conception and birth by the power of the Spirit,
282. and he sanctified him and made him the holy Temple of the Will of his Love.
283. Love dwelt within him from the beginning of his fashioning,
284. and he did not separate from him, and does not separate or go away.
285. In him walks that Will who bound him in the womb,
286. and in the power of his Power, he conquers all powers, and reigns over all.
287. I say that he and the Power that works all in him are One,
288. One, but not one where I mingle distinct natures.
289. One I call the Will of the Hidden One and the unveiled Body,
290. and true though this is, I do not mingle the Hidden and unveiled.
291. It does not confuse me that there is distinction between one and the other,
292. inasmuch as the made nature is less than the Maker.
293. I do not trouble the settled order of the Hidden Nature,
294. nor do I undo the characteristics of the unveiled Body.
295. The Hidden One is hidden, as much as you mingle bodily things,
296. and the Body is a body, as much as you mix in spiritual things.
297. The Hidden One is not mixed with the Body except in Love,
298. and the unveiled one is not mingled with the Hidden One except in Name.

VIII. Unity of Person in Christ

299. In Name it is possible to call them One in Substance,
300. while the one speaking does not forget their distinctions.
301. On these terms I also call the two One Love:
302. the Son of God and the Son of humanity are one Person.[6]
303. The Son of God willed in his Will, through the Son of humanity,
304. and gave him what is his, and received what is his, but not in Nature.
305. In his Begetting without beginning, he honored his birth,
306. and in his unending authority, he exalted his station.
307. He called and established him in the great station of his Divinity,
308. that he may fill the place of the Hidden One to the works of his hands.
309. In place of his Hiddenness, there was the unveiledness of the unveiled Image,
310. that by his unveiledness he may preach the Power hidden from all.
311. His unveiled birth cried out to creatures like a trumpet,
312. regarding the Son who was begotten from eternity without beginning.
313. His is the conception, and his the bodily birth,
314. though the Word of the Father participates in his bodily characteristics.
315. His is the conception, and his the birth, and his the circumcision [Luke 2:21],
316. and he is the one who offers sacrifices to the Hidden One for the sake of his fashioning.
317. He was suckled with milk, and carried by knees, and kissed by a mouth,
318. and he is the One who crawled among infants in the marketplace.
319. He is the one who grew in small increments,
320. and he also accepted the power of wisdom through the power of the Spirit [Luke 2:52].
321. He completed the just acts of the Law of the Spirit at thirty years [Matt 3:15],
322. and he paid the debt to the God of all and reconciled all.
323. He was baptized by John as if in need,

324. and the preacher entombed his Body in a tomb of water.
325. He accepted the Power of the Spirit as the sign of a dove [Matt 3:16],
326. and upon him the voice of the Father witnessed, whose love is true.
327. He fasted and hungered according to what nature demanded of him,
328. and he entered battle in the wilderness with the mighty one [Matt 4:1–2].
329. His is hunger, and his is thirst, and his is sleep,
330. and he tired and sat, and asked for water to sate his thirst [John 4:7].
331. His is the visible Body that accepts sufferings,
332. and his the soul carrying the weight of discernment.
333. His the fear, and his the sweat, and his the prayer,
334. and he was strengthened by the spirit and did not slacken [Luke 22:43].
335. He in the upper room, and he in the judgment, and he on Golgotha,
336. and he accepted impure spit from impure mouths [Matt 27:30].
337. His the cross, and his the nails, and his the spear,
338. and he put down his head on the wood and commended his Spirit [Luke 23:46].
339. His is the Body that was in the tomb for three days,
340. and his the soul that went to Eden[7] and returned to it.
341. He descended among the dead without harm,
342. and he was raised in the Power of the Creator that was hidden in him.
343. In him was hidden the great Power of the Word of the Father,
344. and in the power of his Power, he was empowered to conquer his sufferings.
345. In him dwelt the Word of the Father willingly,
346. and while he was hidden in him, he did not share in his weaknesses.
347. In him completely from when the watcher announced to his mother;
348. in him in Will in a way that cannot be explained, how or how much.

349. In him before the passion and after the passion, without leaving;
350. in him on earth, and in him in heaven, without end.
351. I do not say that the Power of Existence left him,
352. not when in the Body, and not when he stripped off mortality.
353. I count him One with Existence due to his station,
354. One I call the Son of God, and the Word.

IX. Defense against Accusation of Heresy

355. I do not say they are two as the heretic says;
356. One, I say, as much as [the slanderer] slanders deceitfully.
357. No, slanderer, do not slander me as is your custom;
358. you never heard from me that God has a Son and another son.
359. No, you insolent one, do not condemn me falsely;
360. you do not see me wandering off the path.
361. No, you heretic, do not contend with my words;
362. do not think that I have ever departed from what is proper.
363. No, deceiver, do not accuse me before deceivers,
364. you have never examined me, that anyone should accept the witness of your words.
365. What do you have against me, O blinded with envy, without understanding,
366. that you quarreled with my words for nothing as if it were fair?
367. What do I have to do with you, violent and quarrelsome man,
368. who provokes with angry arguments in order to fight with me?
369. I appeal to you, O Hidden One dwelling in our unveiled Body through love:
370. chastise the rebels who revile you with passions.
371. I appeal to your Existence, O Being who is without beginning:
372. silence the voices who enclose you in a womb of flesh.
373. Because of you do the sons of heresy quarrel with us,
374. for we call to you with the Living Name that is fit for your Name.
375. They fight at every hour against your Life, to make it dead;
376. and because it is impossible, they make you dead deceitfully.
377. Those dead in sin deeply desire your death,
378. and they do not consider that your Nature is above harm.
379. O you filled with wrath, why do you want to kill the Living One;
380. is there no chance for life to cease in your own lives?

381. Why do you labor to imprison a Spirit into body parts,
382. when heaven and earth are not enough to contain him?
383. Why do you hate anyone who says that Existence does not die?
384. For whether he says it or not, he does not die.
385. Why do you begrudge anyone who exalts the misery of our body?
386. For whether it is praised or not, it reigns in glory.
387. What do you gain by killing the Immortal One,
388. and what did you lose when our Body reigns with Existence?
389. Is it not clear that Existence is greater than dangers?
390. And who does not know that the passion and death were of the Mortal One?
391. If it were possible for the mute to gain rational mouths,
392. they would agree with us that Existence does not die.
393. If there could be discernment in undistinguishing beings,
394. they would scorn whoever makes the Hidden Nature feel pain.
395. Come, silent things, judge justly with the rational,
396. who hide the open truth through foolishness.
397. Feel shame and modesty, even a little, you who have rationality,
398. and stop positing the suffering of the One who does not suffer.
399. Be silent; do not cry out insolently against Existence,
400. lest you be companions in the judgment of the backbiter.
401. The envy of your minds resembles the backbiter,
402. who also reviled the Adorable Name in the disguise of love.
403. Why are you friends of the evil one, O lacking in mind,
404. and estrange yourselves from the blessings that do not end?
405. O miserable ones, flee from conversing with the killer of man,
406. and come take refuge in the life that is hidden in the Faith.

X. The Permanent Unity of the Word with the Man

407. We believe that the will of Existence put on a Body from us,
408. and perfected him with sufferings [Heb 5:8], and bestowed life to man through him.
409. For the sake of life, he took him from us as a Principal,
410. and called him by his Name, that he may give life to all in his Name.

411. The Will of the Hidden One gave life through a Man from us,
412. and this is the Man who died and was raised, and lives and gives us life.
413. He has undone the binding of Sheol from the deceased,
414. and went out and preached the new Gospel of the life of the dead.
415. He died and lived through the Power of Life dwelling in him,
416. and while he was in death, the Life of his Life was above death.
417. The Will that accompanied him did not abandon him,
418. and did not turn away from aiding him at the time of suffering.
419. With him in judgment, and with him on the wood, and with him in the tomb,
420. and while he was with him in his weaknesses, he did not participate.
421. The mortal nature accepted his natural characteristics in himself,
422. and the Hidden Nature remained with him without changing.
423. He did not change, and again I say that he did not change,
424. and if someone gets angry, let him be angry again, for he does not change.
425. That which changed was the nature of man, which gained life,
426. who took off his sufferings and put on the glory of immortality.
427. It was a mortal who died on the cross, distinct from the Word,
428. and by the Power of the Word, he conquered death and distributed life.
429. It was a mortal, and again I say it was a mortal,
430. and true though this is, One I call him and the Word.
431. In his nature, he bore the humiliations that humiliated him,
432. and in his temptations, he learned to help those who are tempted.
433. Through his vindication, he vindicated our guiltiness,
434. and in his victory, he wove our race a crown of glory.
435. The Power dwelling in him crowned him in great glory,
436. and invited and called watchers and men to glorify him.
437. He showed his glory and his great station to watchers and men,
438. and gathered them to consider him on the day of his ascension.
439. He left him on earth for forty days when he had been raised,
440. to verify any doubt of his race through his embodiment.

441. To verify his race, he showed the place of the nails and spear in his body,
442. and he ate and drank after he became immortal.
443. In all these things, the Hidden Power dwelling in him perfected him,
444. and when they were finished, he brought him above to the heights above all.
445. The day of his ascension was greater than any day,
446. and the path he trod to heaven was gorgeous.
447. Assemblies and assemblies of spirits stood to consider him:
448. how can a Body fly through the air against all custom?
449. Watchers and men saw a new thing in the Head of Humanity,
450. who opened the doors that had been shut against the face of man.
451. The gaze of all was fixed on him spiritually,
452. until he reached the place where there was no chance to see [him].
453. The Hidden Signal passed him through the veil above,
454. and he entered and considered that fashioning that does not decay.
455. He entered to minister the great and perfect dwelling [Heb 9:24],
456. and his great station will not end after any time.
457. With Existence, he holds authority without end,
458. and his staff rules for the ages, over all and in all.
459. Who would not marvel at the great love of God,
460. who has made us with him the heirs of his glory and authority?
461. Who would not confess the true incomprehensible faith,
462. that he has brought him up and placed the work of his hands with his greatness?
463. Who would not praise the craftsmanship of the power of the Creator,
464. who bound the world in one Man and called him by his Name?
465. One Creator engraved his will [in his nature] like an Image,[8]
466. and brought him up and placed him above all, to judge all.

XI. Christ in Heaven

467. He placed him in the heights above all like a spectacle,
468. that by his unveiledness, all may see the beauty of the Hidden One.

469. In his Embodiment, he wished to show his Love to all,
470. that they may not be discouraged from asking requests of his Hiddenness.
471. In him he concluded all in the unsearchable search,
472. and turned the sight of all to him, that will not turn away.
473. He made his Body a second sun in that fashioning,
474. that hc may fill the place of Light and the place of the eyes.
475. He is Light to all who examine his brightness,
476. and the light [of the sun] is like nothing compared to his Light.
477. In the globe of his Body is the Hidden Will that chose him from all,
478. and made him more beautiful than all to those who see.
479. Like rays, the wisdom of truth goes out from him,
480. and instructs all in that knowledge that is incomprehensible.
481. No teacher teaches wisdom to others there [Heb 8:11],
482. for learning has rested from labor, that it may not be doubted.
483. He has made man and spirits dwell in the harbor of life,
484. and they will not again journey laboriously for the rest of time.
485. The course of words and deeds rests in him,
486. and no one asks "what is this" or "why is this?"
487. No one asks, "Where is the Hidden One who is not searched?"
488. For the inquiry about him is searchable by the mind.
489. There, the thing made cannot say of its Maker
490. that the door of his unchanging Will is shut in his face.
491. No one has doubts about where he is or that he is hidden from all,
492. for he has silenced the love of his inclination, that it may not doubt.
493. One sees the Hidden One in the Visible One, not with sight,
494. and in him the desire of his soul is fulfilled without neediness.
495. There what is written is fulfilled, that he is the Image of man,
496. for the Image of Existence is seen in him in the eyes of all creatures.
497. There he will be the Lord over all indeed,
498. and will rule over all and subjugate all under his authority.
499. There the demons who had made light of his Lordship will be ashamed,
500. and will bend the knee and hallow him, though unwillingly.
501. There the divided parties of heretics will end,

502. and will no longer lead astray with the ignorance of asserting change in God.
503. There the war prepared against the Hidden One will cease,
504. and there the battle made against the Unveiled One will rest.
505. There they will truly confess two Likenesses:
506. the likeness of a Servant and that of the Maker, One Person.[9]
507. There, all tongues will confess One Person,
508. and will repeat one hallowing there to the Word and the Body.
509. They will together adore the Hidden and Unveiled One in one equality,
510. and while it may seem they are two, they are preached as One.
511. Through their worship they will there see a great marvel,
512. that with the Maker, the One Made will receive the worship of all.
513. The wonder is equal, and the world too small to marvel at it:
514. how can the creation adore at the temple of a Body?
515. Who is able to consider this precisely,
516. and who can say how great is its Power?
517. The Power of Existence alone is enough to say how great,
518. and it knows how to inspect it wisely.
519. This craftsmanship is true craftsmanship,
520. that of the Craftsman who created the creation craftily.
521. Craftily he fashioned and made it according to his Intelligence,
522. and perhaps from eternity he considered it and then made it exist.
523. In the end he examined it as he knew it from the beginning,
524. and it was seen to him before it existed as it did.
525. In the fullness of time, his Will, perfect in Existence, perfected it,
526. and richly poured out his love upon all and in all.
527. He revealed the great wealth of Divinity to his works,
528. and established a Man to manage [what is God's] through what is his own.
529. He chose one Authority from among man according to his will,
530. and sealed him in his Name, and gave him a station to rule and judge.
531. In the place of his Love, he called and established him before his fashioning,
532. that the place of his invisible Existence may be filled.
533. A Man filled the place of Existence for man and watchers,

534. and in seeing his Body, their sight rests and their seeking is silenced.
535. This is the reason for the greatness of his station and authority:
536. that he may preach the Power of Hiddenness through his Unveiling.
537. Two causes are hidden in his Name, and they are greatly honorable:
538. one of Existence and one of Love toward all.
539. It was impossible for things that are made to see the Secret Being,
540. so he comforted them by an open Vision, lest they be crushed.
541. They had also been cheated from Divine Authority,
542. so he made an incomprehensible opportunity and gave them a share.
543. The Cause of our life is great and incomprehensible,
544. and as much as we speak, we are too small to say how great it is.
545. Heaven and earth, if they became a mouth for us,
546. do not have the power to announce how great it is.
547. Great though the Cause of our life is, and incomprehensible,
548. the sons of conflict do not consider it to be what it is.

XII. Concluding Chastisement

549. Evil upon you, heretics, how wrong you are,
550. for you have cheated the Good One whose blessing has no equal.
551. O beaten who do not leave off conflict,
552. why do you destroy the great height of the building of Truth?
553. O deceivers who are deceived by the evil ones,
554. why do you tear apart the being of man and of Divinity?
555. Divinity desires to honor man in what is its own;
556. why is it bad to you that men are sons of God?
557. The Being has shared his great station with human nature;
558. why is it stupid to you to share in a free grace?
559. Cease, quarrelers, from fighting against this,
560. and look and consider that watchers and men are amazed at it.
561. Look at the greatness of the heavenly who praise this,
562. and do not cease or be silent in glorifying how glorious it is.
563. Well was it fashioned that man may become Divine [1 John 3:2],
564. and no one is able to repay thanks to its Fashioner.

565. Well has the made nature ruled with its Maker;
566. for there is none among things made that is able to find fault with this.
567. Do not find fault, heretic, lacking in mind,
568. with that Existence who does all it does well.
569. Come, if you wish, and praise and exalt with all creatures
570. that Craftsman who shared his greatness with his work.

DIALOGUE BETWEEN THE WATCHER AND MARY

1. O Power of the Father that descended and dwelt in a virgin womb, as his Love desired, grant me a mouth to speak your great and incomprehensible story!
2. O Son of the Rich One who sent down his mercies, and who dwelt in the womb of a poor woman: grant me voice and word to speak while I marvel.
3. The mouth is too small to speak of you, and the tongue to describe you, and voice and word are weak as well, for I wish to tell your story and speak of you.
4. Help me to approach your exaltation, O Lord of all, though I am afraid: the head of the watchers announced to the virgin mother regarding your descent.
5. Come, O prudent, attend and listen to the story filled with all wonders, and sing praise to the One who was brought low to give life to Adam who was lost.
6. The mercies of the Father indicated to the Son to come down and save his construction, and he called Gabriel and commanded him to prepare a path before his coming.
7. His mercies dawned toward the daughter of David, that she may be a mother to him who created Adam and the world, whose Name is before the sun [Ps 72:17].
8. The incomprehensible Will that called and commanded the angel girt and sent him from the ranks to a pure virgin and announced to her.

9. He took the letter of the Perfect One, in a mystery concealed from the ages, and he filled a young girl with peace, and all nations with good hope.
10. The spirit flew, descended, and arrived to the barren one, and he fell down and adored. He gave her a greeting and announced to her regarding her conception that fills all with awe.

Alap

The Watcher said to Mary: "Peace with you, mother of my Lord; blessed are you, mother of my Lord, and blessed is the fruit in your womb" [Luke 1:28, 42].

Mary said: "Who are you, sir? And what is the story you tell? What you say is strange to me, and I am unable to understand its meaning."

Beth

Watcher: "Blessed of women, in you does the Most High wish to dwell. Fear not. In you has Grace been pleased to pour out his mercies upon the world."

Mary: "I wish, sir, that you not insist I accept you without objection. What you say is distant from me, and I cannot understand it."

Gamal

Watcher: "The Father has revealed it to me, and so have I revealed it to you: the Mystery that is between them—between him and his Son—for which I was sent: that from you he will dawn upon the world."

Mary: "You are a flame; do not harm me. You wear burning coals; do not frighten me. O fiery one, why should I remain with you, for all you have spoken with me is a novelty?"

Dalath

Watcher: "It is a wonder that you do not believe—that you would let go the trust that has come to you, for the Begotten of the Most High rejoices to dwell in your womb."

Mary: "I am afraid to accept you, sir, for indeed my mother Eve, when she accepted the snake who spoke to her as a friend, was deprived of glory" [Gen 3:1].

Heh

Watcher: "That imposter deceived, my daughter, when he made her trust him. I am not like him, however, for I have been sent by God."

Mary: "This story you tell me is contentious like that one—do not blame me—for in a virgin has never been found a son, nor in a fruit, Divinity."

Waw

Watcher: "O daughter, the Father pledged me to bring his peace, and [pledged] that I could trust you, for his Son will rise from your womb. There are no words contrary to mine."

Mary: "Your pledge is fair, and even your word. If only nature would not shake me and make me terrified to accept you: all on account of 'a fruit being found in a virgin.'"

Zayn

Watcher: "Angels tremble at his word, and, as soon as he commands, do not act insolently. But you—do you not fear to prevent something that the Father desires?"

Mary: "I was indeed shaken, Lord, and alarmed, and being afraid, I dared not tell you that nature itself has forbidden virgins to give birth."

Ḥeth

Watcher: "The Love of the Father has thus desired that, in your virginity, you shall give birth to a Son. It is right that you accept and be open, that the will of the Father not be constrained."

Mary: "Your visage is honorable, and your story awesome, and your fire ablaze. The Love of your Lord will not be constrained, but it is difficult for me to verify this all."

Ṭeth

Watcher: "I have brought you glad tidings—that the Begotten of the Lord will be revealed to you. O girl, confess him who has made you worthy to be his mother, as he is your Son."

Mary: "I am only a girl and not able to accept a man of fire [Heb 12:29], for your difficult story is not easy for me, nor is it easy for me to examine and confirm what you have said."

Yodh

Watcher: "Today hope has been revealed to Adam—that through you the Lord of all would be seen, that he would descend, unbind, and free him. Accept these things and give thanks."

Mary: "Today I have been astonished and amazed in all the things that you have said to me, but I am fearful of accepting you, for perhaps there is deceit in your word."

Kap

Watcher: "When I was sent to convince you, I heard his greeting, and came to you. My Lord is trustworthy, and desires this: that from you he dawn upon the world."

Mary: "All your words amaze me—I am allowed, Lord, do not blame me. The story you speak to me is hidden from me, and it frightens me to accept you."

Lamadh

Watcher: "He is coming to you, do not turn away. In your womb will he dwell, do not hold back. O full of blessings, sing canticles to him who is pleased to be found in you."

Mary: "No, sir. I am not known of man, and I have not met with copulation, so how can it be as you say, that one without intercourse give birth to a son?"

Mym

Watcher: "By the Holy Spirit, who is without suspicion, will you accept a conception that is beyond understanding, and the power of the Most High will descend upon you, that the King may dawn from your womb" [Luke 1:35].

Mary: "Well, then, O watcher, do not turn away from me. If the Holy Spirit is coming to me, it is easy for me to be his handmaid. Therefore, be it done unto me according to your word."

Nun

Watcher: "Raise up your head, O maiden. Let your heart rejoice, O virgin. The second heaven is pleased in you, and earth is given peace in your Son."

Mary: "My head is raised, sir, as you say, and I will rejoice when I see your Lord. But, if you are his servant, it is thus proper [to ask you], what does he resemble? Do you know?"

Simkath

Watcher: "Our ranks do not dare to look upon him who is so awesome, for he is hidden in the fire of his Father, and flame covers him."

Mary: "This shakes me very much, for if he is a Flame, as you say, how will my womb not be harmed—if a Fire dwells in me?"

ʻe

Watcher: "Your very womb is filled with holiness, and your virginity is confirmed, and the sanctified place is much beloved, in the God who will be seen therein."

Mary: "O angel, reveal to me, now, why it is fitting for him to dwell in a poor woman, for, behold, the world is full of the daughters of kings, so why does he wish me to be treasured?"

Pe

Watcher: "It is easy for him to dwell in a rich woman, as well as in your pure poverty, and it is by friendship that the poor he makes rich by his revelation."

Mary: "Make plain to me also, if you know, why does he wish to come to me? And if, like a fire, he is unseen, why will he dwell in me as he says?"

Ṣadeh

Watcher: "He wishes to come and, indeed, in you to dwell. And while he is not seen, you cannot perceive. Nor do I even dare to look upon you, who are full of fire and do not burn" [Exod 3:2].

Mary: "I wish, Lord, to ask you—make also clear to me the habits of my Son, who dwells within me, whom I do not know: What shall I do for him who will not misbehave?"

Qop

Watcher: "Holy, holy, holy is the Lord. Holy and glorious and exalted his Name. And all that is made is unable to say a word against your Son."

Mary: "Holy and glorious and blessed his Name, who has looked upon the abasement of his handmaid. Henceforth shall call me blessed all the generations of the world."

Resh

Watcher: "Height and depth and all therein, watchers and men, glorify him who has descended and dwelt in a virgin, that he may free all the visible world."

Mary: "Great is his Power and unending, and unable to be spoken upon lips. The sky above does not contain him, but behold: a womb below suffices for him."

Shyn

Watcher: "Heaven and earth are made one, and sing to him with one voice—even the angels and a virgin who serve the Mysteries between them!"

Mary: "Heaven above rejoices in the angels, and earth below in a virgin. And when both sides exult, they bring glory to the Son of their Lord."

Taw

Watcher: "Both sides will mingle—angels and men—and will glorify the Son who has reconciled them who were angry and agitated."

Mary: "Thanksgiving to [God] from all angels of fire who are unseen. From every mouth in the world, the earth sings praises to you!"

Chapter 6

MEMRA 7: ON JOHN THE BAPTIST

INTRODUCTION

This memra is a running commentary on the life of John the Baptist, from his conception to his death at the hands of Herod. Here again we observe Narsai's style of reflective interposition of spiritual meaning while working through a biblical account. The central proposition of this memra, however, does not come from John the Baptist but from Christ, who calls John greater than any man born of woman (Matt 11:11). This cue from Christ prompts Narsai to ask what exactly makes John so special, and this memra is the fruit of that reflection.

John the Baptist is the endpoint of prophecy, which until now has been a violent struggle of doubt and debate (as Narsai interprets Matt 11:12 in lines 3–6). John is not here to debate or doubt, much less be doubted. He is here as the ambassador announcing the coming of the new King (line 35). His announcements come about not only through his words and actions, but by his very being. Indeed, the oddities surrounding his birth of two elderly, sterile people itself announces Christ's entirely supernatural birth from a Virgin (lines 45–46), and even as an infant in the womb, he announces Christ by leaping and teaching his own mother to praise Mary, the mother of the Lord (lines 50, 61–62).

Mary and Elizabeth are fundamentally holy women who, participating in the work of God's Spirit, begin to reverse the damage done by Eve (line 53) and fulfill the promises given to Abraham and

Sarah as their daughters (lines 63–64). This is an important section of the memra, among other reasons because it partially balances out the misogynistic tirade of Section IX, prompted by Narsai's anger at Herodias. The embarrassing section in question is published here for the sake of completion and historical record, and not for imitation.

Returning to John, Narsai examines several ways in which he is the greatest of men. Important among them is his life in the desert, which was laborious and difficult, but spiritual even from his youth (lines 91–92). Indeed, the desert at some point becomes personified as John's own teacher (line 98), and gives him a harsh and chaotic life to teach him how to find peace in the midst of it (line 104). As plant life in a desert is unlikely, John's own life is marked by many unlikelihoods. Indeed, one reason he is greatest of men is because he is the quintessential "underdog." He grew physically strong with little bodily nourishment (line 152); he was intelligent enough to stump the Pharisees without any human teachers (line 101); he battled both his own sinful human inclinations as well as demons, and in both became conqueror (lines 143–144), both as a rugged man of the wilderness and as a vessel of God's Spirit (line 152). In all this, John is absolutely unique (lines 161–182), and his virtue is victorious over sloth, lust, greed, pride, wrath, and envy (lines 184–199; John's victory over gluttony is so obvious as not even to merit mention).

These decades of harsh training in the ascetic life are not an end in themselves, however, but rather for the sake of John's ambassadorship, his spiritual mission in announcing the coming Messiah. He grew in a harsh chaos in order to bring true peace to those who are living in comfort (line 125). The true spiritual desert is a bad culture (line 107), and John living and thriving in the physical desert gives hope of life to those living in a spiritual one. This parallels his birth from elderly parents, which gives hope of life-giving to the sterile (lines 23, 123). John is, to his people, the farmer who pulls the weeds and the sower of good seed (line 113), as well as a voice crying out and waking up the sleeping (line 116).

Despite the fact that John's baptism of repentance is incomplete and does not give the Holy Spirit (lines 266–269), this does not change the fact that John is the greatest of men naturally born. He represents a primordial natural justice, but one held with superhuman virtue through the grace of God (line 212). This places him in direct opposition to Herod, who is extreme in his vice of adultery with his brother's wife, and their conflict is described by Narsai as a war, and John is a warrior (lines 291–318). But bringing the truth to those who resist it is a fight that the just man will suffer and die for (line 319). John's virtue prevents him from being intimidated by political power (line 342), and therefore the conflict ensues. Because John is the greatest of all men, Herod his persecutor is therefore the most evil (lines 353, 429). While this is somewhat hyperbolic, Narsai takes pains to illustrate Herod's viciousness as well as that of Herodias and her daughter. Indeed, according to Narsai, the murder of John was Herod's plan all along, and the event of his birthday and the promise given to his niece was a preplanned ruse (lines 363–398).

In the end, as John's very conception and birth prepared the way for those of Christ, as well as his ministry (especially in its conflicts), so does his death. This makes John both the final prophet of the Old Testament and the beginning of the New Testament, a minister of both and a hinge connecting the age of prophets to the Messiah (lines 505f.).

TRANSLATION

I. John the Baptist as the Completion of Prophecy

1. The voice of prophecy was worn out on a wearisome course
2. until it came to the peaceful harbor of the dawning[1] of our Lord.
3. The just had been going through a laborious struggle in revealing the Spirit [Matt 11:12],
4. until one victor conquered and gave them victory.
5. They were doubting among the laborious mysteries of objections,[2]
6. until the Truth came to the open and gave them rest.
7. They were meditating and musing about this Hope,
8. until they touched it[3] with unveiled senses and were comforted.
9. In every fashion, they longed for that which happened,
10. until it happened, and the course of their contest came to rest.
11. From one to the next, they passed on the hope of their promises,

12. until one revelation to one just man completed it.
13. One revelation completed their revelations,
14. and a Voice testifies that the course of their revelations had come to rest [Matt 3:17].
15. They heard this through him, in an unveiled Voice,
16. that in John, the revelations of prophecy were completed.
17. The Torah and the mystery of prophetic revelations—
18. their predictions received completion through John.

II. The Birth and Upbringing of John the Baptist

19. His birth silenced the course of mysteries and parables,
20. and revealed and declared the mystery of spiritual declarations.
21. Through the birth of the just one, grace revealed the power of his wisdom,
22. and trod the path for man to walk to the promise of life.
23. The son of the sterile was like a guide for the sterility of man,
24. and they began to repay fruits of praise to the Name of the Creator.
25. The Spirit of revelation revealed the mystery of hidden things to his father,
26. and he spoke and confessed: "blest is the Creator" who visited him [Luke 1:68].
27. The Spirit instructed the splendid priest, son of the Hebrews,
28. and revealed and showed that the time had come for the salvation of man.
29. He compared the salvation of man that was declared to him to a trumpet [Luke 1:69],
30. in which rebellious demons who pierced our race were pierced.
31. By means of his birth, he revealed the mystery of the salvation of our life,
32. and named his son "pity that pities the sons of men."[4]
33. The name of John is a name of pity that pities man,
34. and his ambassadorship depicts an image of the King of Kings.
35. The preacher went out before the one to come like an ambassador,
36. and showed his dawning to the heavenly and the earthly.
37. He set out on the path of preaching beyond the natural order,
38. for while he was an infant, he began the works of maturity.

39. O mature one, while immature in bodily senses,
40. the Spirit matured him for his ambassadorship before the King.
41. O immobile one, who had not moved through the study of the Scriptures,
42. whom [the Spirit] instructed above the wise and the readers of the Scriptures.
43. O one who had the measure of an ignorant child,
44. who gained the taste of discernment beyond measure.
45. O John, conceived in nature but not in nature,
46. whose conception preached conception without copulation.[5]
47. The King whose ambassador you were was conceived without copulation,
48. and beyond the natural order, you revealed order in the womb of your mother.
49. While in the womb of your mother, you saw the mother of the King of Kings,
50. and revealed to your mother to call his mother "the mother of the Lord" [Luke 1:44].
51. Your mother called Mary, his mother, "the mother of the Lord,"
52. and returned thanks to the one who revealed hidden mysteries to her.
53. O marvel that occurred among the daughters of Eve,
54. who humbly repaid thanks to the children within them.
55. Who has ever seen pregnant women beyond the custom,
56. who are made to prophesy about the greatness of their children?
57. Who has examined the joyful wonder of two women,
58. who conceived immediately, out of the natural order passing among women?
59. The marvel within them was spoken among the Hebrews [Luke 1:65],
60. and they were amazed at the new conceptions beyond custom.
61. Without hope, the mother of the servant and the mother of the Lord conceived,
62. one in sterility and one in a manner without copulation.
63. Here what was written about Abraham she fulfilled,
64. for while there was no hope, the daughters of Abraham awaited hope.
65. Elizabeth gained good hope through the unexpected son,

66. and her son became the one who gave hope to the hopeless.
67. O one who did not hope to hope a hope of salvation,
68. and who interpreted the manners of blessings that were unseen to him!
69. O John, young in body and mature in soul,
70. whose voice became an instructor to man and the heavenly!
71. O man who was not yet mature in the order of manhood:
72. you became an ambassador from God to humanity.

III. John as Greatest of Men

73. O how amazing is the narration of the account that is spoken of you,
74. and yet no man can relate the ways of your story.
75. I wish to relate the manners of your works before those who hear,
76. and I fear that my mind will not be enough to order your story.
77. It is a great fear to relate the manners of your history,
78. and it is daring to ascend to the height of your story.
79. Your story is greater than all the stories of the sons of flesh,
80. and your account is loftier, because you are exalted above all who are born [Matt 11:11].
81. None among creatures can relate you as you are,
82. except for the One whom you preached before many.
83. Before many, you unveiled the mystery of the salvation of man,
84. and like an image, you depicted the icon of his Sacrifice.
85. The Spirit of revelation dragged you to the desert while you were a youth [cf. Luke 1:80],
86. and I want to know why there is a youth in the desert.
87. I heard that your fellow servants were calling you a youth,
88. and my mind endeavored to attend well to noble things.
89. The image of your works I saw depicted by fishermen,
90. and I gave my mind over to consider the beauty of your labors.
91. The Spirit taught you to be guided through laborious labors,
92. and while you are mortal, you depicted images of immortal beings.
93. The power of the Spirit was a spirit and instructor to you,
94. and it taught you an order greater than the order of those who order.
95. You were a student of a spiritual teaching,

96. and it gave you the great station of doctrine.
97. Come, O hearers, and hear the wonder of John,
98. who was raised without the discipline of teachers.
99. Good habits and order are usually gained from many people,
100. and here is the wonder: while there are no people, there is everything.
101. The order of the one who grew in the desert was more perfect than anyone's,
102. and perhaps even the desert was amazed by him in wonder.
103. The desert, which has no lucidity, was left in great wonder,
104. and it marveled like a discerning thing at the peacefulness of his peace.
105. O John, who brought peace to the imprudent desert,
106. who converted and brought peace to disturbed discernment.
107. The dwelling of man was like a soulless desert,
108. and it lacked the blessings of the love of the truth.
109. Mankind was filled with a thicket of evil and thorns of malice,
110. the life of man was choked, but no one weeded [Matt 13:7].
111. Nature was cut open and the Law of the Spirit was overturned,
112. and demons and men trampled upon it brutally.
113. The voice of John worked the world, a second wasteland,
114. and instead of seeds, he sowed the hope of the forgiveness of sin.

IV. John Battles in the Wilderness

115. The Adamic race had died in dead sin,
116. and it awoke from death, as from sleep, with the voice of forgiveness [Matt 3:3].
117. The guilty, sons of the guilty, heard the voice of forgiveness,
118. and they woke up and tore the bond of evils that had judged them in sin.
119. Adam had written a bond of debts in the land of Eden,
120. and he raised his children with a disgraceful discipline.
121. The race of man had been overturned in disgraces,
122. until it heard the voice of John, and then it became modest.
123. The One who chose him to be an ambassador, in this pretext,
124. made him pacify the quarrel that the evil one had cast among men.

125. With this intent, the desert raised him outside of peacefulness,
126. that he may know how to pacify the divisions of man.
127. He who accomplishes all accomplished this faithfully,
128. that through his servant, he may turn his servants back to his Lordship.
129. The divine command placed a banner of peace for him,
130. that he may see it before him with the senses of the body and the powers of the soul.
131. The Spirit clothed him with the armor of the Spirit entirely [cf. Eph 6:11],
132. lest he be pierced by the arrows of the backbiter.
133. The backbiter was going to war against his thoughts,
134. and he girded himself with the Spirit like a warrior with armor.
135. He gave himself over to battle like a warrior,
136. and he endured the fight against evil until death.
137. The assemblies above marveled at his fortitude,
138. at how much he endured and did not weaken in the contest of his labors.
139. The tyrannical demons were amazed at his courage,
140. how he conquered their power in the longings of his body.
141. The son of mortals was thrown into two difficult battles:
142. the battle of demons and the battle of brutal passions.
143. The demons plotted to weaken him through deceit,
144. and the powers of his soul through the enticements of desires.
145. His body and soul were strengthened by the strength of the Spirit,
146. and through it he prevailed over his desires and the desire of the evil one.
147. Nature sought after him silently with natural things,
148. and demons laid traps of deceit for him deceitfully.
149. Two enemies fought against his freedom,
150. and he alone did not weaken from the fight.
151. His body and soul labored in labors,
152. and the marvel is that he labored, was crushed, inflicted, and conquered.
153. The nourishment of his body was shortened and less than normal,

154. but the work of his life was greater and more exalted than bodily things.
155. He was nourished by miserable locusts and the honey of wasps [Matt 3:4],
156. and the power of the Spirit protected him with the nourishment of the Spirit.
157. The power that empowered Moses the great in intense fasting [Exod 34:28]
158. gave [John] victory of soul against enticements.
159. The same command that gave Elijah power over eating [1 Kings 19:8]
160. gave [John] the strength to conquer the passions of desire.
161. Elijah went forty days with little food,
162. and John thirty years in a desert of want.
163. The just man went on a laborious path for thirty years,
164. and though it was laborious itself, it was restful to him.
165. O man going along a path filled with fear,
166. who was not shaken by the many evils of fear on your path!
167. O heated one enflamed with love of his Lord,
168. whose love did not cool through the fight for his Lord!
169. O soldier who was armored with the armor of labors,
170. who did not take off his armor night or day for thirty years!
171. O athlete who took up a fight against immaterial beings,
172. and did not lose a hair of his body against the prince of the air!
173. O fight that has no equal among the earthly,
174. and perhaps even the heavenly assemblies are smaller than!
175. O conscience, how victorious in labors,
176. which did not weaken the entire time it labored and suffered!
177. O bodily members, how much did they bear the weight of their enticements,
178. and did not weaken in the fight of unusual labors!
179. John went on the path of labors unusually,
180. and the ways of his works are strangers to comparison.
181. No mortal has gone on a path that resembles his,
182. nor an earthly one who has endured the battle that he endured.
183. His soul was occupied in good meditation without conversation,
184. and who would not wonder that sloth did not overcome him?
185. Without comfort, he comforted himself in things unrevealed,

186. and who would not say that the Spirit wrapped him in secrets?
187. Where indeed were the tiresome sufferings of human nature,
188. which were not found before that Power that fought within him?
189. How did the desire of flesh, the second fire, cool?
190. For even the scent of its heat did not touch his pure body.
191. How was the love of money, the source of evils, cut off,
192. and its flow not reach the height of the soul of the one with girt soul?
193. Who bound up the love of glory, the hateful hawk?
194. For its claws did not remain in the mind with small wings.[6]
195. Who calmed the turbulence of turbulent arrogance?
196. For it did not bite or kick the solid mind of the solid man.
197. Who put a bridle of silence upon the passion of wrath?
198. For it did not enflame the soul angrily as it usually does.
199. Who killed envy, the killer of man?
200. For it was dead in John as in a tomb.
201. Disordered passions were dead in him as in a tomb,
202. and while they were alive, they were not alive to his free soul.
203. They went about as nonliving things in his mortality,
204. and the desires did not have power over his body.
205. They had the power to shake him like other people,
206. but the power of the Spirit roared within him, and they trembled.
207. Trembling and fear were in the passions in John,
208. and they were afraid to battle him as they usually do.
209. He suffered them as one suffering with the passions of his soul,
210. but was raised above their sufferings through endurance.
211. Through endurance, he conquered the passions of his body,
212. and man though he was, through his works he became superhuman.
213. The just man was superhuman, beyond human,
214. until the time for the dawning of the King who chose him came.

V. John Preparing for Christ

215. In the fullness of time, the fulfiller of time came suddenly,
216. and began crying out that the time of mortality is finished.

217. The preacher cried out that the time is fulfilled [cf. Matt 3:2] (about the time of the world),
218. and the time had arrived that ends the times that are full of time.
219. The son of Zechariah called to sinners to repent,
220. and taught them to destroy evil through baptism [Matt 3:6].
221. The son of the sterile opened up the baptism of the forgiveness of faults,
222. and began to give birth to new men from within the water.
223. The voice of the trumpet of voices preached the mystery of renewal,
224. and those dead in sin woke up from sin as from sleep.
225. The sons of Abraham were drowning in the sleep of sin,
226. and the voice of the preacher, the son of Abraham, woke them up.
227. The people of obstinate mind took pride in the name of Abraham,
228. and the just man chastised them, that it is not just to take pride in names [Matt 3:9].
229. "Do not be arrogant in the name of Abraham, sons of Abraham,
230. and do not settle on a name lacking fruits.
231. It is your duty to show fruits of works [Matt 3:8],
232. repay your duty purely to the One who loves you."
233. John sowed these words in the ears of the people,
234. and each man began to tear up the deed of his sins.
235. He showed them that the deed of sins is erased in water,
236. until the One comes who erases sin and gives the Spirit [Matt 3:11].
237. He erased the sin of the people with water alone,
238. and taught them about the One who comes after his words.
239. After his words dawned the Dawn that gladdens all,
240. and he began to cry out and show him to the eyes of those who see.
241. He openly showed the greatness of his station, how great it is,
242. and how small he was if compared to his greatness.
243. "He is great and exalted as high as the heaven is compared to us,
244. and I am unworthy even to untie the sandal of his feet [Matt 3:11].
245. He is the King of all, and the Judge of angels and man,
246. and there is no creature that does not adore him as Lord.
247. The Power of Existence gave him names greater than him,[7]

248. and for this I said that angels and men adore him.
249. He did not gain the Name that all adore by his nature;
250. the Nature above all made him to be honored by all.
251. I also marvel at the greatness of his station, who am his servant,
252. and I am preparing to reveal to men the greatness of his station.
253. For the sake of man, the Lover of man honored him with his Name,
254. that he may forgive the sin of man through the sacrifice of himself.
255. The sin of man troubled the peace of the sons of men,
256. and the Good One wished to reconcile men through a Man."
257. The good servant preached these things before the Lord of all,
258. like a debtor pays tribute to a master who chose him.
259. The Hebrew sowed these sounds in the ears of his people,
260. and prepared them to accept the King who had dawned.
261. The just man established these opportunities for the wicked,
262. that they may hate the wicked one, who hates them, at every opportunity.
263. He wished to transform the ugliness of man through the beauty of his words,
264. and he sanctified water and forgave them their debts.
265. The Forgiver of Debts taught him the ritual of the forgiveness of debts,
266. that he may tread the path for that complete and good forgiveness.
267. The forgiveness of debts that John gave was not complete,
268. for he could not give the Spirit to those who were forgiven [cf. Acts 18:25].
269. He only promised to forgive through water,
270. and showed that there is a forgiveness greater than his.
271. "Behold, a man is coming after me who is much greater than I am [Matt 3:11],
272. who forgives sin, and gives the Spirit, and provides life.
273. He will provide immortal life to man,
274. and they will no longer fear the transformation of mortality.
275. Through his death he will destroy the power of death that destroys man,
276. and crush the mighty pride of tyrannical demons.

277. Demons had pulled down the race of man into the chasm they had dug,
278. …[8]
279. Satan had stung the head of humanity with the sting of sin,
280. and a man turned and broke the sting of his bitterness.
281. The gall of his bitterness had spread over our entire species,
282. and from within our species came a Healer for our wounds.
283. The Lover of our species chose a skillful Healer from our species [Matt 9:12],
284. and taught him to heal the wounds of our species with the medicine of the Spirit.
285. The Divine Power gave him the medicine of the Spirit,
286. and divinely, he healed all manner of evils with it.
287. Like the sun, his revelation dawned among the dark [Matt 4:16],
288. and it chased away the error that had been spread upon and within all."

VI. John the Warrior

289. The voice of John resounded on earth about his coming,
290. and error trembled, and the foundations of the building of sin were shaken.
291. The word of the son of Zechariah flashed like a sword,
292. and demons marveled at the sharpness of the word of his mouth.
293. As with a sword, he destroyed the side of error,
294. and the ranks of truth were strengthened by his courage.
295. The King chose a brave worker and sent him before him,
296. and girt him with armor whose might could not be overpowered.
297. The armored worker, son of Hebrews, swaggered in his armor,
298. and did not weaken in the battle against his enemy.
299. He conquered in every fight with his enemy,
300. and was victorious as much as possible in fighting.
301. He ran the course of his labors without abundance,
302. but did not weary of the fight against sin.
303. He carried his armor against evil night and day,
304. and he preferred the struggle of labors more than comfort.
305. The just man hated the evil of hateful evil,

306. and he tried to erase its name from humanity.
307. He loved mankind because of the love of the Lover of mankind,
308. and he longed to bind men in love of his Lord.
309. The love of the good servant was yoked to love of his Lord,
310. and he anticipated hearing the words "good servant" [Matt 25:23].
311. John was a good servant to a good Lord,
312. and the Good One who saw the goodness of his labor stamped him in his Name.
313. He stamped the son of Abraham, who had been stamped with circumcision, in his Name,
314. and placed in his hand the sword of the Spirit to destroy evil.

VII. John and Herod

315. The sin of man had raised a rebellion against justice,
316. and in John, [God] wished to humble tyranny.
317. The just man who hated sin desired to kill sin,
318. and did not cease his fight against his evil.
319. He gave himself over to fight until death,
320. and he died without dying, for his death is the hope of the life of the dead.
321. The righteous man died wrongfully in the fight against sin,
322. and his death was the first witness to his preaching.
323. He was armed against the tyrannical, sinful king,
324. and he raised his voice and exposed and revealed his baseness [Matt 14:4].
325. The base-souled one was turned basely,
326. and the holy one stood up against his sin bravely.
327. He exalted himself against the divine Law,
328. to guarantee that his relationship would not be taken away.
329. The sinner had snatched a relationship with his brother's wife,
330. and John became zealous for the Law that was breached.
331. The zealous one became zealous for the law lawfully,
332. like Phineas who became intensely zealous against adulterers [Num 25:10–13].
333. The Law threatened adulterers through the mouth of the just,

334. and always destroyed the manners of adultery through the hand of the righteous.
335. He killed Zimri who committed adultery with a lawful sword,
336. and Herod with the rebuke of the words of the Spirit.
337. To Phineas he showed the great zeal of the Law of the Spirit,
338. and in John the intensity of rebuke.
339. There he required blood of the sinner among sinners,
340. here with a word sharper than a sword.
341. The just man raised the sword of his word against Herod,
342. and he was not intimidated by the power and crown upon him.
343. The just man remembered the word that David interpreted [2 Sam 12:1–10],
344. and heartily chastised the king hearty in sin.
345. Herod had committed an evil sin worse than all,
346. for he despoiled his brother with a relationship with his wife.
347. The miserable ignorant man was infatuated with the wife of his brother,
348. and because the just man saw it, he became intensely zealous about his infatuation.
349. O upright one, how accurate was the aim of your uprightness,
350. who announced and revealed the lie before the eyes of all who saw.
351. He knew the deception of Adamites,
352. and so [Herod] proceeded to kill him boldly.
353. The one more evil than all imprisoned the just man [Matt 14:3],
354. and plotted how he could fulfill the desire of his soul.
355. He desired to kill him, and he waited for the day of his death,
356. for when the just man died, he would bring his lustfulness to the open.

VIII. Herod's Plot against John

357. Herod and Herodias made an evil plot,
358. to turn off the light that had broadcast the evil within them.
359. The evil crafted an evil secret between them,
360. to silence the sound of the trumpet that silences evil.
361. The deceitful laid a trap of deceit for the upright of soul,
362. and did not know that what they cast for him would catch them.

363. The king kept him for his birthday [Matt 14:6], for the deceit of his heart,
364. that on a feast day he may reveal the deceit he was hiding him for.
365. A foul fraud was hidden in the heart of the Adamite,
366. and he longed for the time when he would fulfill the evil of his inclination.
367. The evil man made an evil party for his troops,
368. and he called and invited the heads of the people to rejoice with him.
369. The evil man spread a disguise of dance over his defilement,
370. and the daughter of the vile one entered and danced to defile herself.
371. The foul dance pleased the foul one before those at table,
372. and he bragged with his promises disorderedly [Matt 14:6–7].
373. The vile one divided half his belongings for the daughter of the vile,
374. but she did not want to receive anything but what she desired.
375. The evil woman desired an evil thing, as always,
376. and she opened her mouth and asked for the head of the hater of sin.
377. O sinner, how sinful are you; you should be ashamed
378. of your hateful sinfulness that is without equal.
379. O how silly is the height of your impudence before your guests,
380. and how shamefully the desires of your lust are fulfilled.
381. The wretch asked, "Give me on a platter the head of the just man" [Matt 14:8],
382. and was not ashamed to speak such an atrocity.
383. A great atrocity and an enormous sin were hidden in her word,
384. and it is a wonder that those who heard it did not wonder and marvel.
385. She requested the death of a just man as a payment for her lasciviousness,
386. and the king was "saddened" to hear the sound of death.
387. O sadness without sadness that the deceiver accomplished,
388. which was folded up in the form of sadness, but rejoiced and was glad.
389. O disguise that was disguised in the form of pain,

390. which hastened to shed blood cursedly.
391. The king was saddened deceitfully about the sad thing,
392. and the Scripture did not wish to reveal the fraud of his deceit.
393. Thus deception knows how to lead men astray,
394. and that the fraud of deceit is obscured with the form of good.
395. The liar spread a lie over his evil,
396. and he sent and cut off the head of the just man as if unwilling.
397. He truly wanted what happened, according to his will,
398. and he hid his evil with a disguise like a garment.
399. He of crooked conscience pretended that it was because he vowed,
400. for it is unfitting for a king to lie about a promise.
401. But which is more fitting, O evil man, entirely evil,
402. for your word to be invalidated, or to spill righteous blood?
403. O deceiver who has no place that is pure or decent:
404. which is more evil, a lie or a murder?
405. Lie, you demon, even if it is a sin for men to lie,
406. and do not dare to spill the blood of an innocent man.
407. The sinner wore the disguise of vows like a garment,
408. and he erred and led astray, though his sinfulness was clear.
409. O deceiving disguise of the deceitful king,
410. who was not ashamed to be saddened at an impure deed!
411. O the cursedness of a heart as hard as a rock,
412. which was not softened by an atrocity worse than all atrocities!
413. O woman filled with impudent lasciviousness,
414. who was not ashamed to shed blood before many!
415. O lustful hands that defiled the soul,
416. which carried the pure head carrying victory!
417. O rebellious pupils of arrogant eyes,
418. which were not ashamed to look upon the blood of the innocent!
419. O countenance of king and woman filled with defilement,
420. which beheld victorious blood of their own their fashioning!
421. They carried the head of a just man along with vessels,
422. and did not tremble from the righteousness hidden within it.
423. How was justice silent in this wickedness,
424. and did not reveal the deception of the deceiver as it usually did?
425. It was able to shake the earth and swallow them
426. if it had visited that place that it judged and exposed.

427. They deserved that new chastisement that happened,
428. indeed, they deserved it because of the incomparable sin.
429. There is no equal to the loathsome sin the filthy committed,
430. as there was no greater man than the one to whom it happened.
431. There is no one among the born greater than John,
432. and therefore the revenging of his blood is greater than any vengeance.
433. I saw the blood of the pure one as I wander among the impure,
434. and fear seizes me: who wins in a crime?

IX. Diatribe against Herodias

435. The impure woman was carrying the head of the pure one,
436. and she mocked him, asking where was the honor of his zeal.
437. She entered with a platter of food, along with food that feeds life;
438. and the atrocity is how they could eat at that feast.
439. O feast in which was mixed the blood of the righteous,
440. where they thirsted for the blood of the innocent along with wine.
441. Herodias did not thirst for a drink of wine
442. as much as she desired to hold the head of the innocent one in her hands.
443. There was no desire that satisfied her lasciviousness
444. as much as the desire to see his blood pour out on the ground.
445. Her beastly desire was satisfied in the shedding of his blood,
446. and like a beast, she bit his flesh with her hands and eyes.
447. O rabid woman, rabid with desire of flesh,
448. which was not satisfied until she ate the flesh of man!
449. O fighter who fought against the truth,
450. who did not rest until she put a true man to rest!
451. O fool who became foolish with desires,
452. who spilled her bile upon the one who stopped her foolishness!
453. Hear, O women, of the atrocity that the rabid woman committed,
454. who became a dog and bit at the body of a just man.
455. Tremble, O fools, at any foolishness that resembles this,
456. lest you be compared to Herodias who killed the just man.
457. Marvel and wonder, O women who are captive to desires,
458. lest the net that captured Eve in Eden capture you [Gen 3:6].

459. The desire for the fruit captured Eve as in a net;
460. run from desire that is hidden with this: desire of sin.
461. The desire within you captured our species from the beginning;
462. and it exiled us from good things like exiles.
463. There has never been an exile that you did not cause,
464. and the evil one has not captured us in desire without you.
465. Who drove out the head of our nations from Paradise,
466. other than the confused desire of your mother Eve?
467. Who destroyed all and everything with fearful waters,
468. other than the lust of the daughters of Cain?[9]
469. Who bound Joseph the modest in binding,
470. other than the rabidity of one of you, filled with impudence [Gen 37:2]?
471. Who advised Job the just to beget complaining,
472. other than a daughter of Eve whose advice resembles that of her mother [Job 2:9]?
473. Who made Samson the warrior a laughingstock,
474. other than the impudent adulteress without reverence [Judge 16]?
475. Who put a stain upon David of pure conscience,
476. other than seeing the vile weak one from among your ranks [2 Sam 11]?
477. Who made Solomon the wise to be stupid,
478. other than the troubling of the lustful women united to him [1 Kings 11]?
479. Who made Ahab a hater of noble things,
480. other than Jezebel, the hateful spring of shameful things [1 Kings 16:31]?
481. Who was the cause of all these things I said,
482. other than the impudence of Herodias that surpassed all?
483. Because of her, I repeated the causes of your actions,
484. to reveal to man how evil is the evil of women.
485. The evil of women presumes and is greater than the natural order,
486. and I mixed the story of your shame with that of the righteous.
487. The story of the just man forced me to tell of the kinds of foolishness,
488. how much more foolish and wily than simply shameful things.
489. The death of the just man called and awoke me as from sleep:

490. "Arise, O man, see a man who died at a feast."
491. A wicked man made a banquet of wickedness wickedly,
492. and mixed the blood of man like wine accursedly.
493. He who chose him to be ambassador saw the mixing of his blood,
494. in the same form that he revealed the blood of Abel.
495. He said: "The sound of the blood of Abel cries out to me" [Gen 4:10],
496. and perhaps the blood of John cries out more than his.
497. John is greater than all the just who were and are,
498. and therefore his tragic death is more valuable than all deaths.
499. The death of the one who died at a filthy feast is tragic,
500. and the lustful daughter and mother derided it.
501. The daughter and her mother carried the head of the modest one,
502. and shamed his honor accursedly.
503. O cursed ones, how rabid and bold accursedly,
504. who mocked and derided the priest who ministered two as one.

X. John as Hinge between Testaments

505. John ministered two as one in his ambassadorship,
506. for he silenced the course of earth and revealed that of heaven.
507. The preacher stood between both and taught the truth,
508. and concluded one and gave the beginning of that to come.
509. With the seal of his word, he sealed the course of the Law,
510. and opened the Scripture of the spiritual Testament.
511. The educated scribe of scribes traded scriptures for Scripture,
512. and preached life in place of the condemnations in the Law.
513. The scribe who concluded the scriptures revealed new life to us,
514. and trod the path before the One who came to give man life.
515. He engraved the image of the Lamb of the salvation of our life like a statue,
516. and he preceded him and called him by the name of Lamb because of his sacrifice [John 1:29].
517. By the sacrifice of his death, he eradicated death and sin,
518. and [John] revealed them before they occurred in deed.
519. O John, who revealed mysteries and unveiled hidden things,

520. who revealed to man that the death of man would destroy death.
521. How great is the great good that was given to you,
522. who revealed the mystery that had been hidden from all creatures?
523. Glorious is the Will who willed to make you a son of his will,
524. and who ministered, through you, the entire mystery of his teaching.
525. He who revealed to you the mystery of his will is worthy of glory,
526. and angels and men together speak glory to his Name.

Chapter 7

MEMRA 21: ON THE TEMPTATION OF CHRIST

INTRODUCTION

This dramatic memra is a theological explication of the temptation account in the Gospel of Luke. It begins by recounting some selected events from the life of Christ, beginning with the annunciation, the words of Simeon and Anna in the temple, the preaching of John the Baptist, and the Baptism of Christ. The thematic connection between these events is brought into strong relief by Narsai in making the observer of them to be Satan. The words of Gabriel to Mary, and of Simeon, and John, and most of all the voice of the Father pointing out his Beloved, taken together terrify Satan and his hosts and force him to ask how Christ can be a mere man when he is spoken of in these ways (line 42). The second section of the memra continues Satan's perspective and asks a series of questions about how Christ can be either God or man, or both. This section (paralleled by a hymn in the Christmas Office of the Church of the East attributed to Narsai and discussed in the Introduction) verifies Narsai's orthodox Christology, since there is a singular Subject spoken of in discussing both the Divine and the human nature of Christ (lines 43f.).

This is an important point here, since much of this memra focuses deliberately on Christ's humanity and refers to him as both "the Son of Man" and "the Man." This focus is necessary in the context of the temptation narrative for several reasons. First, Christ enters the arena to fight against Satan precisely as the Second Adam (lines 90f.)—God sees that his image Adam has fallen and therefore sends Christ to repair what was broken (line 415); second, in his victory, Christ gives the whole human race victory over temptation, since if in the first Adam all of us fell, in the Second Adam all of us rise up (lines 213, 376, 385); third, Christ's battle against temptation is depicted as an example for us to learn from in fighting our own temptations (line 360). These reasons, added to the plain fact that Christ cannot be tempted in his Divinity (line 522), make it clear (on the one hand) that it is Christ the Son of Man who is the focus of the temptation, but also (on the other hand) that it is Christ the Son of God who alone has the Power of the Spirit needed to defeat Satan (line 372).

Indeed, the baptism of Christ reveals not only the Trinity, but also the Incarnation, since there we witness both the humble virtue of Christ baptized by John as well as the voice of the Father announcing his Eternal Son (line 61). But again, Satan is bewildered by this, and sets out to see whether Christ is truly Divine or merely another son of Adam. The memory of the temptation of Adam is still fresh in Satan's mind (line 90), and this is the pattern he takes up as he approaches Christ. The memra is filled with the imagery of gladiators fighting in a stadium, with Christ and Satan as the fighters and the angels (and later the human beings around the temple) as spectators (line 141). Christ, armed with the Spirit, is not only victorious, but gloriously so, making Satan and his armies a laughingstock, which is especially embarrassing because he, a spirit, was defeated by one with a Body (lines 119, 210).

The first temptation is the most like that of Adam, since it involves food and bodily desire (line 173). But the temptation itself, while based on human desire, tests Christ's Divinity, since transforming the nature of a thing would be an act of creation (line 189). Christ is not led into the wilderness to prove anything to Satan, however, but rather to teach us how to defeat him. The way to defeat the enticements of bodily desire, it turns out, is by means of the Law, which Christ quotes (line 224). Through obedience to the Law, Christ, and in him all of us children of Adam, can find the strength to defeat the temptations based on the body's desires.

The second temptation (following Luke's ordering) focuses on the material aspect of the kingdoms that Satan shows to Christ, and Narsai interprets it in terms of love of money and the glory that comes from wealth (lines 241, 252). The drama again is elevated here, and Satan comes across as a clever and experienced conman, telling Christ to merely say a few words of worship in order to gain the whole world (lines 270, 280). He depicts himself as a kind tyrant who asks so little of his subjects and gives them so much (line 282). Christ responds in furious zeal (line 306), first because only God is God and deserves worship, and second because money itself is worthless (line 310).

The third temptation is the most public since Satan in his arrogance wishes for human spectators as he attempts victory again. This is why he takes Christ to the temple (line 324), but the temptation itself is not for Christ to simply show off, but to prove publicly that God rewards the just man (line 350). Christ throwing himself off the temple and being carried by the angels would therefore be a shortcut to coerce faith in those who do not believe. Remarkably, Narsai does not immediately (or even explicitly) narrate Christ's response to this third temptation. It is not until nearly one hundred lines later that we are given an implicit answer: Christ is not simply some messenger to bring the faith of God into people's hearts; he is himself the Temple in which God and Man become one (line 449).

Christ's humanity is stressed in this memra, therefore, not only because it was "one of us" who had to defeat Satan (lines 118, 134), but because the Incarnation that unites God and Man completely is revealed during this trial. In a way, Satan got his question answered, not for himself, but for us—though the full battle, and the full revelation of Christ's Divinity, is not complete until after Christ's death (line 478). The temptation is therefore a prefiguring of the passion of Christ, where his Body truly fulfills its sacrificial destiny in being the Temple of God in which all things are reordered and restored, all becomes what it should (line 487), and God and man are ultimately united (line 491). It is no surprise, then, that the Trinity is also revealed at the temptation: the Spirit, by the command of the Father, leads the Son into the wilderness (line 445) and allows Satan to tempt him exactly three times (line 473), subsuming the ultimate desires of the evil one into the redemptive plan of God.

TRANSLATION

I. Christ's Life until the Temptation

1. Satan heard new sounds among mortals:
2. men and angels speaking of peace for men [Luke 2:14].
3. The rebel heard of the peace of man from Gabriel,
4. and fear seized him—what is this new thing happening?
5. The head of the angels greeted the daughter of mortals,
6. and the envier trembled at the good news to man.
7. "Peace to you, Mary" [Luke 1:28], the spirit said in the ears of Mary,
8. and the evil one lamented and gathered the demons to his laments.
9. "The Lord is with you," the angel called to the daughter of mortals,
10. and the laments of the backbiter doubled at the peace of man.
11. The messenger called the Son of the daughter of mortals "the Son of the Most High,"
12. and the hater was shocked, and his legions sat in mourning.
13. The man of spirit explained these things among the earthly,
14. and the demons shook, and Satan, the head of their ranks, trembled.
15. One spirit preached his conception to one woman,
16. but on the day of his birth, many cried out in hope for man [Luke 2:14].
17. Spirits cried out with good hope to the bodily,
18. and the rebel died at the hopeful things for the life of man.
19. Hopeful sounds were spoken by every mouth,
20. and man and spirits rejoiced, and demons were saddened.
21. Simeon heard the sound aloud of him to come [cf. Luke 2:32],
22. and man was tested in the dawning of his light as in a furnace.
23. Anna the prophetess narrated his various commands [Luke 2:36],
24. and Hebrew women erupted after her words.
25. The voice of the son of the sterile[1] was louder than thunder,

26. when he cried out that the time is fulfilled and has come [Matt 3:2].
27. He prophesied that the time of the Law is complete,
28. and the time for leading a spiritual life has come.
29. The pure one, purifying the impure, named him the pure Lamb [John 1:29],
30. whose sacrifice would erase sin and give life.
31. The ambassador called the One who sent him "master of the threshing-floor" [cf. Luke 3:17],
32. and showed that he is the Lord and Judge who tests all.
33. Men and the heavenly preached these sounds,
34. and the Father added the stamp of his voice and sealed them [Luke 3:22].
35. The rebel, hater of man, heard these blessed words,
36. and became embittered against the words alien to him.
37. New sounds were spoken among the rational,
38. about a Son of Man who resembles man but is above man.
39. Even the rebel looked at him as if a man,
40. and was embittered at the speech about him implying he is not.
41. The hater was between two considerations about him,
42. for he did not know what to call him, man or God.

II. Christological Interlude[2]

43. If he calls him man, things said about him are greater than that;
44. if he calls him God, his embodiment witnesses that he is man.
45. The composition of his body shows that he is fully man;
46. but the power of his words preaches that he is Divine.
47. His conception and birth proclaim his humanity;
48. but those who brought his tidings,[3] the Power of Existence dwelling within him.
49. Even Satan was considering the Power of Existence,
50. how he is man and how his Power is greater than man.
51. The one lacking in intellect was amazed by his great Power,
52. and was consumed by [the thought that] these two can be in one Man.
53. A womb conceived him; organs birthed him; knees carried him:
54. these are of a man who has sensible senses.

55. He was conceived by a Voice, not by a physical union:
56. this is higher than a fleshly man.
57. He suckled milk, and received instruction, and tired from labor:
58. natural things witness that he is of human nature.
59. He was baptized by a man like a man, as if in need;
60. this reveals the neediness according to his humanity.
61. The Holy Spirit descended, and the Father proclaimed "this is my Beloved";
62. here is the Divine Power that empowers the Man.
63. He went up from the water, one Man with body and soul,
64. and the Spirit descended and alighted upon him without moving.

III. Satan's Scheme

65. The Second Adam was led in the power of the Spirit,
66. and the enemy marveled at his power and his Body.
67. The backbiter whipped himself with stiff cords,
68. and considered whether to fight against him or not.
69. He of bitter inclination was dismayed like a child,
70. and thought about ways he could fulfill his inclination.
71. The rebel felt a hateful feeling in his mind,
72. and longed to fight against him as against a man.
73. He thought, "Who will grant me to fight against him?
74. For I will reveal his passions by means of passions if he is [merely] a passionate being."
75. He looked upon the Son of Adam as if upon Adam,
76. and he expected to lead Adam astray like Adam [Gen 3:6].
77. He supposed he could fight with him adamly,
78. but he feared that the Hidden One would overcome him.
79. The vessel of wrath counted him as [merely] one of the just,
80. and was too bitter to speak judgment openly with him.
81. He was consumed by his good works for thirty years,
82. until he heard the sound "this is my Beloved."
83. This sound brought trembling to his armies,
84. and they began to cry out from the sadness of their minds.
85. The drowning awoke as from sleep at the voice of the Father,
86. and they gathered as one to weave a plot against the Mystery of our salvation.

87. The rebel and his armies wove an evil plot,
88. in order to battle against the Warrior who was stronger than they.
89. The deceiver armed himself with an armor of deceit,
90. and began to trouble things as he did in Paradise.
91. He had compared that time to this one,
92. but did not know that one time does not resemble another.
93. He called the Second Adam an Adamite,
94. and like him, he tempted him in the passions of the flesh.
95. He reminded the bodily one of the passions of the body,
96. and he troubled him with various enticements as if a friend.

IV. Christ the Champion in the Arena

97. The lover of conflict wished to face him in a conflict,
98. where the needs of life could not be found by earthly beings.
99. He provoked him to the fight like an Athlete,
100. to see whether he had the kinds of enticements that Adam did.
101. He armed himself with every adamic passion,
102. for he thought he might escape from his temptations.
103. What was said of him shook him to trickery,
104. and he plotted to fight against him craftily.
105. The craftsman prepared his armory craftily,
106. and he gathered opportunities to fight with various attacks.
107. He arranged crafty opportunities in his mind like weapons,
108. and he gathered his strength and tested the weapons of his deception.
109. He sought a time to show the manners of his tricks,
110. and in time he measured which opportunities were best.
111. He prepared the opportunities of his deception for a long time,
112. and as he lied, he feared his deception would be revealed.
113. He fought him before he fought an open battle,
114. and he tested himself before he was tested, lest he fail.
115. He attacked a Warrior mightier than himself,
116. and so he strengthened himself lest he become a laughingstock to man.
117. The hater of man considered these things by himself,
118. and the Lover of man prepared a Man to fight against him.

119. The Spirit armed a Man from us with the armor of the Spirit [Eph 6:10],
120. and sent him to do battle in the war against the mighty one.
121. He prepared the match according to the preparation of the enemy,
122. and wherever the headmaster wanted, there the Athlete went.
123. The Athlete of Justice went out like an athlete,
124. and he was entirely armed with the armor of the Spirit.
125. The Power that chose him sent the armies above along with him,
126. to be witnesses and spectators of his athleticism.
127. The Lord of the world set the world as a theater,
128. and the armies above were spectators of the fighters' contest.
129. That fight was a fight on behalf of the world,
130. so he did well to gather the heavenly to cheer at it.
131. They had been saddened since the time Adam had failed,
132. and were awaiting the time when Adam would conquer in Adam.
133. Those who love our race were prepared for the day of victory,
134. and they longed for our race to conquer through the Son of our race.
135. The fighters stood one against the other for forty days:
136. the prince of the air [Eph 2:2] and a Man from us—an amazing sight.
137. An amazing sight was shown to the eyes of the spectators,
138. as a spirit and a Body fought, but not with hands.
139. The Bodily One fought, but not with hands,
140. and spiritually he held his own against the spirit of the air [Eph 6:12].
141. He chose a laborious fast as a weapon to fight with,
142. lest the backbiter think that the Power was that of food.
143. He came to battle with the mighty one without food,
144. that demons may see that though he is Man, he is greater than man.
145. Through his endurance he taught the savage ones
146. that there is another Power within him, mightier than all.
147. The head of their ranks considered his great Power,
148. and because of this prepared many battles of every kind.
149. The rebel arranged every kind of trap for the Man,
150. lest he escape his tricks and he become a laughingstock.

151. The attack that he made immediately against the Warrior was great,
152. and did not resemble the attacks he had made in any other age.
153. Great fear came upon the one who had put on a soul,[4]
154. and he feared to make battle with the Bodily One.
155. The Bodily One also considered his fear and boldness,
156. and provoked him to a fight through the form of hunger.
157. The Faster fasted for forty days from enticements,
158. and at the end, nature demanded natural things of him.
159. The nature of Adam considered his nature,
160. and because of this he concluded his fast like the fast of his kinsmen.[5]
161. Satan was encouraged by this opportunity,
162. that the amount of fasting did not pass that of those who had fasted.

V. The First Temptation: Stones into Bread

163. The rebel looked at the hunger of the Body of the Bodily One,
164. and he approached him and saw a Body that hunger had overcome.
165. He saw that the senses of his Body had weakened like any body,
166. and he thought in himself that this is the time to entice the body.
167. He remembered that time in Paradise,
168. when he saw that Adam longed to eat the fruit [Gen 3:6].
169. He looked upon the Adamite as upon Adam,
170. and in the same way he brought forth a bodily enticement.
171. He awakened the desire of the body in the Body of the Bodily One,
172. and as if a friend, he moved him to ask for food.
173. He had convinced the house of Adam to go astray with him using food,
174. and he thought that perhaps he could convince him like them.
175. He had previously taken up the argument of bread like a battle,
176. and he began to show the manners of might to his Enemy.
177. The deceiver explained: "Say the word 'let it be bread' [Luke 4:3],
178. and then it will truly be known that you are the Son of God.

179. Command insensitive nature as the Creator,
180. and do a thing appropriate to your Name, for he called you in his Name.
181. Transform rocks from the hardness of their nature,
182. and give them the nature of edible bread.
183. Through actions reveal a proof of the things said about you,
184. and the greatness of your station will be revealed before the eyes of spectators.
185. The Father proclaimed before the eyes of many that 'this is my Beloved';
186. if you are the Beloved, perform a miracle and verify your love.
187. Thousands heard the sound that you are the Son of God;
188. verify the Name by an act that comes from you.
189. Perform an act that resembles your Father for the work of his hands,
190. and the rational and mute will lift their hands at the Name of your authority.
191. Speak a word filled with marvel before the spectators,
192. that those who see the marvel of your powerful words may praise you.
193. You are in the wilderness and cannot find sustenance;
194. command the natures to nourish you as a Lord.
195. You are a Lord according to the Voice that spoke of you;
196. complete your Lordship by a complete word from your mouth.
197. See your need, as the righteous, your friends, also saw,
198. and do a thing that is justified by the need of your body.
199. Your friends also fasted in a fast like yours,
200. and after a time, they turned to fill their needs.
201. The choice of your Name is greater than theirs,
202. so perform a wonder that is fit for one greater than your friends.
203. It is fit for you to change a thing into another thing,
204. that your act may be a verified witness to the word of your mouth."
205. The prince of the air explained these things to the Head of our race,
206. thinking he would entice him through his troublings.
207. The master of error had held this battle before

208. and led many to error, but his claw did not touch the skin of Christ.
209. The skillful combatant had won this fight before,
210. but now a Bodily Combatant made him a laughingstock.
211. By this fight, the one haughty by nature tempted his Power,
212. and the Nature clothed with mortality crushed his arrogance.
213. The spirit brought the Bodily One to a battle of desire,
214. and the spirit lost, and the Body with noble senses won.
215. He enclosed desires with boiling desire,
216. and sent them like scouts to the Bodily One.
217. The miserable one sent miserable scouts to the quick-minded One,
218. and he sent them back in the miserable shame they deserved.

VI. Christ's First Response

219. The Second Adam slapped the scouts of the evil one in their faces,
220. the way the Creator treated the sacrifice of Cain [Gen 4:5].
221. He trampled the advice of the deceiver like garbage,
222. and he mocked and laughed at his boring tricks.
223. He wisely gave a word to the weak-minded one,
224. and with the Law he shut the mouth of the blasphemer.
225. He judged his condemnation lawfully,
226. that he may know that he fought him lawfully.
227. He undid the binding of the many-worded one with a single word,
228. with the Scripture, "Man does not live by bread alone" [Luke 4:4; Deut 8:3].
229. "Man does not live by bread alone," he answered the liar,
230. and he destroyed and brought down the deceitful tricks of every kind.
231. The Creator is able to give life to man without bread,
232. and the word of the Name of the Creator is enough for anything.
233. The shamed one was ashamed of the confidence that had inflated him,
234. and he moved on and ran to devise other tricks.
235. He exchanged tricks for tricks for the Champion,

236. thinking there was hope for his deception.
237. The loser thought he had a vain hope against the Victor,
238. for he did not know that his hope was less than victorious.
239. The shamefaced one was fighting against the Victorious One,
240. thinking there were tricks to entrap the Man.

VII. The Second Temptation: Worldly Glory

241. The deceiver set the deceitful traps of love of money,
242. and hid them with comely beauty that shuts the eyes.
243. He arranged every kind of lovely beauty to shut the eyes,
244. gold and silver, beryl and pearl.
245. He arranged everything illusively, though it was nothing,
246. and held them up, while they were really nothing.
247. He considered the Man from us as merely a man,
248. for this he arranged a likeness of what man loves.
249. The love of money is greatly loved by mortals,
250. and for this he kept its pleasure for the second battle.
251. In the first battle, he fought him with a comely desire;
252. and in the second with the love of money, the sea of sins [cf. 1 Tim 6:10].
253. He saw that the mind of man was drowning in this sea,
254. and he unleashed and made it flow over the land before our Savior.
255. He covered the earth with the garment of money as with a sea,
256. and did not know that the Quick-Minded One derided it.
257. He arranged his shadows in a garment,
258. and saw while hidden that all of his hidings were torn up openly.
259. He arranged all kinds of lovely things while they were naught,
260. and approached the Champion in order to stomp his Power.
261. He opened the theater of his shameful, evil things,
262. and the ignorant one entered and stood among gold that was not gold.
263. The haughty minded one cried out rabidly against the Humble One:
264. "Come, O human, see something that is difficult to show.
265. Come, O man," the evil one said to a Man from us,
266. "the whole world, which I hold under my authority [Luke 4:6].

267. Mine is the world and the glories within it,
268. and I give it to whomever I will if he worships me.
269. Only worship me as a lord almighty over all,
270. and take the world in exchange for the confession of the word of your mouth.
271. Confess my lordship, and call me lord lovingly,
272. and I give you the good reward of the world and its wealth.
273. I give you the world and its wealth with one word,
274. and you return to me the worship of love lovingly.
275. Take the world, you man who is of the world,
276. and give me as a dwelling the word of your mouth, that you worship me.
277. Give me your mouth as a temporal temple,
278. and take the thing that cannot be comprehended by the rational.
279. See how large is the great station of the entire world,
280. and how small is the worship of the word that you repay me.
281. See how overflowing I am in my love to man or the son of man:
282. I do not demand heavy things from those who love me.
283. I ask for love alone from him who hears me;
284. hear me and see how generous I am to him who hears me."

VIII. Christ's Second Response

285. The evil one spoke this to the Son of our race,
286. and the Son of our race became zealous against his deceptions.
287. The One Zealous for noble things put on great zeal,
288. hearing that the servant desired the worship of his Lord.
289. Intensely, he launched the arrow of chastisement into him,
290. he burst his heart, and the bile that was there came out.
291. Evil bile was hidden in the evil-minded one,
292. and our Lord revealed it with the open word of the word of his mouth.
293. He answered the adversary from the Scriptures,
294. and taught him the order that he should have known without this.
295. "Have you heard or not heard, O rebel, that it is written,
296. that the Lord is One, and all worship is due to him [Luke 4:8]?
297. The Lord is One, who has dominion over all divinely,

298. and there is no participation in his Divinity for another.
299. The Name of God is not due to one who is not God,
300. nor allowing the station of Fashioning to a thing that is made.
301. You are a thing that is made, O insolent one, supreme in arrogance,
302. know your nature, lest you try to raise yourself above your Maker.
303. Know that you are made, a work made by a Maker,
304. and you cannot grasp at the station of your Lord insolently.
305. Cease, O insolent one, from your insolent explanation,
306. and do not explain your hateful babbling blasphemy to me.
307. I know you and your deceitful explanations,
308. and the error by which you lead others astray will not fool me.
309. Go fool others, you fool, like you always do;
310. take the fantasy of money gathering and slam it in your own face.
311. You give nothing, and you do not gain what you think;
312. you fight in vain, and your battle is pointless.
313. Go fight your fight against yourself,
314. and receive the reward of shamefacedness for your loss.
315. Go, you loser, and look at how vile you are,
316. and leave off your fights against honest men, lest they cut you apart.
317. Lo, your loss in two battles has been revealed:
318. go prepare a third battle and lose three times.
319. Three witnesses raise their hands in every decree,
320. and thricely I will win against you in the third battle."

IX. The Third Temptation: The Temple

321. The fighter went up from the contest of the second fight,
322. and he changed the place and the manner of fight.
323. He ran away from the war where he thought he would win,
324. and he began to arrange an evil battle before spectators.
325. He wanted to show his battle in a peaceful place:
326. "When I win, there will be men to witness my victory."
327. The fault-filled one fought for victory,
328. and did not know defeat upon defeat would increase for him.
329. The impure one went up to the holy temple to fight,

330. where everyone could plainly see his loss.
331. The lowest of the low brought the Exalted One to a great height,
332. and he stood there and became mad with his usual madness.
333. "Throw yourself from this height to the depth below,[6]
334. and if you remain uninjured you are the Son of God.
335. God called you the Son of God before the eyes of many;
336. fly on the air as is fitting to the Son of God.
337. You are a just man, and what was said about you witnesses this;
338. descend from the heights and the assemblies above will receive you.
339. It is written about the just that they will proceed on earth without injury,
340. being protected by spiritual angels.
341. You are one of the just, and indeed your station is greater than the just;
342. prove your justice with diligence regarding your justice.
343. Test your Power through the diligence of the heavenly,
344. who would bear you upon their hands, as it is written.[7]
345. They will not leave you among difficulties, as difficult as they are,
346. for they are commanded by God to protect you.
347. Prove the help of your guardians through deeds,
348. and the portion of the just will be encouraged to continue in justice.
349. Tread a path by a trial through difficulties,
350. and show man the crown of the reward that comes from justice."

X. Litany on Christ's Victory: Man Defeats Satan

351. O deceiver, how deceptive you are in laying traps;
352. O Quick One, how well you jump over the hidden traps.
353. O cunning one, how cunning you are in weaving tricks;
354. O Wise One, how wise you are in cutting them up.
355. O battered one, how much did you fight to fulfill your inclination;
356. O Thoughtful One, how thoughtful you were to win in order.
357. O spirit, how quickly your tricks flew away;

358. O Bodily One, how robustly your senses passed over them.
359. O uncustomary fight upon earth,
360. which made it custom for the world to fight against spirits.
361. One Bodily One fought against the spirits,
362. and men began to fight spiritually.
363. A Bodily One conquered the one with great power by the Power of the Spirit,
364. and the heavenly assemblies marveled at the victory of man.
365. Assembly upon assembly of spirits stood at this fight,
366. and were amazed at how a Body can overcome a spirit.
367. A great marvel was spoken of among their assemblies:
368. "what is this new thing that has happened among mortals?"
369. They saw the Son of mortals fighting against a mighty one,
370. and they were amazed and dumbfounded that mortality overcame the tyrant.
371. They considered the victory of man and the loss of the evil one,
372. and they glorified the Power of the Creator that gave man victory.
373. Spirits cried out in glory to the Power who gave man victory,
374. and who reconciled the world to his Greatness through one Son of Man.
375. One Man fought against Satan,
376. and Satan lost, and the Man won, and gave man victory.
377. The Son of Man won in the battle he made against the mighty one,
378. and the mighty one lost in the battle against the Son of Man.
379. The assemblies above considered this fight,
380. and wondered at the unusual victory.
381. They saw the unusual victory and loss,
382. and praised and exalted the One who had exalted the race of man.
383. The race of man had lost and been conquered by Satan,
384. and the Son of Man rose and paid the debts of the sons of his race.
385. Adam was guilty in the desire of the fruit through the advice of the evil one,
386. but the Son of Adam conquered the one who had conquered man.
387. Adam sought the uprising of Adam against the hater of Adam,

388. and he humbled him and threw him down from his tyrannical throne.
389. He openly held a battle against him before the spirits,
390. and he picked him up and tossed him, and made him a laughingstock and a byword.
391. He entered with him into a stadium filled with sufferings,
392. and he kicked the difficult passions with the legs of the mind.
393. The rebel had arranged every suffering for the Bodily One,
394. and he divided them into three battles.
395. The ignorant one held three battles against the Wise One,
396. and in all three, the Son of Adam won and Satan lost.
397. In the desire for bread every desire that man desires was contained,
398. and the Son of Man despised human desires.
399. In the love of money he had arranged all forms of money,
400. and the Athlete of the Truth considered them as nothing.
401. In the love of glory he hid all the traps that entrap man,
402. and the Man jumped over them and passed by them without injury.
403. The Athlete went up from the contest without injury,
404. and was extolled by the spectators of his athleticism.
405. The Bodily Athlete won victory victoriously,
406. and the spirit, the head of the air, lost like a loser.
407. The head of the air fought against the Son of Man,
408. and the Man won and the mighty one who had beaten man lost.

XI. Christ Redeems Adam as God's Image

409. Now that all kinds of fight and loss had ended,
410. he asked where was the fight, and what was its cause.
411. Its cause was the battle that had happened in the land of Eden,
412. when man had lost, and the evil one had won until now.
413. The Adamic race had been bound in the loss of losses,
414. and the tyrannical demons had become haughty over its loss.
415. The One who had called it his image [Gen 1:26–27] saw its loss,
416. and did not like it that demons stomped on his image.
417. Now he has renewed the same image [cf. Col 3:10] that had lost in sin,

418. and returned and fashioned it in that original form.
419. He had formed Adam from the dust without copulation,
420. and without the union of sharing he formed the Last One.
421. He undid sin through the same race that had lost to sin,
422. through the Son of Man that he fashioned through the Spirit without copulation.
423. He fashioned the Son of Man from the daughter of man by the power of the Spirit [Luke 1:35],
424. and filled him with the Spirit and called him in his Name—the Son of God.
425. God called the Son of Man the Son of God,
426. and Satan trembled at the Name of the Son of Man that was greater than man.
427. These names made him come to the fight,
428. and he was consumed about when there would be room for his desire.
429. He was scorched with the fire of his desire as in a fire,
430. and did not know how to cool off the furnace.
431. "Who will grant me to fight against him?" he thought,
432. and he feared the divine command.
433. "Who will let me bring all kinds of enticements to him,
434. and learn whether he also is a man full of enticements?
435. Who will bring him out to the wilderness, far from humanity,
436. that I may go out with him and test his strength by the passions of man?
437. He is a man entirely, of the humanity filled with passions—
438. but what is this, that he treads on passions while being a passionate being?
439. Who will disregard the Power of the Creator that helps him,
440. and give me a chance to come before him as against Adam?"
441. The hater of man considered these things,
442. and the Lover of man anticipated his shameful desires.
443. He saw that he prepared to do battle against the Son of Adam,
444. and he armed Adam with the armor of the Spirit and sent him against him.
445. It is written that in the Spirit he left a peaceful place for the outer wilderness [Luke 4:1],
446. so it is clear that he was led by the Power of the Spirit.

447. The Power of the Creator signaled that he should go out to where he went out,
448. and because the hater saw it, he went out with him to see the ending.
449. The Spirit revealed to the Temple of the Spirit that he would do battle,
450. and taught him the way to destroy the tricks of the backbiter.
451. He showed him that the hater who defeated Adam would fight against him,
452. and he anointed him with the Spirit, that the hand of the spirit would not strike him.
453. He instructed him how to hold battle spiritually,
454. and how to overcome in a stadium full of sufferings.
455. The Athlete of the Spirit did all he did in the Power of the Spirit,
456. since the will of his soul was united to the Spirit he had accepted.
457. He with the Spirit, and the Spirit with him, made battle,
458. and he repaid the debt of the eviction from Paradise.
459. He repaid the eviction that fell upon Adam to the evil one,
460. that he may know that Adam has the power of victory.
461. The Son of Adam won, and gave Adam victory over his debts,
462. and Satan lost, and the army of demons lost along with him.
463. The Son of Adam answered a tough answer to his envier,
464. and it was not enough for the hater to give a word in response to a word.

XII. The Trinity Revealed in Christ's Temptations

465. The deceiver asked the Mindful One three times,
466. and he exposed his responses with one word.
467. He held three battles with the Champion,
468. and three times he beat him into the dirt like death.
469. The Son of Adam kicked the son of Gehenna three times,
470. and he mourned and cried out, and the legions of his armies trembled.
471. The Archer of justice shot three arrows,
472. and three times he completed the fight against his envier.
473. He was destined to preach three Names among the earthly,

474. and he preached them mysteriously in the battles he fought.
475. Through the Mystery, the Power hidden within him won in battle,
476. and he depicted it in mystery before he showed it after his death.
477. This is the reason why he battled with Satan:
478. to save his race, and to reveal the Mystery of the Name of his Existence.
479. Mysteriously, these things were hidden in him:
480. the salvation of man, and the Power of Incomprehensible Existence.
481. By the Power that chose him, he revealed both of them through the battle he fought,
482. and verified them through the victory he won over the evil one.
483. By the Power that chose him, he defeated the tyrant that had defeated man,
484. and the Good One declared the victory in favor of his might.
485. By his might, he strengthened the habits of the passions of man,
486. united to the Will that chose him over all.
487. The Will of the Hidden One dwelt in the Temple of the construction of his Body,
488. and accomplished in it whatever was appropriate to order all things.
489. It was appropriate to accomplish all [John 19:28] to order all things,
490. and for the Son of Man to complete the love of his Sender.
491. The Hidden One sent the Son of Man with this intention:
492. to save man, and to reveal the love of his Sender.
493. Man was captive to the hater of man from the beginning,
494. so a Man went out and returned the captive to the house of his fathers.
495. The Lover of his race went out to visit his race in the wilderness,
496. to the place where the captor wished to capture his race.
497. The Son of Man saved the captivity of man from the rebel,
498. and his Power shamed him and made him a laughingstock before all creatures.
499. This very Man defeated the tyrant who had defeated man,
500. and by his victory, he exalted man and humbled demons.

501. He humbled demons by the battle he made with the head of demons,
502. and took from them the armor they had taken from his fathers.[8]
503. He made the haters of his race stand naked,
504. that they may no longer be armed to make battle with man.
505. The Son of Man fought a great battle with their ranks,
506. and the spiritual assemblies marveled at the power of his victory.
507. The spectators of the contest saw the power of his victory,
508. and they gathered to him to praise him as King.
509. They weaved and offered a crown of praises to the Athlete of mankind,
510. and they praised and thanked the Power that empowered him in the contest of passions.
511. The Athlete of justice won against all passions,
512. because the evil one had brought forth all three battles.

XIII. Christ Victorious in His Humanity

513. The Son of our race was mighty in three battles against the mighty one,
514. and he humbled the hater that had taken over our tribes.
515. He humbled the mighty one who had humbled our race,
516. he and the Power that empowered his weakness.
517. The Power of the Creator made him victorious over the enemy,
518. while the Creator was hidden in his constant glory.
519. The Hidden One was constantly hidden in his constancy,
520. for the Power from him upheld the Man from us.
521. A Man from us fought against Satan,
522. not the Creator, as the hard of heart pretend.
523. …[9]
524. the Creator could not fight with bodily passions.
525. The demons even witnessed whom they fought in battle:
526. with a Son of Man, whom hunger overcame after his fasting.
527. Hunger overcame him after fasting for forty days,
528. and the hater knew that hunger witnessed to his humanity.
529. He saw that the fashioned Flesh was weakened by need,

530. and thought that perhaps he could lead him into error through the desire for bread:
531. the Second Adam was aware of the desire for bread in his body,
532. in the way that he led Adam into error by the desire for the fruit.
533. His tricks lost, and his opportunities were broken, and his lies were destroyed,
534. and there was not found a place in the Pure One with faults.
535. The rebel and his armies lost entirely,
536. and the Son of Man won and gave victory to his race entirely.
537. Henceforth, the race of Adam must give due glory
538. to him who exalted the race of Adam through the Son of Adam.

Chapter 8

MEMRA 37: ON THE THIEF

INTRODUCTION

This memra is a soteriological exposition on Luke's account of the criminals crucified with Christ (here called "thieves" following Mark 15:27). The overarching theme of the repentance of the "good thief" is expressed through the image of iconography. The first section of the memra, indeed, begins with a description of Christ's crucifixion as an image of salvation—both in the sense of Christ being the most beautiful work of God and in his sufferings being the perfect depiction (as a result) of human sin (line 10). If Adam is the first image of God, Christ crucified is the renewed Image, and indeed renews by means of his crucifixion (lines 11–12). Looking upon this Image heals our wounded nature, as looking upon the bronze serpent lifted by Moses healed the Israelites (line 17).

Vision is indeed the primary sense referred to in this memra. The good thief sees a series of events: the injustice of the innocent Christ crucified, the earthquake, and the darkened sun, and then looks inwardly to see his own sins and repent of them (lines 38–42). Vision moving from outer sights to inner reflection naturally leads to an exercise of reasoning, and the thief makes use of his rationality to wonder what the chances are that an earthquake and an eclipse would happen at the same time (lines 52–65), and wonders whether perhaps there is something special about the human crucified with him, about whom he has heard rumor (lines 76–81). Reflecting on Christ's earthly deeds leads him to a condemnation of his own evil deeds, which leads to his repentance depicted as a battle in the midst of his bodily suffering (lines 86–96).

While the bad thief imitates the language of Satan during Christ's temptation ("If you are...," lines 115–124), the good thief becomes a teacher after his repentance, even though he did not know he was instructing or being instructed (lines 153–156). His repentance is a "dying to self," but his renewed, repented self still retains the cleverness required of his previous life of thievery, but now pointed to greater treasures (lines 167–184). He is still bold, shameless, and greedy, only now these vices turn into virtues as he pillages the kingdom of heaven (lines 185–190). He is rhetorically clever, asking Christ to use him as an example for others; he thereby gains salvation but also becomes a living symbol (lines 198–200), like that of the prodigal son (lines 207–208).

Clever though he is, it is still impossible that the good thief understood Christ's Divinity through his own reasoning, and Section V of the memra discusses the necessity that the Holy Spirit granted him private revelation at the moment of his death. Though his senses and reasoning had helped him begin the process, both had to be elevated for him to know what he knew and implicitly said through his words to Christ (lines 225–263). The Holy Spirit accomplished what he had requested, and made him an example or symbol of repentance so that others might learn from and have hope through him (lines 272–276). Thus the good thief, "erring in his error," makes a double-negative reversal (lines 227–230), and thereby becomes an icon as Christ himself was described at the start of this memra: God reveals salvation through him, and therefore he becomes a Christ figure, whose death is also for our sake (lines 279–282). God thus works through nature and through sinners (lines 295–306).

Yet again Narsai's Christology is shown to be orthodox, since the Son of God is crucified in his humanity (lines 313–322). The memra ends clarifying why Christ promised "paradise" when the thief asked for the "kingdom"—because the kingdom was not opened until the resurrection (line 351). Thus the thief breaks the command forbidding Adam to return to Eden, making him also a second Adam (line 368), and Satan mourns his loss, but especially the fact that God has become man (line 398).

TRANSLATION

I. The Crucifixion as Icon of Redemption

1. The Creator created a new creation upon Golgotha,
2. and showed the power of his craftsmanship through a crucified Man [cf. Acts 4:10].
3. The earthly and the heavenly saw a crucified Man,
4. and gathered to him to see the marvel spoken about him.
5. The entire creation gathered and came from all corners [cf. John 12:32],
6. to observe the Craftsmanship that was upon the wood.
7. He depicted [cf. Gal 3:1] the Lord of the world craftily for the world,
8. and brought him up and placed him upon wood, so that everyone might see him.
9. He engraved all creatures upon a bodily tablet,
10. So that the speaking and mute might consider his craftsmanship.
11. In the human being, he completed the works of his hands in the beginning of time [Gen 1:26–31],
12. and he perfected his fashioning in the fullness of time through the Son of Man.[1]
13. He chose a Man by whom he would renew the weary world,
14. he scoured him with sufferings, and showed his beauty before the eyes of all creatures.
15. He fastened him to wood as a mirror before the eyes of spectators,
16. So that they might look upon him and see the stains of their own souls.
17. He raised him up like the snake that Moses raised up [Num 21:9; John 3:14],
18. to heal man from the bites of tyrannical demons.
19. Demons had bitten the human race brutally,
20. and so he hung a Man upon Golgotha to give life to man.
21. He turned the gaze of everyone toward him lovingly,
22. so that whoever looks with the fondness of love may overcome demons.
23. The rational and the mute looked upon the crucified Body with love,

24. and they suffered over his suffering and gained hope for human salvation.
25. The world looked upon him lovingly for the salvation of its life,
26. for it saw that the time for the renewal of its decrepitude had come.
27. It saw that he stood among thieves in great disgrace [Luke 23:32],
28. and it was extremely sad over his lawless humiliation.
29. The mute and rational natures marveled at his love,
30. for he accepted to die on behalf of the renewal of their natures.
31. The hidden signal instructed them to marvel
32. at the crucified Man in whom the world and its iniquity were crucified.
33. O marvel of the indescribable Power of the Creator,
34. who crucified the world and its desires in one Son of Man!
35. Creatures saw a great marvel in one Son of Man,
36. for they were crucified with the Mortal upon the wood.

II. The Thief at Christ's Right Side

37. The thief on the right side marveled at this marvel,
38. and terror at the lawless deed seized him.
39. The vicious one had put on great suffering due to his vices,
40. for he saw the creation mourning passionately.
41. He saw the natures mourning at the time of the passion,
42. and he suffered and lamented his innumerable vices.
43. He saw the luminaries that were wearing the garments of mourning [Luke 23:44],
44. and he was confounded at the change of order among them.
45. He saw that an earthquake shook the earth enough to make it fall [Matt 27:51],
46. and he shook and was stunned at the harshness of the beatings of his mother [earth].
47. He saw that hard rocks were ripped open and the people were confounded,
48. and instead of a garment, he tore himself over what had happened.
49. He saw that the insolent mocked the Man who was crucified with him,
50. and he thought about what the cause of his death was and the cause of his mocking.

51. He considered wisely and he thought discerningly:
52. "Why have the luminaries darkened and why has the earth quaked?"
53. He thought: "Why then are the darkness and the earthquake together?
54. Why are there two extremely unlikely things in the same hour?
55. Who then can shake the mute natures from their roots,
56. and, behold, they are stunned like a woman in travail overcome with pain [Rom 8:22]?
57. Who has transformed the clarity of light into darkness,
58. and who has made the face of the earth tremble with an earthquake?
59. Who has bridled the path of the swift-moving sun,
60. and who has changed the happy moon into mournful blood [Joel 2:31]?
61. For whom do the mute natures lament unusually,
62. and why do they weep, as for a firstborn with bitter lamentation?
63. Why does the earth thunderously weep tears,
64. and why do the eyes of its face let down its quaking tears?
65. Is perhaps the Man crucified with us righteous,
66. and for his sake the mute natures dress for mourning?
67. Perhaps envy has iniquitously crucified him though he is not guilty,
68. and a backbiter has fastened nails into him, though he is undeserving.
69. Perhaps the priests have envied and begrudged him iniquitously,
70. because he accomplished miracles loftier than their stations.
71. Perhaps they threaten and revile him as someone evil,
72. But, behold, the reputation of the help he has distributed is famous upon the earth.
73. Why does he drink insult and mockery like a guilty person,
74. for, lo, the dead whom he has raised carry on his victory?[2]
75. If my own iniquity has crucified me according to my crimes,
76. why is he iniquitously condemned who has done no wrong?
77. If the crimes I have committed against justice have bound me,
78. why is he who is innocent lowering his head upon the wood?
79. If the traps I set upon the earth have entrapped me, a sinner,
80. why is he, by whose words sinners have been saved, dying?

81. I have heard the reports of the powerful deeds he has done on earth,
82. he whom men have repaid with the pangs of death unjustly."
83. The one at the right thought these things within himself,
84. and like a judge, he tested the reality he saw on the wood.
85. He entered into just judgment against his inclination prudently,
86. and he condemned his own wrongdoing, and vindicated the just man crucified with him.
87. As in a furnace, he tested the truth and rejected the fraud,
88. and showed the beauty of the word of truth before the eyes of the spectators.
89. And although the suffering of the body's suffering tormented him,
90. he did not lose or weaken in the fight against iniquity.
91. An armor of truth strengthened him at the time of suffering,
92. and like a warrior, he fought and defeated against all odds.
93. A difficult battle came upon him suddenly upon Golgotha,
94. and like an athlete he gave himself over to the battle.
95. He placed himself as against death, although he was dead,
96. and he made light of and despised all suffering as one who is impassible.
97. He fought two fights as he stood upon the wood:
98. against his iniquity and against the mockery from the insolent.
99. He who had plundered man stood at the cross like an athlete,
100. and took on a fight against his vices and the mockery of the people.
101. Iniquity and the people were raised up[3] against him like a tent,
102. and he alone defeated sin and the crucifiers.
103. O how marvelous was the battle done by the weak-minded one,
104. who at the time of despair gained vindication.
105. At the time of death, he entered the fight without armor,
106. and naked he defeated all the sufferings within and without.
107. The people wore an armor of mockery against our Lord,
108. and cast words of cursing against him like arrows.

III. The Thief at the Left Side of Christ

109. He who sanctifies the impure was mocked by the mouth of the impure,
110. and was put down like a vicious man by the insolent.

111. Even the thief on the left side jeered at him,
112. and more than the people cast the arrows of cursing at him.
113. The insolent one insolently acted in foolish blasphemy,
114. and instead of a sword, he pulled out his tongue to shed cursing.
115. "If you are indeed the Christ to come," the stubborn one said,
116. "save yourself and save us also from torture [Luke 23:39].
117. If you are a King, and the throne of David is yours,
118. command your troops to take up arms against your crucifiers.
119. If you are the Son and the Son of God, as you say,
120. descend from the cross and, behold, the Name of your Sonship will be verified.
121. If the miracles you performed for humanity are true,
122. show your power in reference to yourself, and you will be believed in.
123. If you are innocent, and men have crucified you upon wood for no reason,
124. call upon God and let him repay this obscene injustice."
125. O how the rabid dog barked at the Kind One,
126. and the small-souled one was not ashamed before the Holy One.
127. O how much the mouth of the insolent one blasphemed against the Humble One,
128. and the cursed one was not ashamed either by his sin or his suffering.
129. O how patiently did the Hidden Signal bear his insolence,
130. and did not bring the fire of wrath upon him intensely.
131. The one at the right side became zealous and intense at the sound of these curses,
132. and he forgot his pains and began fighting against his insulting.
133. The just man made a righteous war against the evildoer,
134. and wisely cast arrows of remorse against him.
135. The wise man repeated the Name of God to the godless one:
136. "Do you not fear God, whose testing is just?" [Luke 23:40].
137. He spoke to the one condemned to death as in judgment:
138. "Why do you cast the evil of your mouth upon an Innocent One?
139. Why do you insolently mock the One without blemish,
140. and increase the tortures of the judgment upon your stupidity?

141. Do you not know that our own evil has hung us upon the cross,
142. and our own insolence has made us die without forgiveness?
143. The Hidden Signal has condemned us justly,
144. and has repaid us the payment of our deeds with a shameful death.
145. This Man is innocent, holy and pure of stains,
146. but a people blind with envy has crucified him without understanding.
147. Why do you want to be a partner in abusive bloodshed,
148. and to mingle yourself in condemnation with murderers?
149. Is not the first blood you gratuitously shed enough for you,
150. without adding a double sin upon the first?
151. Is not your temporal death on behalf of your evil sufficient,
152. without also dying a hidden unending death?"
153. O new teacher who preached the truth on earth,
154. and exposed and chastised tyrannical evil with the word of his mouth.
155. O wicked one who exposed the evil to which he was accustomed,
156. and preached the truth he did not know he was studying.
157. He chastised his companion who unjustly mocked the Righteous One,
158. and turned to beg on behalf of his own crimes thunderously.

IV. The Repentance of the Good Thief

159. The memory of his evil entered his heart at the time of suffering,
160. and he began to judge himself for the sins he had committed.
161. The one asleep in sin awoke from his faults as from sleep,
162. and saw that he had been stripped of good works as of garments.
163. He saw that his body and soul were exposed nakedly,
164. and he suffered and groaned bitterly over his crimes.
165. In great suffering, he beat himself passionately,
166. and with thunderous lamentations he cried over his wickedness.
167. He made a house of mourning[4] alone upon the cross,
168. and his emotions became lamentations and he composed melodies.[5]
169. His soul wept upon the wood as for a dead man,
170. and he wrapped and entombed himself with regret.

171. He made a double mourning over himself and his torture,
172. for he saw that he was dying, but also that he would be resurrected to judgment.
173. He justly considered two thoughts about two deaths,
174. and terror seized him because his faults had bound him in two judgments.
175. The judgment to come terrified him more than the one happening then,
176. and he reckoned the death on the wood as nothing.
177. He remembered that torture without end,
178. and he saw it with a hidden mind as with eyes.
179. He secretly saw that fashioning of the kingdom above,
180. and he desired and thought perhaps mercies would make him worthy to enter.
181. His mind focused narrowly upon the promised blessings,
182. and he gained boldness like a poor man about his neediness.
183. The bold one gained great boldness as before,
184. in the same form by which he would boldly steal.
185. He spread the immodesty of thievery over his own face,
186. and he struck his aspect[6] and began to burgle the palace.
187. In this manner he shamelessly asked our Savior
188. if it were possible for him to despoil the spiritual treasury.
189. The old habit drew the greedy one to be greedy,
190. and he trampled all voices and entered to pillage like he owned the place.
191. "Remember me, Lord" [Luke 23:42], he began to say to the Lord of the treasury,
192. "in that kingdom above that is hidden from spectators.
193. Pity my neediness with one spiritual penny,
194. and let me live in grace through one small drop of your Gift.[7]
195. Forgive my crimes, erase my debts, cleanse my stains,
196. and in mercy erase the deed of my guilt before your Justice.
197. Save my lostness, pity my neediness, resurrect my mortality,
198. and engrave in me the type of death's eradication and of evil's undoing.
199. Through me, tread the path of repentance for the ages to come,
200. that they may come after me in regret toward forgiveness.
201. May the light of your Faith dawn within my darkness,

202. and let the darkness of evil that dwells in me flee from my soul.
203. Turn me toward you, away from the captor that captured me from you,
204. and free my slavery, that I may work with you, and be yours.
205. I was yours, but I was kidnapped from your Lordship;
206. save the son of your house, that all may know the power of your Lordship.
207. It is enough that I have worked among strangers until now,[8]
208. and my days were lost in the work of error without benefit.
209. The day has ended, and the sun has passed on the Sabbath of my life,
210. and if your Aid does not catch me, I will become nothing.
211. Lord, let me not perish through conversing with the dirt of Adam,
212. nor be estranged from sharing in the life of the dead.
213. Sprinkle the dew of mercies hidden in your words upon my mortality,
214. that I may be moistened and repay glory on the day of resurrection.
215. Make me worthy to go with the few upon the path of the just,[9]
216. and enter and rejoice in the delight that does not decay."

V. Private Revelation to the Good Thief

217. Who revealed to you, dead in his sins, to know these things,
218. and who made known to you that the Man crucified is King over all?
219. Who showed you that Man has authority above,
220. and how he is able to rule over the things to come?
221. Who taught you that he can free man from evil,
222. and from where it is that he can give immortal life?
223. Indeed, man, when has a human resurrected a human,
224. and when have the earthly distributed the kingdom above?
225. Granted that it is written that a human has resurrected a human,[10]
226. have we ever heard that humans have distributed the kingdom above?
227. Who led you into error,[11] you who err in the straying of desires,
228. that a crucified Man gives life and forgives sin?

229. See, O son of error, how perhaps your conscience has erred in error:
230. investigate well and then you will be asking things too great for you.
231. Indeed, you went astray and were troubled by the heaviness of the passions of your body,
232. and like a dream, your conscience roamed about in things not revealed.
233. It is not that the thief erred in his supplication:
234. fitting words together, he erred and mocked his own deeds.
235. The speaker remembered the greatness of his sin and his crimes,
236. and wished to mock the way he had forgotten the truth.
237. Who then taught the entirely stupid one to know the truth,
238. and who trod for him the path going above?
239. Who wrote out the new scripture to the false disciple,
240. and who became his teacher in meditating on things to come?
241. Who interpreted for him the meaning of the revelation of guarded things,
242. and who told him there is a kingdom that does not end?
243. Who became the advisor to the one erring in error,
244. that at the time of terror, he might make his soul rational?
245. With what eyes did the seer of hidden things see
246. that fashioning that the eye of flesh had never looked upon?
247. With what ears did the one who attends to sin hear the Honored One,
248. the sound that is not heard by the senses of the body?
249. With what mouth did the mute one, stuttering the truth, speak
250. those halleluiahs that are not spoken by the tongue of flesh?
251. With what palate did the bland one taste the Sweetness of life,
252. and how was he able to accept the Food of the Spirit?
253. Granted he reckoned there is a kingdom hidden above,
254. what authority does a crucified Man have over its delight?
255. Granted he has considered that that mercies have pity on sinners,
256. how is a Man able to help man?
257. And granted he has believed He could accomplish the things he considered,

258. who has placed in him the consideration of things that are unseen?
259. The fleshly one did not consider with fleshly thoughts,
260. and it was not his to ask for what is above so lovingly.
261. The Hidden Signal dragged him hiddenly to see hidden things,
262. and he exalted him to the revealing of guarded things.
263. The Power of the Spirit spoke with him spiritually,
264. and explained to him the hidden mysteries hidden from him.
265. He made the power of wise and of future things dwell in him,
266. and he revealed to him that there is a kingdom and a judgment.
267. He told him: "The crucified Man crucified with you:
268. his are the kingdom above and the judgment to come."

VI. The Good Thief Becomes an Icon

269. It was he who revealed to him that He could erase the sin of man,
270. and that he writes in his name the decree of freedom instead of slavery.
271. He wished to tear up the decree of the guilty through his instruction,
272. for if a guilty one can be vindicated, who can doubt?
273. He opened the kingdom above to the earthly through his exaltation,
274. for if a thief enters first, who is the one who will remain?
275. He revealed the exaltation of our species through the promise promised to him,
276. for if a son of our species gains the kingdom, blessed is our nature.
277. He showed the undoing of our foolishness through his soul that entered Eden,
278. for we are destined to enter with him the kingdom above.
279. Like an image, he engraved in himself our sin and our repentance,
280. and he brought it up and fastened it upon Golgotha before spectators.
281. For this reason, he left behind his sin at the time of suffering,

282. that we ourselves might learn that for our sake, he suffered on the cross.
283. In this form, he chose a man who sinned more than all,
284. that through a sinner he might show his power that can accomplish all.
285. He promised the kingdom in a shedder of blood who was filled with evil,
286. that he might tread the path of repentance for those who are wicked.
287. He came to repay the decree of debts of the race of Adam,
288. and first freed one debtor who owed so much.
289. He wished to renew the nature that had been wrecked by mortality,
290. and he cared for [mortality] in a man who was entirely dead in ugly evil.
291. At the time of suffering, he showed man the renewal of man,
292. and with unveiled deeds, he revealed his greatness.
293. He signaled to the natures, and saddened them at his humiliation,
294. and they showed that he is Lord and Son of God, almighty over all.
295. Through the silent and the endowed with speech, he preached his Power,
296. and like preachers, creatures cried out about his authority.
297. He saddened insensible things like they were sensible,
298. and he endowed sensible things with a spiritual mind.
299. He clothed the sun and moon with garments of mourning,
300. and he forced the thief to preach the greatness of his Power.
301. The silent cried out by their transformations as with a mouth,
302. "We suffer for the sake of the Man who hung with us."
303. The earth spoke with the sons of earth through an earthquake:
304. "my sons, you have greatly hated the Blood that bandaged my wounds."
305. The voice of the thief thundered in creation more than thunder:
306. "Look, O mortals, at the salvation[12] hanging upon wood."
307. Heaven and earth have already heeded the trumpet of his voice,
308. and the people alone shut its ears from hearing.
309. The miracles happened for the chastisement of the hard of heart,

310. and because of them the luminaries darkened and the earth shook.
311. He constrained the thief because of his iniquity and he repented from his iniquity,
312. that [the people] might see and repent, and beg, and plead for its foolishness.

VII. The Son of God Crucified

313. [Christ] revealed his Divinity through his humanity before the eyes of all creatures,
314. that even if he suffers like a son of man, he is the Son of God.
315. The Jews crucified the bodily Son of God—
316. not God, the Word of the Father begotten of him.
317. They fastened bodily nails into the bodily composition,
318. not into Existence whose Nature is higher than injuries.
319. The thief saw an unveiled Body upon the wood,
320. not the Hiddenness that is invisible except to the mind.
321. The Spirit of revelation showed the one at the right in his mind,
322. that the Man the people were mocking with insult is the Son of God.[13]
323. The truth chanted in him for the shame of the people and the overcoming of demons,
324. that the hater and the members of his party might be shamed by his preaching.
325. In the sound of his confession, the rebel who had captured Adam was shamed,
326. for upon the wood, [Christ] snatched back from him the captive [Satan] had captured.
327. He shamed him through one human being whom he turned toward himself,
328. and [Satan] was not able to persist nor did he prevent [the thief] from confessing him.
329. [Christ] exposed [Satan] through the promise that he promised [the thief],
330. and for his salvation he sealed the word of his mouth with "amen."[14]

VIII. The Promise of Paradise

331. The Word who is the seal of the truth vowed with an "Amen,
332. today you will be with me in Eden in the life of the soul."
333. "You will be with me in the land of Eden," he said to him,
334. but why "in Eden" and not "in heaven" as he had asked?
335. The thief wanted the kingdom above, not Paradise;
336. he asked him for the promised blessings, not the trees.
337. Even the thief could have said, "What is this?
338. For I have asked for the kingdom from you, not Paradise.
339. If you are the Lord, and yours are height and depth,
340. why do you delay completing the promise of your words?
341. I asked you that I might inherit the unending things above;
342. why do you give me the inheritance of earth, such a humble dwelling?
343. Paradise is still a part of earth, as beautiful as it is,
344. and the food of its fruits is still corruptible, as tasty as they are."
345. He who judges the truth did not judge this way in his mind,
346. for the Signal that pitied him did not ask him to seek this.
347. He who revealed to him the mystery of the invisible kingdom
348. placed a harness of silence that was not divided.
349. In faith he had asked for the kingdom from the One who chose him,
350. but because it was distant, he brought him into Eden until it was revealed.[15]
351. It was not possible to enter with him at this time,
352. lest the great order of that fashioning be troubled.
353. That entrance will be orderly, at the end of time,
354. and angels and men will enter together—a great assembly.
355. And so because it was unfitting, he did not allow him to enter with him,
356. he brought him in in hope, in a symbol of entry into the kingdom.
357. He brought him into the land of Eden in soul, not in body,
358. by that man who is able to accept spiritual things.
359. He gave a pledge of future things to his rationality,
360. that he might know that the hope that entered him did not lie.
361. Through Eden, he gave the son of mortals a pledge of life,

362. that death, which had subjected Adam and his children, might be undone.
363. In the place where the head of humanity sinned and death killed him,
364. there he brought the one who wanders on a thief's journey.
365. The son of the thief entered to abide in the land of his father,
366. and the hater saw him and mourned and cried, for it was unpleasant for him.
367. The land that transgression of the commandment shut off in the face of Adam,[16]
368. Adam entered through the thief that entered with our Lord.
369. The soul of our Lord and that of the thief entered together,
370. and opened the door for the souls of the just and modest.
371. The wall of wrath had been built against us, lest we enter,
372. and our Lord opened it and brought us in with him through his entering.

IX. Satan's Shame

373. He opened Paradise to mortals, to the shame of demons;
374. so that those who rejoiced in our expulsion might be saddened now through our entrance.
375. He exposed the prince of the air and shamed him through what he did,
376. for he had cast out Adam from the inheritance that his Lord had given him.
377. The envier thought that Adam would not return to his land,
378. but he was ashamed suddenly for he saw him in Eden through two souls.
379. Two entered first: one Just and one sinner,
380. that he may know that both the good and the evil certainly enter.
381. He suffered and lamented more over the thief than over our Lord,
382. for how could a shedder of blood break open the wall he had built?
383. Based upon his own counsel the arrogant minded one thought that Paradise had been closed off,

384. and when he saw that they had opened it, terror and despair took him.
385. He saw that the path to Eden had been trodden for humans to walk,
386. and he lamented and cried that he remained alone in his disgraces.
387. The bitter one said to himself, "What will I do?
388. For the king I cast into exile has returned to his kingdom.
389. Where can I go?" the evil one asked his evil inclination,
390. "for Adam has seized height and depth through his children.
391. I had cast him out at first from Paradise that he might not inherit it,
392. but now there is no place on earth that he has not inherited.
393. I was blessed with the earthly inheritance he had owned on earth,
394. and not because a new report had come to me that he would ascend above.
395. I had doubly desired for him to gain the earth,
396. but be named the heir of the heights and son of the kingdom.
397. I would even have settled if he had inherited height and depth together,
398. but had not been elevated to the great station of Divinity!
399. The One whom I crucified upon wood was one of his tribe,
400. and now heaven and earth have been promised to his kinsmen.
401. He hung on the cross, and nails were fastened into his Body,
402. and he vowed with an 'amen' that he could give the kingdom above.
403. He had gone into a contest of passability and approached death,
404. but one wretched man stood and begged: 'Give me life.'"
405. Doubled tortures were given to the backbiter,
406. in the phrase "Remember me, Lord, when you come."
407. As much as the thief begged upon the wood,
408. so much [Satan] increased his bitter lamentation.
409. As much as the Life Giver to all promised "You will be with me,"
410. so much [Satan] burned intensely with the fire of his inclination.
411. As much as [Christ] vowed and sealed his word with "amen,"
412. so much [Satan] whined like a sick little girl.
413. The envier was wounded by these events like by arrows,
414. and more than anything, the voice of the thief was pricking him.
415. For if the thief, his own student, could prick him so,

416. what would he do when heaven and earth cried out against him?
417. If the one sharing his secret exposed and revealed his craftiness,
418. where would he go when watchers and men mocked him?
419. If a murderer received the promise of the kingdom above,
420. with what eyes would he look when his entire race entered?

X. The Good Thief, Example and Hope of Sinners

421. O thief who cut off the hope of the enemy,
422. and gained hope for the hopeless through the forgiveness of his sin!
423. O condemned one who pledged his soul for disgraceful things,
424. who received his debt forgiveness for free with a word!
425. O entirely impure one in his filthy sin,
426. who sprinkled upon all of it the pure water of repentance!
427. O one who plundered and defrauded earthly things his entire life,
428. who plundered heavenly blessings on the day he died!
429. O one from whose evil wayfarers have hid,
430. who trod the path of repentance before sinners!
431. O lazy one who spent his days in emptiness,
432. who spoke a word and received the reward of the kingdom above!
433. O how much and in what way can I depict the image of the forgiveness of your sin?
434. For the One who gives ranks sealed the rank you reached with "amen."
435. My tongue is not enough to depict your story, O burglar,
436. and I do not know how to reveal the wiles of your craftiness.
437. You are entirely cunning, and you lived your life craftily:
438. you sinned as you wished and returned and pled as you wanted.
439. The Forgiver of your sin alone knows the secrets of your heart,
440. and the One who knows you does not count the greatness of your sin.
441. Wisely did he depict your story in the tablet of his own sufferings,
442. that he may teach all to travel through sufferings to the things to come.

III

Theology and Prayer

Chapter 9

MEMRA 16: ON HUMAN NATURE

INTRODUCTION

In this masterful memra (which is sung in the Chaldean, Assyrian, and Malabar churches during the liturgies of the *Ba'utha of the Ninevites* before Lent), Narsai sets out to describe human nature under several different aspects. His theme, though often overlapping philosophical ideas, is still fundamentally theological. He examines human nature within the context of God's creation and the history of salvation; indeed, the entire homily is one long prayer addressed to God.

The theological nature of this treatise does not water down the philosophical themes, for example, of human greatness and human misery, which have been described by secular thinkers for centuries. On the contrary, Narsai understands that seeing the human being as God's creature and pinnacle of physical creation is the best way to underscore the greatness of human nature as well as the depth of its misery and need of redemption and salvation. We are truly a marvel in our nature, and our sin is therefore truly catastrophic, and salvation is therefore truly spectacular.

The memra begins, as do many of Narsai's, with an invocation for strength and wisdom as he takes up his theme. In the first section, God is given twelve different titles and addressed according to each of them in poetic harmony. God having been addressed and named, Narsai introduces the larger theme by asserting that the human being somehow resembles God and is named after him as an "image" (beginning with line 27). This honor given to us at our creation, however, is something that we can mar with our sins and failings, which is exactly the story of human history. The whole creation is somehow fulfilled and even contained in the human being (line 51), and the human failure to live up to our calling is all the more disastrous because of this. Even at our best, human life has a large portion of misery, and despite the Name by which we have been called, there is an aspect of our existence that is still connected to the dust of earth (lines 95–140).

It is exactly this that launches the need for prayer (line 149), and on behalf of the whole human race, Narsai prays for God's mercy before turning to the parables of the Good Shepherd and the Prodigal Son, which become his theme (beginning at line 173). We are lost, both in our animal nature as sheep and in our human wills as sons, but God pursues and forgives us nevertheless. This becomes the basis for prayer, since without this kind of mercy, even addressing God leads to logical absurdities, reflecting the weakness of human language (lines 221–260). In response to God's incomprehensible mercy, the right human response is pure gratitude. Because "our age" is bereft of a great prophet as in times of old, we are left without a just man to plead on our behalf (line 328). God himself, then, must take up that role and be merciful without anyone deserving to ask for mercy; and yet this is exactly the situation with creation itself, since no one was able then to ask God to create (line 337). Everything, in the end, returns to God, from the creative act to the merciful act of redemption, to human dignity itself. Thus Christ, who is perfect God and perfect man, is the pinnacle of history (lines 389–412).

TRANSLATION

I. Opening Supplication

1. O God[1] Divine, O hear our pleading heard before you,
2. and in your mercies, answer the permitted request of our soul.
3. O Overflowing in his mercies, show forth your love as is your custom,

4. lest the hater of man mock the work of your hands.
5. O Richer than all, open your treasury to our neediness,
6. lest we be impoverished and hire ourselves out to the deceiver.[2]
7. O Mighty of ages, sustain your order by the force of your power,
8. for lo, it is shaken by the severity of pains and demons.
9. O Being of whose Essence heaven and earth are filled,
10. may your Will fulfill us, and in us your holy Name be hallowed.
11. O Hidden in his Nature from physical and spiritual,
12. reveal your power in us and show forth the riches of your Sweetness.
13. O Fashioner of all, who created creation from nothing,
14. pity what you have made, lest it decay because of our malice.
15. O Free Sustainer, gracious Life-Giver to rational and irrational,
16. extend your right hand and fill our soul with your Gift.
17. O Un-Wanting One, of whose Fullness his construction is filled,
18. open the door of your Will, which is closed in our face, to our pleading [Matt 7:7].
19. O Perfect in his Essence, whose constancy has no beginning,
20. perfect in deed the promise of your words to our race.
21. O Painter of the world in the paint of his love that does not dull,
22. scour the filth of ignorance from our image.
23. O Fashioner of bodies and Breather of the soul into members,
24. tighten our inclination, lest we slacken before enticements.[3]
25. O Honorer of man as surpassing all else due to his love,
26. have pity on your Honor's image lest it be shamed.

II. Man's Composition

27. You have named our composition after the Name of your Uncomposed Existence,
28. may your honored Name not be made dull by our dullness.
29. In us you have shown your great love toward your works,
30. show not in us a sign of wrath against your handiwork.
31. In us you concluded the great Name of your workmanship,
32. and within our composition you have bound up the earthly and the heavenly.
33. In us you composed the height and the depth as one flesh:
34. irrational in our body, rational in our soul—a great marvel!

35. May you not, O Lord, unravel this composition your Love has composed,
36. and may the great bind your signal has bound not slacken.

III. Taking Up the Theme

37. At this composition my weak rationality gazed,
38. and sought to journey through the rational path bound within it.
39. In this bind my meager mind was bound,
40. and wondered at the craft of the command that bound it.
41. Through this structure did my short thoughts wander,
42. to prepare words to compose the story before listeners.
43. In this hope did my rationality seek after words,
44. that I may go out and bring good tidings of your Name to your handiwork.
45. With this intention I journeyed among the verses of your Scriptures,
46. to explain to men the great story of your workmanship.
47. In this way my mind painted with the pen of my tongue,
48. that I might paint, for everyone, the gorgeous image of your making.

IV. Creation Contained in Man

49. I saw that the image you composed was decorated wisely,
50. and I wished to uncover its gorgeous beauty before spectators.
51. Within the image of our image I saw the whole creation tied,
52. and I called to man to come and see all in our nature.
53. Our nature drags me to examine the natures that are bound within it,
54. and how indeed this frail thing was able to hold everything!
55. In our very own nature, I saw the sciences of your Divinity,
56. and I reflected that there is hope for man, sinner though he is.
57. I saw the Name of your Essence dwelling in him[4] as in a temple,
58. and wondering seized me—how can the wretched suffice for the Hidden One?
59. He is wretched indeed, yet you honor him without measure,

60. and who would not marvel at this wretchedness you chose over all?

V. Levels of Honor

61. If your Love has chosen him from all and named him in its Name,
62. we can therefore be sure that you will not despise the one you have chosen.
63. And if your Lordship has made him lord over all that is,
64. who would not join himself to the yoke of his life's work?
65. If your Knowledge has called and appointed him to a high position,
66. who would not confess that his position and the name of his authority are true?
67. If your Hiddenness reveals itself to your handiwork by his uncovering,
68. who would not gather his vision from all else toward his construction?
69. If you have shown in him the great mystery of Son and Spirit,
70. who would not approach the sciences hidden in his name?
71. If in him you have shown your sweetness to angels and men,
72. who would not take refuge in his body, which pleads on his behalf?
73. If that Word begotten of you dwells in him in love,
74. who would not call him the Emperor of height and depth?
75. If in him you have completed your provision for all,
76. who would not labor for his own provision without weariness?
77. If through him you will judge the earth at the end of time,
78. who would not fear the trial that is in his hands?
79. If through him you will grant blessings to the good and punishments to the wicked,
80. who would not beg you to let him be an advocate for his debts?
81. If he is the one with authority over this world and that to come,
82. who would not believe that he is the Second [Person] of Divinity?
83. To these levels I saw our miserable nature raised,
84. and my mind was stirred to journey mentally toward his authority.
85. The greatness of his rank forced me to dare go out of order,
86. and to proceed on a path whose inquiry is greater than my words.

VI. Request for Aid

87. Toward your Hiddenness that is in his uncovering I wish to be drawn,
88. extend your hand to me as to Simon who approached you and pleaded [Matt 14:30–31].
89. To the rational sea about our life do my thoughts descend:
90. let your command draw me out, lest I sink into what is improper.
91. I approach pleading for the sake of my defects and those of my friends;
92. empower my faculties, lest they weaken before they are heard.
93. Your servants knock at the door of your mercies, who wills our life,
94. open to us, that we may enter and receive alms like the poor.

VII. The Misery of Mankind

95. Poor and lacking is our miserable race of all good things:
96. sustain this miserable thing with a small crumb of your Gift.
97. He is far too weak to gather temporal sustenance,
98. and he is unable to work the land with his strength without your Strength.
99. His work is filled with great fear, as much as he works,
100. and there is no security for his sustenance, as much as it multiplies.
101. Sufferings and griefs accompany his toil summer and winter,
102. and all perils are constant for him—for him, and for what is his.
103. Much is his work, and little the reward returned to him;
104. great is his weariness, and miserable and lacking, the sustenance of his life.
105. He plants so much and harvests little of the much,
106. he is beaten and crushed, and by the time he can rest, death has swallowed him.
107. In fear he plants, and in trepidation he gathers his produce,
108. and his heart does not rely on enjoying his labor or his gathering.
109. He casts his wheat upon his field, that it may be returned to him,
110. and he is afraid and distressed that perhaps he perish and his life pass away.

111. He works his land and he thinks that perhaps it may fail to produce;
112. he walks on the path, and death sits and waits for him.
113. Like a mother, he waits for produce like a newborn,
114. and the whips of death strike at his mind at every hour.
115. He stands in a contest of sufferings every day and night,
116. and there is no end to the battlefield of his emotions.
117. A great battle is poised at all times against his inclination,
118. and if he falls asleep, temptations enter and plunder his freedom.
119. The wretched one is cast before two calamities, each worse than the other:
120. the twofold scourgings of the passions of his body and the sustenance of life.
121. As if with leather cords, he beats himself with his inclinations,
122. and there is no place in him not filled completely with the passions.
123. He is suffering and weary regarding his passions and regarding his labors,
124. and there is no time when he does not rest with bitterness.

VIII. Twofold Wretchedness

125. If the sun grows hot, his mind grows hot regarding his crops,
126. and if the rain stops, his thoughts dry up along with his plants.
127. If heat gains the upper hand, thirst has killed him;
128. and if cold increases, he is consumed by frost.
129. If he is impoverished, he conceives depression and begets complaining;
130. and if he is made rich, he puts on pride and arrogant spirit.
131. If he is justified, he derides and mocks sinners;
132. and if he sins, he despairs and decides there is no hope.
133. If he is made wise, he forgets the clay of his wretched nature [Gen 2:7];
134. and if he glorifies himself, he becomes a beast without understanding.
135. In great and in small, his sufferings increase and his malice grows,
136. and what can he do, where can he run, who has such a brief life?
137. He is stuck wanting between neediness and excess,
138. and so how is it possible for him to keep his life without harm?

139. It is exceedingly difficult for men to live well,
140. and the course of righteousness is not made easy for the bodily.

IX. God's Temple

141. Flesh—he is flesh, as much as he desires spiritual things,
142. and even that desire is not his, but an Other's.
143. An Other dwells in him, in a temple of corruptible clay,
144. and in his living, he blossoms a little before he decays.
145. He is corruption entirely, although there is in him a portion of life,
146. and even this life is small compared to his afflictions.
147. So if the living that is in him is less than life,
148. how can he live a life without corruption?

X. Supplication for the Human Race

149. May your mercies come, O Lord, to the aid of our miserable race,
150. for its life's strength is burned away and wearied in the trial of suffering.
151. Stretch out your hand to the weak-hearted athlete,
152. for he realizes and admits openly that he cannot enter the match.
153. Cry out and encourage the mortal warrior,
154. for the fingers of his hands are too weak to hit the mark.
155. Command the intellectual natures to come and help him,
156. for his hand falls short of grasping even a straw of truth.
157. Call forth the heavenly legions to assist him,
158. before he falls and becomes a laughingstock to his enemy.
159. Write and send him an epistle of your Name above all,
160. that he may be strengthened to carry his sufferings through hope in your Name.
161. Lift [your] hand in writing of his life's salvation,
162. and lo, sufferings and demons will be terrified to look upon him.
163. Rebuke the ranks of warriors who threaten him,

164. and lo, they will be dismayed by the command of the Name of your Essence.
165. Send a watcher, as in the time of the Assyrian [2 Kings 20:1–7],
166. and lo, the powers of the evil one who surround him will be scattered.
167. Send your command, as Isaiah toward Hezekiah,
168. and instead of figs, let it place mercies upon our wounds.
169. Let us hear the voice that was heard by Hezekiah,
170. "Instead of life, lo, I increase the forgiveness of iniquity."
171. Yes, Lord, return us to health of body and soul,
172. lest we be torn apart by the wounds of our disgraces.

XI. Parables: The Lost Sheep and the Prodigal Son[5]

173. Come out in search of us, like the parable your Love composed,
174. and let us enter and graze in the sheepfold of spiritual life.
175. Brighten your Face, and seek our straying in your mercies,
176. lest the beauty of our clay, stamped in your Name, decompose.
177. Rejoice in our repentance, as in the story of the younger son,
178. and interpret, through us, the sound of hope signified in it.
179. With the deceitful one, we have worked for free and lost our pay,
180. and have lived wickedly on the swine-pods of desire.
181. We have sinned and enraged you (though, in fact, you have never been angered, nor are even now);
182. and we are unworthy to call ourselves the sons of your Name.
183. Let us become as hired hands in service to your house,
184. and let us receive what is just from your table as poor men.
185. And, if it is possible, fulfill in deed the meaning of the parable,
186. and bring to light the symbol you composed for our sake.
187. Tell us, "From death, you now live,
188. and from the corruption of ignorance, you have turned to me."
189. Command your pity to conceal our shame with a robe of glory,
190. and place a pledge of life on our hand as a ring.
191. Let your signal persuade you and prepare before us the Sacrifice of your Son,
192. and in eating it, may we banish the bitterness of death from our members.

193. And if there is one who envies our life's salvation and our repentance,
194. let your love pacify his bitter disposition with the sweetness of life.

XII. Reconciliation with the Angels

195. Call the angels and gladden them in our repentance,
196. that those once saddened by our sins may rejoice in our justification.
197. Appease those who were angered because of our malice,
198. and turn them toward the service of our life's needs.
199. Let them shake the air with the power that is from you, as is their custom,
200. and make it firm to carry the waters upon its back.
201. Let them place bridles of silence and reconciliation in its mouth,
202. lest it become fierce in disorderly seasons.
203. May they themselves be as charioteers above its back,
204. and may they watch over the vehemence of its course over the face of the earth.
205. May they watch its course like viewers in a gymnasium,
206. and weave, for your Name, a crown of thanksgiving by which you may gladden us.

XIII. Pleading for Hope

207. Yes, Lord, accept the formation of our words, miserable though they are,
208. and grant reward to our soul's study, dull though it is.
209. Yes, Lord, make the word of our mouth worthy to respond to the Word,
210. and let us hear from you, "Repent, O sinner, there is hope!"
211. Yes, Lord, gladden the air that was saddened by our malice,
212. and place a crown of dew in its mouth, that it may be pleased in us.
213. Yes, Lord, may the sounds of our mouth be keys to your treasury,

214. and may we open and receive forgiveness of sins and sustenance of life.
215. Do not, O Lord, turn away from the pleading of our poverty,
216. lest our hope in you be weakened by despair.
217. Do not, O Lord, turn your face away from us in a time of wrath,
218. lest tyrannical demons mock us, as is their custom.
219. Do not, O Lord, cast us away from your aid, as you do to the evil,
220. lest the evil be exalted in our abasement, as before.

XIV. Impossibilities

221. Be not, O Lord, unmerciful, for you are the Merciful One
222. (forgive me, Lord! You cannot be unmerciful; I spoke in weakness!).
223. Let not, O Lord, the Name of your Greatness be reduced because of our malice
224. (though it can never be reduced, even if we are wicked a million times!).
225. Be not, O Lord, lacking in help and poor in treasure
226. (oh, what I said of your Essence is a lie!).
227. Be not, O Lord, as a sojourner in your creation,
228. nor like a guest who turns in to slumber in what is not his.
229. Be not, O Lord, like a human, for you are God,
230. and not like a mere man who cannot save, for you are the Savior.

XV. God's Goodness vs. Human Wretchedness

231. And if our sins have prevailed more than the sins of every age,
232. may you forgive because of your honored Name upon which we call.
233. If our vices have made the face of the clear air vicious,
234. may you not show an angry face unbecoming of you.
235. If our wickedness has withheld benefits because of our malice,
236. may you not, O Lord, change the Name of your Goodness, which is unchanging.

XVI. Weakness of Human Language

237. You are all Good, and you are all Just, and you hate evil;
238. and neither can your Goodness nor your Justice be measured.
239. No one knows how to call you by a name that is fair to your Name,
240. for all names are small compared to the greatness of your Glory.
241. If we call you Good, the sound of your Justice thunders on earth;
242. but if Just, heaven and earth are filled with your mercies.
243. If we call you Hidden, your works are unveiled before the eyes of all creatures;
244. if we call you Unveiled, there is none among things made able to see you.
245. If we call you the Hearing One, our voice is heard by you before we call,
246. and the Gracious and Forgiving One, your Love precedes us and our malice.
247. We know neither how to pray nor how to glorify,
248. and we are afraid to speak words unfit for you.

XVII. Weakness of Human Prayer

249. How can we pray to one who needs nothing and is completely perfect?
250. And how can we glorify him who exists in glory from eternity?
251. If he is glorified, does he then increase through our glory?
252. And if he increases, is he made perfect by praise from us?
253. If he is dishonored, is his dishonor greater than his glory?
254. If he is hallowed, does he increase his glory through our mouth?
255. If he is angered, was the wicked man's shame hidden from him?
256. And if he is appeased, did we show him the way to reconciliation?
257. If he notices something in remorse after a time,
258. did time constrain him from knowing something he did not know?
259. If he did not know (that which is blasphemy to say),
260. what more did he gain in knowledge of his own construction?

XVIII. God's Perfection

261. No, earthly ones, do not be content with earthly things;
262. there is nothing in Existence lacking from Existence.

263. The name of every being is a declaration of his Constancy,
264. and insofar as he is, his knowledge is with him.
265. He is before everything, and he is what he is,
266. and there is nothing missing from him, neither what was nor will be.
267. Thus should what is made think of the Maker,
268. and thus is it owed by a rational creature to repay the Giver of rationality.

XIX. Man's Response

269. We owe a debt of love to our Fashioner,
270. come, let us attempt to repay a little of so much.
271. But he does not need repayment from us like a needy person,
272. he arranges pretexts that we may be enriched from his treasures.
273. He possesses an unending treasure of life in his Nature,
274. and he longs greatly to give of it to the sons of his household.
275. He has called our nature sons of the inheritance of the love of his Son,
276. because of this he chastises and instructs us lovingly.
277. Let us therefore endure the methods of discipline from his Lordship,
278. and never become weary of the scourgings of hunger and sickness.
279. If the name of "sons" truly applies to our mind,
280. let us be sure, then, that our discipline is also to our benefit [Heb 12:5–11].
281. Let us accept scourgings from our Maker without discouragement,
282. and let us know the struggle of seasons without murmuring.
283. This alone do we ask of him in the time of scourgings:
284. do not, O Lord, reprove us in stern anger, according to our deeds.

XX. King David

285. Like the son of Jesse, let us plead thunderously regarding our wickedness,
286. and in the way of his words, let us proceed to the promise of repentance.[6]

287. Yes, Lord, let us be worthy of that word to David,
288. and let us turn back to the rank of forgiveness of sin in his likeness.
289. Yes, Lord, pass over the faults of your servants as with your servant,
290. and let them hear the voice of forgiveness as the just one did.
291. David was just, but the evil one envied him and made him evil;
292. but he admitted he sinned and erased the name of evil from his heart.
293. So if confession erases evil things and writes good ones,
294. then there is hope for the evil to become good.
295. O Kind One who forgave adultery and murder with a word of the mouth,
296. forgive our disgraceful crimes as you see fit.
297. It was you who forgave that lawless crime:
298. forgive now also the sins we have committed against love.
299. It was you who loosened the execution given to murderers,
300. stop now also the tortures prepared for our injustice.

XXI. Patriarchs and Prophets

301. You are the One who mixed mercy with wrath in every age,
302. and you gave no room for the haters of our people to mock us.
303. You are the One who reckoned the greatness of your Love upon the just,
304. and made them worthy to appease you though you do not require it.
305. By your Love, you absolved the faults of our people from the beginning,
306. and you gave the will of the righteous the reward of your Kindness.
307. Because of the just, you forgave the faults of the first generations,
308. indeed, you forgave before they persuaded your Kindness.
309. You cast out Justice that the sons of men may persuade you,
310. that when they persuade you, they may realize that they can defeat evil.
311. Moses prayed, and you forgave the sin of the calf-worship,

312. and you told him, "Lo, I have forgiven as you have persuaded" [Exod 32:30].
313. Joshua prayed, and you stopped the course of the sun and moon,
314. and placed in the book of the deeds of Joshua that "their course was stopped" [Josh 10:12–14].
315. Samuel prayed, and your command answered him in the sound of thunder,
316. and you responded to him through the unseasonal rain that came [1 Sam 12:18].
317. David prayed, for he saw the watcher that would destroy the people,
318. and the spirit stood in awe of his pleading as he stood in awe of you [1 Chron 21:16].
319. Elijah called to you, and you hardened the winds and they carried the rain,
320. and you aroused the people to zeal whom the just man's words had bound and unbound [1 Kgs 18:41—19:8].
321. Elisha called to you, and by his hands you turned a dead man alive,
322. and you reckoned his prophecy a victory from the mouth of death [2 Kgs 4:8–37].
323. Hezekiah called to you, and you destroyed thousands of Assyrians,
324. and as this was truly happening, he won victory against the destruction of the watcher [2 Chron 32:1–22].
325. Daniel also, by the power of your aid, revealed hidden things,
326. and the Babylonians wove a crown of praises for his will [Dan 6:10–28].

XXII. The Logic of God's Mercy

327. In every age, the just ones prayed and you answered them;
328. in our age that is deprived of the righteous, may you persuade yourself.
329. The persuasion of your Kindness is greater than all the just,
330. and the treasury of your mercies is incomparable to that of things made.
331. Your Love provoked the will of the just to persuade you,

332. so if there are no just, send your Will without the just.
333. Yours are persuasion and the words of persuaders,
334. whom would you load with your own grace to the sons of your household?
335. May Goodness be entirely yours, as it is indeed,
336. and so grant us what you granted at the beginning of time.
337. Who convinced you to create creation when it did not exist?
338. And who advised you to bind up the world in the construction of man?
339. Who was it who advised you to call us your image?
340. And who showed you how to complete your work in our construction?
341. So if in our very existence, and all existence, you needed no help,
342. what help do you need regarding our wickedness—a miserable gnat?
343. Our wickedness is a gnat compared to the greatness of your Divinity,
344. and it is only a cup if compared to the sea of your mercies.
345. Your great Pity is a great sea, and greater than a sea,
346. and height and depth are quite small in proportion to its greatness.
347. "Your Pity is great": thus do heaven and earth cry out,
348. for when they were not, you spoke and they came to be from nothing.
349. You created everything out of nothing for our sake,
350. and so how could it be that you would turn away from us in a time of anger?
351. And, what is even greater and immeasurable by the rational,
352. we have put on your Love and our portion has been raised to the level of your Name.
353. You have called our name in the assumed name of the Name of your Being,
354. and now that it is so in actions, may it be for its station.

XXIII. God Honored in Man

355. Our dirt has ascended to a high station with your Essence,

356. may it not be lowered from its exaltation by means of our wickedness.
357. Our body is sitting at your right hand and clothed in glory,
358. may its glory not be shamed by the shame of our presumption.
359. May the rational natures not dishonor it because of its weakness,
360. for you have honored it with the great Name of your Divinity.
361. May you not, O Lord, become a boast for rebellious demons,
362. for they wish to rule, but their hands fall short of dominion.
363. May those who despise our people not rejoice, as is their custom,
364. for how is it that it rose to the great station of the immortals?
365. It is enough that they make light of and mock the name with which you honored us;
366. silence them, lest they become haughty to your Majesty.
367. Through us, they wish to mock your great Name,
368. and thus they think they will prevail over your Greatness.
369. The vain despisers of your Name despise our image,
370. and because they cannot defeat you, they defeat you through us.
371. Do not, O Lord, be disrespected by the foot of deceivers,
372. and let not the deceitful building they boast of be completed.
373. Chastise the arrogance of their minds and they will fall to the ground,
374. and lift up the head of our humbleness to the level of your Name.
375. Save our nature from the hands of the corruptors,
376. for it is enfeebled and brought low in the difficult fight against their ranks.

XXIV. Angelic Assistance

377. Send down your hand upon our encampment lacking in power,
378. for lo, the number of the lovers of truth has been reduced.
379. Brighten your face in our miserable grief-filled dwelling,
380. for lo, the bright light of justice has passed away from it.
381. May your command set up a guardian over our weakness,
382. for lo, it has scattered the treasure it received from your Gift.
383. Call to the spirits, and command them to support us,
384. for lo, demons and grievous pains enter and plunder our storehouses.
385. Send the watchers, let them wake us from our sleeping,

386. for lo, we are immersed in our disgraces as in sleep.
387. Send the angels, let them pacify our disturbance,
388. for lo, all ranks are set in wars of unworthiness.

XXV. Christ Our Mediator

389. And if the powers of the heights are insufficient to wake us,
390. persuade the Son of our race, and let him reconcile us with your Greatness.
391. He is able to help our disturbance in the contest of labors,
392. in that he is both your only Son and our Mediator.
393. He knows how to plead on behalf of the guilty lovingly,
394. in that he took on the test of the suffering of mortality.
395. Indeed, he was tested in all that the nature of mortals had,
396. and he better knows how to help those who are tested [Heb 4:15].
397. For the sake of peace, you chose him from all to reconcile all,
398. complete in act the choice of his Name for the sake of peace.
399. Now is the time for him to show in us the greatness of his station,
400. in that he show it at a time when our guilt has increased.
401. If, when we were haters of your Name, you reconciled us in him,
402. how much will he reconcile our unworthiness through his mediation!
403. If you have saved us by his hand from death and the backbiter,
404. how much more will he redeem us from enticements—miserable gnats?
405. If Judaism and paganism were uprooted in his cross,
406. how easy is it for him to rebuke the sufferings that irritate us?
407. If he will accomplish the reckoning of all at the end of time,
408. how much more is he able, before the ages, to dull the severity of scourgings?
409. If he has authority over the treasury of your Divinity,
410. he has therefore power to pity the sons of his race for free.
411. Pity our weakness, O Kind One, as is your custom,
412. and grant us a portion through the Son of our race, who has hold of your treasury.

Chapter 10

MEMRA 81: ON CHRISTOLOGY[1]

INTRODUCTION

This semi-polemic memra is a brief christological commentary on the Prologue to John's Gospel. It begins with comments on the first verse, that the Word was "in the beginning" with, and was, God. The Father and the Son are therefore equal *Qnome* (lines 7–10), with no time elapsing between them, the way there is no time between the existence of the sun and its light (line 20). Indeed, time itself does not apply to the *Qnome* of the Trinity (lines 28–31).

Narsai notes that John's use of *Word* in describing the *Qnoma* of the Son already treads the path to the incarnation, since in the soul, a word can be spoken and go out to the world while still remaining in the mind (line 37–41). Indeed, a word can even be written in ink on paper, visible to all, and still be present in the soul that first spoke it; thus Christ's Body is the ink that our eyes can see, though the Word remained and remains always in eternity with the Father and thus is not contained or limited by it (lines 45–53).

The controversial question is the interpretation of John 1:14: "and the Word became flesh and dwelt among us" (in the Pshyṭta, "in" us). It is obvious that "became" cannot mean that God the Word changed from one kind of being into another, which would be blasphemous and contradict the first verse of John's Gospel (lines 73–86). No, the Word cannot change either in entirety or in part (lines 85–86), for then the Father could also change, since they are of the same Nature (line 88), and if it is possible for the Will of the Word to change his Nature, then Divinity becomes a slave to Will (lines 93–97). Indeed, if humanity can limit or constrain God through the incarnation, then it is greater than God, which is also blasphemy (lines 103–104).

Narsai therefore sees that "became" must be interpreted in terms of the next phrase, "dwelt in us" (lines 109–112). He sees his opponents, the Monophysites, who assert "two natures become one" in Christ, to be crypto-Arians in asserting change and suffering in the Divine Word, making him less than the Father (lines 117, 146–154). On the contrary, the flesh that the Word took was from Mary, for he had to save Adam's race as the Son of David (lines 133–136), and therefore the Word and the Flesh assumed from Mary are distinct: there is a Word, and there is the Man whose Body is the Temple in which he "dwelt" (lines 141–143). The Word dwells in Flesh without being limited and remaining, as God, in every place and eternal (lines 168, 184); thus he dwells in "Will" not in Nature, for if he dwelt in the Body by Nature, his Nature would no longer be in every place (line 185). Narsai sees this theological conflict a battle to secure the dignity of God as well as to affirm the salvation of human nature, which was assumed at the incarnation (lines 175–176).

Narsai understands that the Word became flesh and dwelt among us so that "we may see his glory." The invisible God is shown through the visible Christ (line 188). Christ's Body is the Temple where God dwells, where the Will of the Word works everything it wills, but which does not limit or contain God's Nature (lines 194–196). The unity of Christ is that of the One Person (consistent with Narsai's other works and the terminology of the Church of the East in general—lines 203–206). This is somewhat analogous to the unity between soul and body, only in that this is an example of two distinct principles being unified in a single person (line 204), of an entity being "in" another but having effects outside it (line 208), and of a body suffering but having within it an element that is impassible (lines 213–214).

The Word took on our lowliness so we can share his glory (lines 219–220); when we see Christ's Body, we know the invisible Word (lines 234, 237, 249). Thus Christ is the final and ultimate Image of God (line 250). We see the outer "holy place" in his Flesh and through our flesh, and the "holy of holies" of his Divinity through the powers of our soul (lines 261–262). The Word took on flesh so that we can see him in the way we are able to as physical creatures (line 263).

TRANSLATION

I. John's Prelude

1. The word that John wrote trod us a new path,
2. and he journeyed on it first and became a guide for us.
3. He trod the path to Existence and showed that there is one Equality;
4. for the Father and his Child are one, and there is no time between him and his Child.
5. [John's] voice was like thunder, and it resounded to the four corners;
6. well did [Christ] name him a son of thunder, who preached "the Word in the Beginning."
7. "Hear, O peoples, and attend, O nations, the new Gospel I preach:
8. the Father who begets from his womb, the Son who is not younger than his Begetter.
9. In the beginning was the Word, and he was with God,
10. and the Word was God, in Individuality and in authority."[2]
11. O Mystery hidden from the ages and generations,
12. which the son of thunder showed and revealed to those above and below!
13. O John the preacher, of the race of feeble Adam,
14. to whom the Holy Spirit gave keys, and who opened the treasure of Existence!
15. He ascended and reached the height of heights, above the spiritual assemblies,
16. and the power of grace brought him near to speak regarding Existence.
17. He received power and authority and preached the Word in the beginning,
18. that the Son was in the beginning, eternally with his Begetter.

II. Equality of the Father and the Son

19. He was eternally with his Father, like radiance with the sun,
20. for the sun is not there before its radiance, nor radiance not in its company.
21. Radiance is with the sun, and there is no time it is not with it;
22. the Child is with the Father, and there is no time he is separate from him.
23. The Father is a true Individual, and the Son an Individual like him,
24. and though he is indeed named Father, there is no time between him and his Child.
25. He is a Nature existing from eternity, and there is no beginning to his Existence;
26. neither did the Father begin to exist, nor was there a time for the Son's birth.
27. The Father is an eternal Being, and there is no time when the Father was not.
28. The Son is perfect, lacking nothing, for there is no time when the Child was not.
29. The Being is distant from times, and times and generations are from him;
30. for how could it be that Being be limited by the times that he fashioned himself?
31. As much as thought seeks, it finds him on the other side of time;
32. neither did the Father begin in his begetting, nor was there a time of the begetting of the Son.

III. The Word Spoken in Flesh

33. John called him the Word, which is eternally with the Father,
34. like a word with a soul, from which it is, and with which it is.
35. A word is with a soul, and goes out from it, and is in it:
36. the Son was with the Father, and came to the world, and was [still] with him.
37. Never has a word gone out from a soul and departed from it,
38. nor has the Son gone out from his Begetter, and become distant from him by moving.

39. A word goes out to all the corners and does not move away from the soul,
40. and while on its mission, it is in the soul where it was.
41. The Word also went out from the Father and came to our mortal dwelling,
42. and while he was dwelling in our nature, he was entirely in the Father.
43. A word that is from a soul is not visible openly,
44. but when it is written in ink, it is seen through letters.
45. And though indeed one confines it in letters, and limits it in garments of ink,
46. it is in letters in name, but entirely dwells in the soul.
47. The pupils see ink when they look at the letters,
48. but the word does not give its nature over to be limited by pupils.
49. The Son was hidden with his Begetter from the lofty and lowly,
50. and he was shown to us by his Will, in the ink of the Body of Adam.
51. While he truly was clothed with the garment of our nature in his Divinity,
52. his Will dwelt in our nature, and his Nature remained hidden.
53. The Body he wore was not a limit to his Nature, which is unlimited,
54. and the eye of flesh did not see his Hidden Divinity.

IV. Life and Light

55. "Through him," says John, "all things that exist were fashioned,
56. and there was nothing without him, for he willed and ordered all that was" [John 1:3].
57. He is the Fount filled with life, who possesses Life in his Nature,
58. and from the Life in his Nature, he distributes life to the things he has fashioned.
59. "The Life was Light, which pursues darkness from life,
60. and the darkness of ignorance has not overcome the course of the Light [John 1:4–5].
61. He was already in the world, and the world was fashioned through him,

62. and though the world was his, the world did not want to confess him.
63. The Creator came to his own, and his own did not accept his word;
64. but those who obeyed his commands gained the authority of sons" [John 1:11–12].
65. He named us his own sons, in the mercies that he showed to our race,
66. for he begat us spiritually through baptism of water and Spirit.
67. The Good One showed us his will, who honored us with the name of sons,
68. and he verified the name of sonship because he chose himself a Dwelling among his sons.

V. The Word Became Flesh

69. "The Word," says John, "became flesh and dwelt in us [John 1:14],
70. and we have seen the glory of his Hiddenness, in the curtain of our humanity."
71. He became flesh and dwelt in us and showed us his hidden glory,
72. and though he was hidden in his Nature, he showed us his glory through our body.
73. He did not descend in order to become, where it says "he became flesh,"
74. but rather to fashion himself Flesh and dwell in it through his Will.
75. It is not possible for the Creator to come to be a new being,
76. nor for the Existence without beginning to set itself a time to be born.
77. If indeed he was from eternity, how can he come into being?
78. And if he came into being, he is far from eternal being.
79. There is no beginning or end for the Existence that is from eternity,
80. but for a thing that comes into existence, its existence precedes its nature.
81. If he was with the Father, he cannot be limited in his Nature,
82. and if he limited himself in a womb, he is not a Being like his Begetter.

83. If he is in every place, and he now comes into being,
84. how can he accept fashioning, whether a part of him or all of him?
85. If he is entirely limited, he does not have unlimitedness,
86. and if he is limited in part, then he could be entirely limited.
87. If he can be limited, whether entirely or in part,
88. then the Father too can be limited, for the Son is of his Nature.

VI. The Word Dwelt in Us

89. How was he in his Father and dwelling in a womb of flesh?
90. This is the question being asked: how can he receive a dwelling place?
91. Perhaps the heretics say that he is in height and depth,
92. because he is able to divide his being and be in a womb and in heaven.
93. In this case, his Will is prior to his eternal Nature,
94. for his Will subjugates and limits his Nature.
95. If his Will is able to constrain and overcome his Nature,
96. then he could be changed at every hour, according to what his Will wills.
97. And if his Will leads his Nature according to what it wills,
98. where is his Existence that has its Nature eternally?
99. Let this complaint go after the impudence of the heretics,
100. who lower the Being to miserable things and limit him in the womb of the daughter of man.
101. O deprived of light, and journeyers on the path of darkness:
102. how can the Nature of Being be limited in his works?
103. If he is limited in his actions, according to the word of the heretics,
104. the thing he has fashioned is greater than he is, for it is able to limit his Nature.
105. How can the Nature more subtle than wind accept composition,
106. whether he is in his Nature, or in a nature that is not his?
107. Come explain your secrets, O uncircumcised of heart [Rom 2:29],
108. and teach us how we can confess the Word who became flesh.

109. Either explain to us how the Word can dwell in body parts,
110. or prepare your weapon and fight, and let us see who is victorious.
111. Gather all your arrows, and stretch the strings of your bows,
112. place "the Word became flesh" as your target, and let us see who hits it.
113. The whole fight is over the Word who became flesh;
114. and I ask you to prepare your weapons regarding this.
115. You wish to fight with us with the weapon of your teacher,
116. who forged the armor and clothed you with it, against the Word that is from the Father.
117. Come with your teacher the Egyptian,[3] and seek out the power of the phrase;
118. let us see how there can be becoming or beginning for the Creator.
119. While he was, did he fashion himself, or did he now begin to exist?
120. Then for what reason did he fashion, he who is distant from being fashioned?
121. If he came into existence, then he was not, and if he was, then he did not come into existence now;
122. for the Being is not able to accept becoming after his Existence.
123. He became flesh, according to your word: a part of him or all of him?
124. But how can the Nature without composition be divisible?
125. If he was entirely fashioned, then he was entirely limited,
126. and he is limited from every place and dwells only in the womb.
127. If it is this way, whence do we say he is unlimited?
128. For his limit is a womb of flesh, according to the deception you constructed.
129. If a part of him was fashioned, and a part remained in his Nature,
130. whence do we say there is equality? For he is divided in his Nature.
131. If the Word became flesh, let us ask whose flesh it was;
132. did he bring it down from above, or was it the flesh of a man?
133. If his Individual became flesh, and the flesh was not taken from Mary,
134. how does it help our nature, if it was his own flesh?

135. Therefore the promise is empty that was promised to David,
136. and the "Son of David" is named with a putative name since he is not so.
137. How are mortals helped by the Word who became flesh,
138. if he who became flesh [did so] in his Nature, and our nature remains in its fall?
139. How then can he erase the judgment of death from us,
140. if he did not take a Body from Mary and help our mortal body?
141. But if the Body is from Mary, the Word took it and dwelt in it.
142. This is fitting for those who know, and witnesses the truth of their words.
143. Therefore the Being is not able to become flesh in his Individual,
144. and becoming flesh is far removed from the Existence without beginning.

VII. The Arian Heresy

145. The secret of your scheme of words is obvious.
146. Reveal the goal of your minds, and interpret things like Arius.
147. Your words empower him, and your phrases support him
148. who denied the Existence of the Son and called him a servant and minister.
149. This is the entire fight of Arius, the disciple of deception,
150. who made the Son less than the Father and counted him among creatures.
151. You are aiming at his target as well, O heretics,
152. who hide the impiety hidden in your words as in a disguise.
153. Leave the sheepfold, O rebels, and do not lead astray in the costume of lambs,
154. for you have corrupted discernment [by saying] two Natures became One.
155. The wickedness of your blasphemy assaults and is brought up to the height of heights,
156. and it lowers the Being from his end and binds him in the cords of body parts.
157. Heaven and earth, attend and hear the impiety that the heretics speak:
158. they limit and imprison incomprehensible Existence in a womb.

159. They hold on to this phrase like a shield in battle:
160. "The Word fashioned his being and became flesh, as it is written."
161. How can it be that you accept this, O teachers of new things,
162. and you forget that "he dwelt in us," and do not examine its meaning?
163. John said "he dwelt in us"; who dwelt in whom?
164. Lo, it is shown to us openly: the dwelling of two who became One.
165. If he speaks of dwelling, which is what we were inquiring about,
166. he is therefore able to dwell, even without becoming.
167. If he dwells in another, "becoming" is therefore improved,
168. and this is fitting to his Nature: to dwell without being limited.
169. So come, O you who hear, test if my words are fair,
170. and with the measure of your mind, measure whether my words are measured.
171. Hearing my words, which are spoken as answers, will not disturb you,
172. nor are they for speculation, but rather for seeking benefit.
173. This is a beneficial inquiry, and in it is hidden the hope of our lives,
174. for it brings him close to our nature, for the honor of the image that was destroyed.
175. Our fight is over this: that the Word may not lessen in dwelling,
176. but rather he took on our nature and honored it in the glory of his Greatness.
177. This is the discussion regarding dwelling, which we investigate with the rebels,
178. that Existence may not be diminished in dwelling with humanity.

VIII. Christ the Temple

179. That "he became" is that "he dwelt," and that "he dwelt" that "he took a man"
180. and hid the splendor of his Greatness in the garment of a mortal Body.

181. The Existent Word fashioned a Temple of a Body for himself and dwelt in it [John 2:19];
182. he did not accept fashioning, as in the impiety of the heretics.
183. He did not become limited in his Nature when he descended for fashioning,
184. and even the Temple that he fashioned himself was not enough to limit his Nature.
185. It was not in his Nature that he dwelt in the Son of Man he took from us,
186. but rather the dwelling of his Will in an undivided unity.
187. The Word wove a garment of flesh in which to hide his Greatness,
188. that men may see in the Son of Man the Image of the glory of his Greatness.
189. He promised an undeceiving promise to Abraham and to David,
190. and he has now completed it in deed, through the Principle from the house of David.
191. The Word is not a son of David; heretics, why are you arguing?
192. The Son of David is a son of our race, whom the Word took and dwelt within.
193. The Word accomplished his entire Will in the Body and dwelt in it,
194. and while his Will is contained in it, his Nature is not limited by it.
195. He was entirely in it in his Will, and in his Nature he was in it and in every place,
196. for it is appropriate to the Maker not to be limited by what he has made.
197. The Body was his creature that he willed to be his Dwelling,
198. and while it did not limit his Nature, he dwelt in it entirely in his Will.

IX. Christ Is One Person

199. You might argue, O heretics, with my words as you always do,
200. "how can you call the Maker and the made one Person?"
201. We call the made a Temple that the Word fashioned for his dwelling,

202. and Maker the Only-Begotten who willed to dwell in what he made.
203. "One Person" I call the Word and the body in which he dwelt,[4]
204. like a soul and body that are equal and are named one person.
205. The soul is the nature of life, and the body the mortal nature,
206. the two that are distinct from each other are called one Person.
207. The Word, the Nature of Existence, and the Body, the nature of humanity:
208. one made and one Maker are one in Unity.
209. The soul is contained in the body, but its acts are outside the body:
210. while the body is in one place, the powers of the soul are in the four corners.
211. The Word dwelt in the Body and was in height and depth,
212. and his humanity was limited, while his Divinity was in every corner.
213. The soul does not suffer in the body when parts are beaten,
214. nor did Divinity suffer in the suffering of the Body in which it dwelt.
215. If the soul does not suffer, which is made as the body is,
216. how can Existence suffer, whose Nature is above suffering?
217. The soul suffers with the body in love, not in nature,
218. and they are called the passions of the body, but also of the soul putatively.
219. He made the Man he took from us one with him in glory,
220. and because of his love for him, he took his lowliness upon himself.
221. The soul dwells in a body, and spectators do not see it,
222. and while it is limited in its nature, the eyes of flesh do not contain it.
223. The Word also dwelt in our nature and was not limited by our nature,
224. for it was a Dwelling of his Will, and not a dwelling of nature.
225. Come, example in our nature,[5] in which two natures become one:
226. one living and the other mortal; one hidden and the other unveiled.
227. Come then, O heretics, ask a fitting question;

228. humble the height of your words and know your wretched nature.
229. Leave off the question of Existence, for Existence is incomprehensible,
230. and speak about the Son of our race, whom Being took and dwelt in.

X. Christ the Image of God

231. He dwelt in him but his being was not limited, for his Nature cannot be limited.
232. The Mortal suffered in his nature, but sufferings did not approach Existence.
233. He fashioned himself a rational Image to show his authority in him,
234. that when the rational see him, they may honor the Hidden One through the Unveiled.
235. In the Holy of Holies of his Hiddenness, the Being dwelt hiddenly,
236. and through the mediation of the Son of our race, we see the Image of his Glory.
237. For this reason he chose and dwelt in him: that the Hidden One may be shown in the Unveiled,
238. and at the curtain of his Unveiledness we may adore his Hidden Nature.
239. He made him Lord over his house, and Authority over his possessions;
240. he subjugated height and depth to him, rational and mute together.
241. In him the fashioning of our image, which had wasted away in sin, was renewed,
242. and his naming us his image was fulfilled in deed through him.
243. Watchers and men adore him as an unveiled Image of the King,
244. as they are awestruck at seeing him in place of the Hiddenness of the Only-Begotten.
245. O hearers, listen and understand what I say clearly,
246. lest your thoughts be troubled by "the Word became flesh."
247. I have trod the path in words; come follow after my phrases,

248. that you may find the Fount of Life at the end of the path I trod.
249. Glorify the Being in his Hiddenness, through the Unveiled whom he took for his Dwelling,
250. and honor the King through his Image, for the King is honored in his Image.
251. Because it is difficult to walk the path to the Existence without beginning,
252. he trod us the path to his Hiddenness through the Son of our race, our leader.
253. Because the nature of made things is unable to understand the secret Being,
254. he showed us the beautiful glory of his Hiddenness through the Image that he fashioned.
255. He tied the love of creatures to the Pledge that he took from us,
256. and through the Mediator, the Son of our race, he reconciled us with his Greatness.
257. This is the cause of his coming: that he may come and renew our fashioning,
258. and bind up the peace that had slackened through the mediation of our Principal.
259. For our comfort, he fashioned a Temple of Flesh and dwelt in it,
260. that we may adore the outer Holy Place and him who is hidden in the Holy of Holies.
261. We see the outer Holy Place of his Body through the eyes of flesh,
262. and the Holy of Holies of his Hiddenness through the spiritual powers of the soul.
263. The lofty and the lowly are stopped at the veil of the Body of Adam,
264. and creatures do not have the power to see the Truth of Existence.
265. Lo, the path to life is trodden: come, heretics, and walk on it,
266. and do not stumble on the path of the divisions of your minds.
267. Do not mingle division into the confession of Existence,
268. for the Son is equal to his Begetter: do not bring him down to weaknesses.
269. We confess that the Word put on Flesh and willed and dwelt in our nature,

270. while the Temple of Flesh he dwelt in did not limit his Nature.
271. He dwelt in him entirely, in his Will, and remained entirely in his Existence,
272. and took on, in name, his humiliations, and shared his glories with him.
273. Come, O guilty sons of Adam, let us repay thanksgiving
274. to the Good One who shared the glories of his Greatness with our nature.

Chapter 11

MEMRA 44: ON THE NEW CREATION

INTRODUCTION

In this eschatological memra, Narsai calls our attention to the renewal of creation at the end of time and, in doing so, illustrates the spiritual benefit of reflecting on this. The memra begins with a set of parallel contrasts between God and creation, since even by this contrast, God's works reveal his hidden nature. The labor of creation is contrasted with God's rest; the passage of time reveals God's eternity; the constant change in nature reveals God's "constancy" or immutability (lines 7–26).

A second contrast is then painted between the beginning of time and its end. Though creation and the "renewal" that is the theme of this memra are both sudden acts of God (lines 33–35), the renewal of creation is greater than its beginning because it will never end (line 38). Narsai notes that God will not change his mind or have a new thought in enacting the new creation (lines 47–50), but rather that he has planned this from eternity (lines 39–42). This will have special implications for the humanity of Christ by the end of the memra.

As work is related to time, rest is related to eternity (lines 59–60), and this obvious Sabbath imagery is read by Narsai the schoolmaster in terms of intellectual activity: study, the tedious work of the mind, is a temporal task, while meditation is akin to rest and therefore to eternity (lines 61–62). The connection between the two, time and eternity, becomes clear in this intellectual turn: the promises of

God that we accept in faith (line 67). In believing God's promises of the world to come, we who labor through time have hope and encouragement in the thought of eternity. God's initial promise to creation was made in Genesis when he took clay from the earth and breathed life into it (line 73). The sense here is that a dead thing was given life, revealing God's power to do such a thing. Almost immediately, this is likened to how the whole world rose to new life through Christ's resurrection and ascension (lines 74–77).

It is in Christ that God's promise is made clear to the creation, and the world eagerly awaits his return, for its own sake, for then will it rest from its weariness (lines 101–104). This weariness includes the labor done by the angels for the sake of humanity (lines 111–116), but also the work of human beings, the passions, sin, and even death (lines 131–135). The "work" done by all these entities will cease under the rulership of Christ, when creation is given new life through him like a child being born from its mother (lines 139–150). Taken in isolation, this memra even suggests a universalism on the part of Narsai: not only do the angels rest but the demons as well, and all together glorify God in Christ (lines 163–170).

Narsai is clear that the new creation will not be *ex nihilo* as the first creation was, but rather a transformation of the current existing world (line 195). Again, this was God's plan all along from the beginning of time (lines 197–198), and it is therefore not in any sense a destruction of this world (lines 207–208). This is the case not only for the renewal of angels and humans in their move from labor to rest (line 202), but the stars will cease their motion and return to the primordial "light"; air and water and the elements in general will cease their movements as well and return to the earth in peace (lines 217–231). These elemental movements will end because they were, from the beginning, for the sake of man, and after the renewal, man will no longer need any of it (lines 247–262). Thus light, air, darkness, and the seasons will return to their primordial nature, remaining still what they are but finding rest in glory (lines 269–288). The same goes for seeds, fire, gold, and mute animals, who will still exist but no longer reproduce (lines 292–308).

The one exception to this is the "son of perdition," who will be completely destroyed in both body and soul (lines 313–320). This is consonant with other works of Narsai, such as Memra 34, which details the end times and final judgment. The son of perdition's ultimate destruction is meant to teach creatures that they are always upheld by God's creative act, and also how evil sin is (lines 330–332); it reveals the fullness of both God's mercy and his justice (lines 335–336); and it punishes Satan, who attempted to harm creation through the "temple" that he occupied (line 352).

The theme of teaching continues, as Narsai points out that the renewal itself is an example of Divine Pedagogy, revealing God's love and power (lines 388, 397). Learning and reflecting on this is worth the labor (line 391), and indeed Narsai's own pedagogy is learned from God's, since he speaks of the beautiful things in the renewal in order to give us, his readers, hope (lines 411–412). It is worthwhile to meditate on future things and, in various ways, healthy and good for the soul (line 422).

God's teaching occurs primarily through Christ the Son of Man and Mediator between the Creator and his creation (lines 441–450). Christ in his own Person trod the path to renewal by rising and ascending (lines 459–462), and the renewal of all creation will also happen through Christ (lines 469–472). Christ is the Temple where God is worshipped by creation (line 477) as its Lord (line 517). Indeed, Jesus Christ worthily and truly bears the Name of the Maker (lines 521–522), though he is in his humanity a portion of creation (line 529), even in the elements that make up his Body (lines 535, 588). God foreknew and chose Christ from eternity (line 543) to be the Mediator between himself and the world, meaning that in Christ the creature and the Creator are one and equal (line 566).

TRANSLATION

I. God's Unity and Immutability

1. One Creator created creation from nothing [Gen 1:1–2],
2. and he will renew it from what is worthless to what is glorious.
3. One Will fashioned the world weary with toil,
4. and he will free it from subjugation to labors.
5. One is the Lord who began the labor that had no labor,

6. and he will complete it in perfection without anything lacking.
7. One is the Nature who constituted the universe as rational and mute beings,
8. and he will give what he has made rest in the harbor of his Love, lest they be wearied.
9. One is the Signal who sustains the world with visible things,
10. and is going to give life by what is invisible to visible things.
11. One is the Authority who orders the course of watchers and humans,
12. and from his treasure he distributes gifts to their wills.
13. One is the Hidden whose Nature is hidden and whose work is unveiled,
14. and though he is hidden, his works cry out regarding his Hiddenness.
15. His works witness to his Hiddenness, which is incomprehensible [Rom 1:20],
16. for since they came into being, they could not see him who is constant.
17. He is constant Existence without beginning,
18. and he has willed for the works he made to remain without end.
19. He has willed to make the works he made participate in his Constancy,
20. that while they remain, they become witnesses to his Constancy.
21. It is fit that the Being and his labor remain constantly,
22. that as he is, his constructions may also be constant.
23. It is not that the Creator of creation created creation for time,
24. but that by its constancy, it might also maintain time itself.
25. Lo, times proceed from when they came into being along with its fashioning,
26. and times will pass, but [creation] does not pass from what it is.
27. The orders of its constancy proceed without end,
28. and even if it ends, along with its end there will also be its renewal.

II. Creation and Its Final Renewal

29. My mind dragged me to explain [creation's] end,
30. for I saw how much more lovely it is than the time in its beginning.

31. Its end is lovely because its renewal is united to it,
32. and I have said that the renewal is more lovely than the beginning.
33. Its beginning is lovely, which was fashioned suddenly out of nothing,
34. and greatly lovely is also its renewal, which will be sudden.
35. In the same fashion that it came about suddenly from nothing,
36. will it be in the end, something more lovely than the first thing.
37. It is lovely for the Good One to renew the creation he created,
38. so that in its renewal it may remain with him without end.
39. He desired it to be without end from the beginning,
40. and he will perfect the desire of his love on the day of its end.
41. Behold, he had this will eternally without beginning:
42. that it may first be temporal, and then forever.
43. He knew this will before everything,
44. and he did not will newly to fashion, and then fashion again.
45. He was quite able also to renew after time,
46. and no thought has forced him to renew when he renews.
47. There is no thinking for that Thought that cannot be thought,
48. nor willing for that Will that did not will and does not will.[1]
49. What he did was thought by him before he did it,
50. and what that Will willed was willed by him.
51. It was not newly that he did all he did, or will do,
52. for he had everything that came into being before it came into being.
53. Wisely did he make a beginning for the work of his hands,
54. and gloriously he will renew his work at the end of time.
55. The Glorious One in his work made times and orders for his works,
56. and his handiwork cannot say how glorious and ordered it is.
57. The order he made for the two worlds is glorious and ordered,
58. for he gave one a fixed time, while one is forever.
59. In one he placed order that all may remain in labors,
60. and the other he made without labor, giving rest to the weary.
61. In one he piled up different kinds of laborious studies,
62. and the other he filled with unwearying meditation.
63. He looked at both with his hidden secret eye,

64. and ordered them as was fitting to the Knower of all.
65. He knew that the temporal dwelling place was corruptible,
66. and he encouraged it in advance through the renewal that he promised it.

III. God's Promises in Christ

67. Through promises he enticed and dragged it to knowledge of himself,
68. that when it knew him, it would believe that he could straighten its fallen state.
69. He held it with a fleshly hand as one who fell,
70. and he sustained and upheld it and its vision hung upon the surface of the heights above.
71. The Lord of the world held the world through a human hand,
72. and called out to it, "Stand," and it stood and was strengthened in its sickness.
73. He seasoned and gave it clay from itself as a medicine [Gen 2:7],
74. and it drank from it and dusted the bile of mortality off.
75. The dead world came alive and was resurrected mysteriously,
76. and learned of the order that will again be resurrected in actuality.
77. He trod the path for expecting the fashioning above,
78. and sent before himself One of its own like a guide.
79. He sent an Ambassador from the world to the other world,
80. to prepare for the exhausted world a perfected world.
81. Like a High Priest, he ordered him to enter the sanctuary above [Heb 9:24],
82. that through him he might forgive the debts of the exhausted world.
83. The Lord of all took a Pledge of Peace from all,
84. that when he is with him, all might believe that they will return to him.
85. He determined a time when it would turn from his love,
86. and lo, the earthly and heavenly await him.
87. The world wearied in sin awaits that delight,
88. to receive from it freedom from its debts which it owes its God.

IV. Christ's Return and Creation's Eternal Rest

89. It daily awaits that Messenger that he sent before him,
90. to come and proclaim the renewal of its decrepitude.
91. The Light of the world will suddenly dawn from that world [cf. Mark 13:36],
92. and chase out of it the darkness of earthly labors.
93. By the light of his face, he will make its sad mourning pass,
94. and will lighten from it the severe weight of the passability.
95. With the sound of trumpet, he will awaken the sleepiness of its ignorance [Matt 24:31],
96. and [the world] will awake and rise as from a bed of its grievous wounds.
97. In all and in all he will renew suddenly, without delay,
98. and there will not remain any place that remains without renewal.
99. All creation will be renewed in that renewal:
100. heaven and earth, and all that are contained within their limits.
101. The rational and mute will rest together from their labors,
102. and will no longer be wearied in the labors for their needs.
103. That world will give rest to all and all from all burdens,
104. and there will be none among creatures not given rest from its weariness by his rest.
105. That is the rest that was signified in the Scriptures of the Spirit:
106. and in it rest the wearied voices of prophecy.
107. In its rest, there is no labor that wearies the one who rests in it,
108. nor in turn will any fear the change between good and evil.
109. There is no change between good and evil in that renewal,
110. nor one who awaits with expectation of another hope.
111. In it are bound all expectations of watchers and men,
112. and in it are closed up the first things and the last things.
113. In its peaceful harbor, the heavenly assemblies rest,
114. and are not wearied in leading heaven and earth.
115. In it they are given rest from their labors for humankind,
116. for the course of humankind and their works will cease as well.
117. Humankind will rest from the toil of human things,
118. and will not need to think of earthly matters.

119. The freeing of humankind will give rest from labor to the spiritual,
120. and humans and the heavenly will be in one manner of life.
121. The spiritual are engaged in crushing labors on behalf of the human being,
122. but when they are freed, both commanders and the commanded will rest.
123. Because of his need, they now command and also are commanded,
124. but when he is enriched, they will no longer command or be commanded.
125. He promises the wealth of immortal life there,
126. and with him, the ministers of his life's needs will also rest.
127. The weary one will receive perfect unchanging rest,
128. and the natures will no longer crush or be crushed on his behalf.
129. All creation will rest with him, and he with all,
130. and the rational and speaking will be in quiet and silence.
131. The passions of the soul and body will be silent,
132. and he will not struggle nor will his passions struggle against him.
133. Sin will be extinguished, and death which swallowed him as well,
134. and the tough battle he fights against it will be settled.
135. Even the rebels who despise him for nothing will rest in his rest,
136. and will be with him in the one Will of the One Creator.
137. One Will will rule there over all and in all,
138. and there will be no opposition or hindrance, or anything like that.

V. The Rule and Judgment of Christ

139. One will rule along with the Will which established the crown for him,
140. and he is the one who will judge in that Will which gave him judgment.
141. The Son, a son of our race, has received all judgment from the Father,
142. and he is the one who will give gifts to the good and punishments to the evil.
143. On the day of his revelation, he will show the power of his headship,

144. and he will subjugate all and renew all by the power of his authority.
145. Creation awaits that renewal that will take place by his hands,
146. And groans for when the time of its renewal will happen [Rom 8:22].
147. Passions strike its passability like birth pangs,
148. for when it will bear newborns of immortal life,
149. like a mother carrying the weight of mortality,
150. and that day will give rest to its pain and let pass its aching [John 16:21].
151. It will suddenly wear a garment of renewal by a hidden signal,
152. and like a bride it will stand in indestructible glory [Eph 5:27].
153. It will see itself in great glory—how glorious,
154. and it will not be satisfied with seeing itself with the eyes of the soul.
155. That joy will be without satiation for the one who rejoices in it,
156. and even more the humans and heavenly angels who have ministered well.
157. Humans and watchers will rest there in that delight,
158. and they will be heirs of blessings without end.
159. Watchers will rest from service on behalf of all,
160. and will not be wearied by the constant course of the change of seasons.
161. Their mental faculties will rest from change,
162. and they will not again have an ugly desire like the demons.
163. The course of those prone to evil will cease from their ranks,
164. and all of them will be reconciled to the one Will that fashioned them.
165. The demons will cease from the madness of their blasphemies,
166. and in place of cursing they will repay praise, although unwillingly.
167. They will no longer arrange mocking war against the human being,
168. and no longer dare to revile the Name of Existence.
169. There will be one will of love for all and with all,
170. the heavenly and the earthly, the good and the evil.
171. The good and the evil will gain love that does not grow dull,

172. and although they are divided due to their deeds, they will be reconciled in love.
173. Watchers and humans will be reconciled in one perfect love,
174. To reward one glory to the one Creator.
175. The good and the evil will cry out glory wherever they are,
176. and there will be no end to the sound of the glory of the glorifiers.
177. Glory is their constant meditation always,
178. constancy without break and without labor.
179. Everything that comes into being will be without labor there,
180. and the mouth inasmuch as it is mortal cannot say how this will be.

VI. The Indescribable World to Come

181. How is it possible for mortality to relate with words
182. the providence of that immortal fashioning?
183. How can a tongue of corruptible flesh be able
184. to depict the type of that beauty that has no equal?
185. That providence has no equal in this providence,
186. nor is there a display that can show it accurately.
187. It only resembles itself in an accurate image,
188. and it can relate the beauty of its great glory.
189. Its glory incited me to relate its gloriousness with words,
190. how glorious and how glorified to those worthy of it.
191. I saw that its glorifiers were destined to glorify,
192. and wonder seized me at the great indescribable glory.
193. The glory of that day is indescribable,
194. for how can there be another creation in place of the one that exists?
195. It is not that there will be another creation at that time,
196. nor still a different thing standing in place of the first.
197. That is the thing that was in the beginning from nothing,
198. and the same will be the being more glorious than the first.
199. It is the nature of the spiritual that will acquire glory,
200. and naturally they will remain as one without change.
201. It is the race of embodied that will inherit life,
202. and in their nature they will gain immortal life.

203. The raising of those who are raised will give rest to body and soul,
204. and without ceasing they will sing glory to the Renewer of all.
205. Those renewed will repay thanksgiving to the Renewer of all,
206. for there will remain nothing of the universe that is not renewed.
207. Everything will be renewed while its first nature is not destroyed,
208. and all will be changed, but its change will have no change.
209. The rational will be enriched with blessings loftier than those capable of speech,
210. and mute things[2] also will rest in an order that is not disturbed.
211. The heavens will remain in the same manner in which they were fashioned,
212. while they will not move and their columns (that hold them up) will not be moved.
213. The course in which the sun and moon are constant will cease,
214. not while they themselves cease, but rather they will rest from their courses.
215. Mute things without understanding will rest from their courses,
216. and they will again become that luminary that came into being in the beginning.
217. The gathering of the spheres' light will become light again,
218. and in its own nature the light without end will remain.
219. That is, nothing will be lost from the luminaries, not one ray,
220. and nor will anything be reduced from the beauty of its illumination.
221. There is nothing in its nature that will destroy anything that exists in its nature,
222. nor anything that will remain in that thing once it exists without change.
223. That change forces all to be changed,
224. and once it has been changed, it remains in an order that does not change.
225. The sound of the rushes of fast-moving air will cease,
226. because the use of its blowing will not be useful for earthly beings.
227. It will enter and rest from its changes as into a harbor,
228. and will no longer weary the spiritual to move it.

229. The density of its subtle substance is not needed if flesh no longer needs its subtlety,
230. not even to receive fluid water to sprinkle the earth.
231. The nature of fluid water will also be absolutely silenced,
232. and will no longer rage ragefully as before.
233. The blowing of the winds will no longer vex the fluid substance,
234. nor will the fluid thing run in its pouring order.
235. The vexed natures will no longer be vexed in their changes,
236. for nothing will need the change which derives from the elements.
237. There are no elements in that spiritual arrangement,
238. nor one to serve or be served by his partner.
239. One is the Power that will keep the all without the all,
240. and on the power of his Power the earthly and the heavenly will depend.
241. By his Power he will empower rationality not to change,
242. and mute nature to keep the order of silence and peace.
243. Mute things will remain in their natures in silence and peace,
244. and no longer be required to honor those possessing speech.

VII. Creation Resting with Mankind

245. Those possessing speech will acquire power without need,
246. and there is no need for anything from the silent.
247. What is the use of the rising of the sun to those without labor,
248. and what benefit is the course of the moon to those without time?
249. What good are the rays of the stars of light
250. to the one who does not need light from the luminaries?
251. Why would there be the blowing of the movements of the air to those without breath,
252. and why cold or hot to those who suffer neither?
253. Why would there be both the falling of rain and the dew for those who do not need it,
254. and why times and moments for those without time?
255. Why the changes of winter and summer for those without change,
256. or the counting of months and days for those without end?

257. Why the growth of seeds and fruits for those without food,
258. and why the creeping things and beasts for those without walking?
259. Why would there be anything edible
260. for one who does not need sweetness from eating?
261. Why ambassadors and emissaries to the human being,
262. wherever the loose inclination is bound in the fondness of love?
263. Humankind is bound in fondness of Love in that fashioning,
264. and has no authority to change before his opponent.
265. Along with humankind, the all will rest from all labors,
266. and in that rest everything will be kept without destruction.
267. Let no one say that anything has been lost from everything that has come into being,
268. for, behold, everything will remain and be kept in its own nature.
269. Light will remain in the nature of its illumination,
270. not in a sphere but rather in the order in which it was fashioned.
271. Air will remain in the nature of its subtlety,
272. not as it blows but rather in stillness without change.
273. Darkness will be preserved in the nature of darkness,
274. not in the order of this distinction, but rather in another.
275. There is no distinction between the light and the darkness,
276. for there is no sun to distinguish night from day.
277. There is no daytime, for there is no labor for those without labor,
278. nor still a night, for there is no sleep for those without sleep.
279. Humankind will live without sleep or labor or suffering;
280. therefore they do not need the guidance of night and day.
281. These things that have come into being came into being and were fashioned for the need of his life,
282. and in his delight the course of their ministers will rest.
283. Earth will rest from the work of summer and winter,
284. and will no longer be wearied in giving fruit to the one who works it.
285. It will remain in that order in which it came into being in the beginning when it came into being,
286. and will not be destroyed or decay from its construction.
287. In the construction by which it was constructed when it did not exist,

288. in the same will it be preserved along with the natures constituted within it.
289. With it the weary natures will rest from weariness,
290. and with it they will preserve the order of stillness without change.
291. With it the worn-out seeds will be still from growth,
292. for the food that is from them will not be useful to those who eat.
293. With it will be silenced also the bearing forth of all trees,
294. and they will no longer grow or be wearied through maturation.
295. In it will be hidden the nature of fire, wherever it is,
296. and while its usefulness will cease, it will not.
297. Upon it will be poured the flowing waters as they are,
298. while they will not run or be moved by the blowing of the air.
299. In it will be restrained the various species proceeding from it,
300. and they will be with it in silence and peace without use.
301. To it will return every construction that comes into being from it,
302. gold and clay, glorious and miserable, will be buried in it.
303. In it everything, and upon it everything, and it with everything,
304. and in its keeping is kept everything without any loss.
305. In it everything that is constituted to walk upon its surface:
306. creeping things, beasts, and birds as well, possessors of wings.
307. In it will cease from life the mute natures,
308. not in destruction, but in ceasing from generation.
309. The mute species will silently cease from generation,
310. and this is the rest that will give the world rest, not that of destruction.
311. There is no destruction in a thing that is destroyed, or at all,
312. For, behold, everything will return to the earth and be protected in it.

VIII. The Destiny of the Son of Perdition and of Satan

313. There is none among the rational or silent that will be completely destroyed
314. except one rational nature and one silent one.
315. The one who is destroyed entirely, in body and soul,

316. is that human being who will be a vessel for the backbiter [John 17:12].
317. One will vanish from the life of the rational,
318. and he will be alienated from the revival of the dead that will take place for the body.
319. That lost one will be destroyed completely in his body and his soul,
320. and his destruction will be a spectacle for all creation.
321. All creation will consider his destruction,
322. and marvel at the mercy that has kept it in mercy from destruction.
323. Through that one who will be destroyed it will learn the power of its Maker,
324. who fashioned it in mercy and kept it in his love and renewed it in grace.
325. Through his destruction it will see a spectacle that has never been seen:
326. a living soul in which life will vanish from life.
327. The soul possesses characteristics of incorruptibility in its being,
328. and this is the marvel: that suddenly its source of life will fail.
329. Spiritual nature is not corrupted in any way,
330. so who would not marvel at what will come to pass by the power of the Creator?
331. It is the power of the Creator that destroys the soul of one man,
332. that men may learn how evil is the evil of man.
333. The evil of the evil of that man will teach the all
334. that if man does not live by mercy, he will not live.
335. The power in [God's] grace is shown by the mercy that is for everyone,
336. and in one who is destroyed, it will preach the truth of his justice.
337. Two things he will teach through the destruction of body and soul:
338. that he is good and he is just to the rational and to the silent.
339. The rational and mute will together learn about both,
340. that neither his goodness nor his justice will be subdued.
341. In justice he will condemn that condemned one who has condemned himself,

342. lest his compassion be confused in its order.
343. He will show all great order through the destroyed one,
344. not to show but rather to make known that he deserves to be destroyed.
345. He does this not to show the power of his justice,
346. but rather to shame the hater who thought he would overcome all through him.
347. That man will be completely destroyed to shame thc hater,
348. lest he pride in that he began and ended in a human being.
349. Through a man he led man astray from his beginning,
350. and through a man he will perfect error while not perfecting it.
351. The desire of the soul of the one bitter of soul will not be completed,
352. because the temple he wished to dwell in will be destroyed.
353. He erected a tower of flesh for the misery of his bitterness,
354. but his tower will be destroyed and he will be bound with the cords of fire.
355. He will fall into fire the seething of which is hotter than any fire,
356. and into darkness whose darkness is greater than any darkness.
357. In the evil of his punishments the new creation will see
358. that although he is not capable of suffering, his sufferings crowd in and his punishment is double.
359. The earthly and heavenly marvel at his punishments,
360. how insolent he was, and how just is the penalty for his malice.
361. Maliciously, he presumed to steal the honored Name for himself,
362. and so also justice even more justly judged his case.
363. Just is the Creator and just the testing of his judgment,
364. for he has punished little and shows much mercy in order to instruct all.
365. He acts justly in that he has punished the evil who have spurned his commandments,
366. and wisely gives gifts to those who keep his love.
367. Wisely he destroys from all one human being,
368. and mercifully, he gives life to all through his Life.
369. He gives a sign to rationality and muteness,
370. that they may see that he can do all things as the Lord of all.

IX. God's (and Narsai's) Pedagogy in the Renewed Creation

371. He is Lord over all, and all is his, rational and mute,
372. and to him is fit the Name of Existence and Divinity.
373. It is fit to the Being alone to create creation from nothing,
374. to keep the order of his creatorship without confusion.
375. It is a great order which renews his creation,
376. that through its renewal it may show a vision of his sweetness.
377. He shows his sweetness to all in renewing all,
378. to teach all the providence of the Lord over all things.
379. In his providence everything came to be from nothing,
380. yet the works he made did not want to know his providence.
381. He wished to instruct his works in the fullness of time,
382. and for this reason he accomplished the renewal and the just judgment.
383. Through the renewal they learned the power of his creation,
384. that he created and he renewed creation again.
385. Because they did not want to learn his fashioning from the beginning,
386. they learned the power of his Divinity on the day of the ending.
387. This is the goal of the renewal at the end:
388. to teach creation the power of the Creator who created creation.
389. Great is the teaching that creation learns in that renewal,
390. and through which it marvels how much greater it is than it was before.
391. It considers the time of that learning as nothing,
392. when it is compared to that second fashioning.
393. Even that it does not exist in its own estimation (though it indeed exists),
394. when it is considered compared to the constancy of eternity.
395. Its mind gazes at its constancy without end,
396. and its love is never satiated by its sweetness.
397. My mind, wandering in wilderness, also marvels at its sweetness,
398. and it commands itself to look well at its comely beauty.
399. So look well, my mind advises the mind,
400. and begin to walk the path you have never seen before.

401. My thoughts go forth on the new path of renewal,
402. and it marvels and wonders at how marvelous these things are.
403. They stand in awe, though they did not see what they saw,
404. and they fail and give up, for they cannot see the sight they seek.
405. Good hope encourages them lest they weaken,
406. and they begin aiming at the target they want to resemble.
407. I placed a target for the rationality of my mind to aim at,
408. and I wish to aim well if I can.
409. The mind is able to see beautiful things well,
410. and there is nothing that can impede it if it wills.
411. I wished to relate beautiful things before the beautiful,
412. that they may aim to see beautiful things well.
413. I related the beautiful things of the day of renewal as I related,
414. and again I relate, that I may give men zeal to relate them.
415. Who would not love to relate words filled with wonder,
416. and who would not muse on glorious things that glorify him?
417. The conversation of those who meditate on this are glorious and marvelous,
418. and so I muse on the musing of these things as well.
419. I am compelled to muse on these things insatiably,
420. that perhaps my mind may abstain from considering disgraceful things.
421. Through trial I gained trial in my mind,
422. and learned that good musing is good to the muser.
423. Come, mind, and muse orderedly upon fashioned things,
424. and relate in love the relating of words of the renewal of all.
425. Come, look well at how beautiful is the renewal of all,
426. and praise and exalt the Renewer of our decay.

X. Christ the Mediator

427. He who created us looked upon our decay before he made us,
428. and he prepared and depicted the day of our renewal along with our fashioning.
429. Like to a youth, he wished to comfort the youth of our soul,
430. lest the laboring world be saddened by its decay.
431. He engraved invisible images as in a statue,
432. and showed them to the hidden mind hidden in our soul.

433. Through the mind he showed us that renewal and that end,
434. and though it was distant, he placed their revelation in nearby things.
435. In nearby things, he showed us the power of distant things,
436. and in revealed things he taught us the order of hidden things.
437. Unveiledly, he revealed to us his hidden Divinity,
438. and he made a tongue of Flesh the preacher of his secrets.
439. Through a tongue of Flesh, he interpreted future things to us,
440. despite the fact that the flesh is used to hearing fleshly things.
441. He taught the Fleshly one a spiritual mystery,
442. and Flesh chanted and the fleshly ones attended to the new chant.
443. A Fleshly One chanted a new chant among the fleshly,
444. and perhaps the one hearing would ask who is chanting.
445. O hearer, you want to hear who it is that chants:
446. hear from me and learn, that it is a Man who chants with humanity.
447. It is a Man to whose soul the Spirit chants, and he to man,
448. and he attended to secrets and interpreted them through a Man.
449. He is as a Mediator between man and the Creator,
450. and through his ambassadorship, he reconciled the Lord with his creatures.
451. Through his mediation he undid the conflict between all and in all,
452. and preached on earth the Gospel of peace that is unchanging.
453. This is the Man who reconciled all with the Lord of all,
454. and he it was who trod the new path of the renewal of all.
455. He showed us the renewal that will be at the end,
456. and he revealed to us the path of the teaching of faith.
457. He taught us that our decay is renewed in him,
458. and depicted for us a type to resemble him mysteriously.
459. He, in his Individuality, showed these things to our people,
460. lest we doubt the secrets that were promised to us.
461. He was the first who took off the garment of mortality,
462. and in his nature ascended and was exalted above death.
463. As with a finger he showed man the renewal of his Body:
464. "Look, O mortals, at the Body that became immortal."
465. For this purpose the Divine Power resurrected him,

466. and in his resurrection depicted the vision of the renewal of all.
467. He renewed all creation with him mysteriously,
468. and in him he will renew it at the end of time truly.
469. In him the renewal greater than words will occur,
470. and in him also the unspeakable judgment will be spoken.
471. The Lord of all chose him from all as a Principal,
472. that he may fill the place of his Being to the works of his hands.
473. He fills the place of Being for all through his unveiling,
474. and like a harbor, creation rests in the senses of his Body.
475. In him the loose movements of rationality are concluded,
476. and are not wearied in seeking after the hiddenness of the Hidden One.
477. He is a Holy Temple of the Almighty for all,
478. and in him the adoration of all is offered to the Lord of all.
479. All creation enters with him to the Lord of all,
480. and offers him one undivided thanksgiving.
481. The goal of his election and his exaltation is
482. that he may be a harbor giving rest to creatures from their labor.

XI. Christ's Second Coming

483. He gives rest to the weary world from its weariness,
484. and with the wind of his mouth he chases away the clouds of sufferings.
485. On the day of his revelations, he reveals the power of his greatness,
486. and creation will see the Power of Existence that is victorious in him.
487. Suddenly, the light of his dawning will dawn on all creatures,
488. and none among creatures will not marvel and take refuge in him.
489. The Lord of all will turn the sight of all toward him,
490. that they may see when he judges and renews all.
491. Quickly, he will make his command about the things that will be done,
492. and perhaps the deed will precede the command without delay.
493. He will cry out with one word upon earth, and all will hear,

494. and before it is completed, all things are completed and rest in order.
495. The command which renews all by the power of the Lord of all
496. resembles the command that called creation suddenly in the beginning.
497. That same Power that made everything from nothing
498. also renews heaven and earth, the rational and mute.
499. The rational and mute find rest from their labor and from change,
500. and they will no longer labor or be wearied in labors.
501. He began that renewal that is incorruptible,
502. and he perfects it in a perfection that is without end.
503. He was before, in life that is greater than dangers,
504. and he gives power to give life also to others.
505. The Mortal inherited the possession of immortal life,
506. and in his inheritance he shares with man and spirits [Rom 8:17].
507. It is written that we are sons of his inheritance, and indeed we are,
508. therefore the promise of his words is true and does not lie.
509. Spirits saw the unveiled truth through an Earthly One,
510. and they rejoiced and glorified him who revealed his hidden Truth through him.
511. The assemblies above chanted a "glory" upon earth [Luke 2:14]
512. to the Hidden One who showed his love openly to the sons of his house.
513. He revealed his great love to creatures through the Son of Man,
514. and taught them that there is none among creatures greater than man.
515. He made man the teacher of teachers for the works of his hands,
516. and lo, the natures and orders of servants fulfill his needs.

XII. Christ's Divinity

517. Creation adores his Mastership as the Lord,
518. and honors him because of the Power that is extolled in him.
519. The Power of the Creator wished to exalt him to the height of his Name,

520. and lo, he is named by the Name that has no equal among others.
521. There is no Name of the Maker among creatures, not at all,
522. and the marvel is that a creature is worthy of the Name of the Maker.
523. His creation honors the Creator of creation in what he has done,
524. that he took from her a portion and honored it with his glory.
525. The Son of Man is a portion of all these things that were,
526. and in honoring him, all things are honored along with the Lord of all.
527. His soul is a portion of spiritual and impassionate things,
528. and they are near to him in companionship and exaltation.
529. His Body is a portion of all corruptible bodies,
530. and they aim for him in the manner of bodies and renewal.
531. Among all creatures, he has the portion of our life in the beginning,
532. and in his exaltation, there is also the exaltation of all creation.
533. How therefore can anything be lost from creatures?
534. For all things are contained and kept in One from our race.
535. How can it be that when the Principal dwells in glory,
536. the flesh of which he is the Principal remains in misery?
537. No, O hearer, do not doubt the love of all,
538. and do not tear the complete Flesh from its fullness.
539. Do not doubt how this could possibly be;
540. believe that the Power of the Creator has the power to do all things.
541. Everything hidden and revealed is easy for the Power of the Creator,
542. and he is not resisted when he wills to do something.
543. It is appropriate to the Creator to act this way,
544. and it occurred to the Will of his Love before it occurred.
545. He did not choose one Man for the renewal of all newly;
546. for he chose him before he created creation in the beginning.
547. What would happen was with his Existence,
548. not that it existed, but that it was not hidden from him.
549. He had verified this decree from the beginning,
550. and it was with him as it came to be after a time.
551. If the True One is this way, which he is,

552. do not doubt the fact that exists eternally.
553. The Being who brought all into being is eternal,
554. and in him were hidden all that were when they were.
555. The world was created in relation to him before he created it,
556. and was renewed before he revealed its renewal.
557. He who wills our life twice renewed the will of his Love,
558. and taught us the order of his constancy and his creativeness.
559. He taught us through these things he did for us
560. how much he loves us, and how much he honors us in his glories.
561. He loved us who created us, while knowing we hate him,
562. and he renewed us and persuaded us greatly, though we are unworthy.
563. We are unworthy, and as much as he says it, we are unworthy
564. to receive the station greater and more exalted than creatures.
565. The Nature of the Creator cannot be compared with creatures,
566. so who would not wonder that he made us equal through One whom he exalted?
567. His Will willed One from men, and was greatly pleased in him,
568. and placed his Will through his will to provide for all.
569. Through his will he established his Divine Will,
570. and there is no willing that was not contained in him willingly.
571. In him stand the world of time and that of eternity,
572. and he provides for the earthly and the heavenly.
573. He sustains all from the treasury of him who chose him,
574. and he orders all as the Will which established order.
575. He orders all, and gives life to all, the creature, Son of our race,
576. and while he is Man, he has the Divine Station.
577. His nature teaches that the station he received is greater than he is,
578. and witnesses also that his station is greater than his fashioning.
579. Come and marvel at the station which our miserable race has reached,
580. and repay thanks to him who raised us to the height of his Name.
581. Come and wonder at the power of authority of the Son of our race,
582. who renews all and judges all as the Lord of all.
583. Come be amazed at him who showed us all he is,

584. who dawns suddenly and contains light in his Light.
585. Come, remember that descent that came down to earth,
586. and who returned and ascended while all creation was with him.
587. I said that all creation ascended with his ascension,
588. for the rational and mute are bound within his Body and Soul.
589. Come prepare for that Preparer who prepares for us,
590. and wait for that waiting that comforts us.
591. In love let us keep the pledge of life of that renewal,
592. lest we be reproached when heaven and earth are renewed.

Chapter 12

MEMRA 13: ON PRAYER

INTRODUCTION

This relatively long memra begins with the image of Christ the Divine Physician and ends poignantly with the unutterable mystery of grace. In between, Narsai moves between several different ideas and images, such that the overall structure of this work is difficult to decipher. Despite this, we can discern a larger argument toward which Narsai builds.

The initial image of the Doctor healing our wounds contains much of what follows: we are weak and sickly, due to our "evil inclination" (*yaṣra bysha*) and the inescapable troubles of this world, and are therefore in need of healing. A sequence of other images follows, invoking Christ as the Kind One who pities us, the King who frees us from slavery, and the Power who defeats the devil. Rather than focusing on a single image depicting our need of God's grace, Narsai deliberately mixes metaphors, illustrating how no single angle can give us a full view of the picture. This theme is in the background of most of this memra.

One extensive image that follows is that of a sea voyage (lines 13–44). Our life is a journey toward the harbor of heaven over the tumultuous sea of this life. Our inclinations and the enticements of this world, as well as the constant fear of death, are constantly threatening to destroy us like the wind and waves of a storm. Christ is the anchor (line 37), but his grace also provides oars for our journey and guidance like a pilot. The whole image evokes the several accounts in the Gospel of Christ journeying on a boat with the disciples.

The enticement to sin and the fear of death lead to another overarching image in this work, that of debt (lines 73–96). Our sins are like debts in that we gain pleasure without the payment of the responsibility and work that earn it. The moment of death is one of reckoning, and we fear that when we face the Judge, we will be called to account and be found lacking. Moreover, the devil, who has loaned us this debt, charges an inordinate interest, promising temporal pleasures in exchange for an immortal soul.

God, however, is never diminished, no matter how much we borrow, and his Divine Immutability (lines 97–122) is the foundation of our hope. His Name (as spoken to Moses) is Being, in an unqualified way, and therefore he is not limited by any further qualification. And so our words can never do him justice, but at the same time, God has given us the distinct honor of naming us after himself. This opens up the possibility of God's Name being dishonored by our sins.

The image of the unjust judge (lines 123–148) contrasts God with the judge in the parable. Where the unjust judge is forced by the widow's insistence to grant justice, God does not need us to teach him righteousness. And while the unjust judge does what is right for his own benefit, God does what is right because it is his own Nature, and out of love for us. Though we are named after him, his true Name can never be dishonored, and nothing we can do can hurt him (lines 154f.). Because of this, God often threatens punishments in order to correct us, but his punishments are always mingled with mercy, as is shown through many examples in the Old Testament (lines 163–184).

If the misfortunes of this life are interpreted as chastisements meant to teach us, then God is rightly seen as a Teacher. We are, however, stubborn and difficult students, and God needs to teach us even the basic alphabet (lines 227f.) and other elementary lessons. Despite this, we still refuse to learn and continue to sin and accrue debts. The ultimate solution, then, requires not only teaching but redemption. Christ is not only the Teacher but the Savior; he not only brings us knowledge of God and our debt to him, but he also erases the debt. In fact, through his resurrection, Christ frees us from fear of death, and from the bonds of our inclinations (lines 277f.).

Because of Christ the Redeemer of our debts, we have the ability to plead to God, to take away first our earthly punishments (lines 333–376) and then the spiritual punishment of sin itself, which is significantly worse (lines 377–404). Especially tragic is the fact that through sin, we lose our spiritual reward without ultimately gaining even a physical inheritance (lines 395f.).

The ending of this memra might seem surprising, since Narsai seems to suggest that good works and prayer should cease. But this is not the case. Good works are what is expected of us, but because of our inclinations and weakness, they are too difficult and we constantly fail to do them. A wise man is one who chastises the lazy (lines 435f.), and it is a good thing both to do and to hear. But for those who are still too weak to work, there is supplication (lines 461–480). Unfortunately, we are on some level too weak even to supplicate God for forgiveness, and we become weary even of prayer (lines 543f.). In the end, God is all in all, and the mystery of salvation belongs entirely to him and his Mercy.

TRANSLATION

I. Introductory Supplication

1. O Doctor who healed the wounds of our race with the medicine of his mercies,
2. pity our debts, as is your custom, and come visit us.
3. O Kind One who pitied our evil inclination although we had not asked him,
4. perfect the will of your Sweetness in converting our lives.
5. O King who saved us from slavery to the evil one and death,
6. save our race from the damage of the debt of our debts.[1]
7. O Son of God who won back our dwelling from the marauder,
8. free our lives, lest we return again to the slavery of the evil one.
9. He had bound our race to the yoke of death from the beginning,
10. and One of us died and tore away the yoke of death from us.
11. O Power who defeated the evil one and death through the Son of our race,
12. grant us the power to overcome in the contest of labors.

II. The Earthly Journey as a Sea Voyage

13. We are thrown into the contest of labors of bodily passions at every hour,
14. and there is no time when the fight of our desires is silent.
15. A spring of savage passions pours out from us,
16. and it confuses the journey of our lives by its agitation.
17. Enticement dwelling in us shakes like a tempest,
18. and troubles our soul as much as a storm troubles the sea.
19. It resembles the sea as it blows about savagely,
20. and it brings forth the noise of its desires like a storm.
21. Its turbulences run through the middle of man like floods,
22. and the body and soul are shaken by it, fearing they may drown.
23. The second sea is the enticement of the body that dwells in our body,
24. and like a wind, it shakes the boat of our embodiment.
25. The boat of our mortality journeys through a turbulent sea,
26. and the clashing of its winds makes it tremble intensely.
27. Our race, which is filled with dangers, fears its dangers,
28. and always pleads a pleading filled with pity and mercies.
29. The race of mortals always asks for pity and mercies,
30. that it may be protected from the threats that are always there.
31. I saw the varieties of threats crowding increasingly,
32. and composed words to journey with it to the harbor of peace.
33. I wish to arrive at the harbor of the peace of the forgiveness of debts;
34. may your pity be a pilot in guiding our lives.
35. May the oars of your mercies be oars of man's honor,
36. and draw him out lest he drown in the passions of his soul.
37. He ties his life to your great Name as to an anchor
38. and in you is protected from the waves of troubling passions.
39. Troubling passions trouble his mortality at every hour,
40. and hold him back from the journey of your Name's promise.
41. The one weakened and powerless seeks to find refuge in your Name;
42. give him a hand, that in you he may be drawn out from his debts.
43. He is drowning in the debt of his debts, and cast out as in the sea,
44. and lo, he longs to be lifted up by your mercies.

III. Man's Weakness and Mortality

45. He looks to your mercies, that they may support him in the contest of his labors,
46. for he knows that his miserable nature is weak before enticements.
47. I also, weak in my thoughts, look at his weakness,
48. and gave my mind to journey with him to the promise of mercies.
49. May your mercies be like a leader before his steps,
50. and show the path of forgiveness to him who seeks it.
51. He who journeys through danger seeks and longs for forgiveness of debts,
52. forgive his debts, that he may be heartened in his life's journey.
53. Life is short—the life of a debtor with many debts;
54. pity his debts, lest the lamp of his life go out.
55. The course of life is a lamp for one whose life is short,
56. and the oil of mercies blazes quickly in him and is extinguished.
57. The fire of enticements exhausts his life as if it is oil,
58. and the light of his rationality suddenly goes out and vanishes.
59. Savage death defeats the cave of his body,
60. and he becomes a rotting corpse without life.
61. He abides, lifeless, in decaying Sheol,
62. until he hears the voice that quickens the dead.
63. He remains and is tested in this decaying at all times,
64. and he reflects and is saddened, that he may go there in the debt of his debts.
65. He reflects on his debts, and for them asks for pity and mercies:
66. pity his debts, before he journeys to the house of his fathers.
67. The fathers of the son of mortals have journeyed to the house of death,
68. and in the same way, he also makes provisions for his path.
69. The path of death is a large path for the sons of Adam,
70. and they travel it daily, nor is it ever lacking travelers.
71. They are crushed daily on this constant journey,
72. and they reflect that perhaps they will go to Sheol while still in debt.

IV. The Debt of Sin and God's Redemption

73. O Pitier of debts, pity the debts of our indebtedness,
74. for the debt of our debts is greater than that of any age.

75. We owe enormously, and there is no counting our indebtedness,
76. and the interest of our debt's bond has doubled over what we have borrowed.[2]
77. We have borrowed an evil debt of malice from the evil one,
78. and lo, he increases it with the interest of disgraceful things.
79. Our race had begun in disgraceful things from the beginning,
80. and it wants to complete the days of its life in the same manner.
81. Habit conquered and still conquers its entire life,
82. and it is hateful in its eyes to hate its own disgraceful habits.
83. O Lover of man, forgive the man who hates his life,
84. and give him the strength to conquer the battle of his desires.
85. May you grant strength, that his weakness may gain strength,
86. lest he weaken before enticements and rebellious demons.
87. The miserable and wretched one is thrown into two battles:
88. the passions of the soul and the demons that lead him astray in his weakness.
89. Strengthen the powers of the powerless one who begs and entreats,
90. and cast out from him the evil demons who thirst for his blood.
91. Do not, O Lord, allow the desire of the evil to come to pass,
92. lest they be exalted and mock your great Name.
93. O Kind One from the beginning, you have called us by your great Name;
94. perfect in deed the call of your Name through the misery of our race.
95. You placed the names of your Name upon our head when you fashioned us,
96. verify them through acts that are worthy of your Name.

V. God's Immutability

97. Your Name is honorable and cannot be spoken by the speaking:
98. may your Name never be reviled by our frivolous names.
99. If we do wrong, we do wrong to ourselves and do not deprive you;
100. neither deprivation nor increase ever approach you.
101. You are as you are, and you are unchanging;
102. and your command walks with all creatures while never wearying.

103. The malice of the evil and unjust does not weary you,
104. nor does the praise of the just and the righteous glorify you.
105. Neither do reproaches rebuke the name of your Righteousness,
106. nor do exaltations exalt the station of your Perfection.
107. In reference to your Greatness, praise and insult are one,
108. in that the Nature of your Being does not receive either of them.
109. Your Nature does not even have a Name,
110. and from a lack of names, we bring about the name of the Nature.
111. O Bringer-About of Creatures, no other Nature has brought you about;
112. and so no name can be brought about that is fit for you.
113. We call you Bringer-About of Creatures alone, as is right for you,
114. and do not besmirch your Name with assumed names [of things] brought about by you.
115. There is no name that is fit for the Name of your Constancy,
116. rather than one: Being who Exists without Beginning.
117. With this naming it is right for everything made to name you
118. that which you taught to the works of your hands to call you.
119. To Moses your servant you revealed the Name of your Constancy,[3]
120. and thus it is revealed that there are no other names for your Name.
121. Glorious is your will that loves the works of your hands so much,
122. in which you indeed show the power of your Constancy.

VI. The Widow and the Unjust Judge

123. My rationality, lover of words, gazed at this will,
124. and began to beget words of suffering over sinners.
125. My rationality offers a sacrifice of words on behalf of the rational;
126. accept its sacrifice, O Accepter of Sacrifices and Prayers.
127. Its sacrifice is a pleading filled with thundering words;
128. forgive its words if they are too miserable to accept.
129. This thing lacking in power begs you thunderously,
130. like the widow to the accursed judge [Luke 2:14].
131. You composed the parable to make known the weakness of our race,

132. and painted a picture of one who is destitute whom a tyrant attended.
133. If pleading overcame the cursedness of that cursed one,
134. how much more will your mercies descend toward sinners?
135. If an accursed one became merciful as you showed,
136. show unveiledly the power of the parable toward our wickedness.
137. If the unjust one demanded justice for her who had been oppressed,
138. how much more will you, O Just One, judge justly with our oppression?
139. We have been oppressed, O Lord, by enticements and by Satan;
140. demand restitution for us that is fit for your Judgment.
141. Two adversaries are for us a cause of all evils:
142. our evil inclination and the evil one who hated us from the beginning.
143. The evil one became an advisor for us of shameful advice,
144. and men went out to seek a goal of shameful things.
145. Through his shameful things, he shamed the beauty of our comely image,
146. and the heavenly and the earthly became ashamed of us.
147. They had been amazed at the comeliness of our image before our folly,
148. and when we became foolish, they turned and were shocked at our shame.

VII. God's Mercy Is Greater Than Our Sin

149. O Constructor of our image in the Image of his unconstructed Image:
150. forgive our image for the sake of your unconstructed Image.
151. You do not have an Image that possesses construction like mortals,
152. and the marvel is that you have brought us about without [using] natures.[4]
153. You have named us after the Name of your Greatness, O Good One who is entirely Good;

154. may the Name of your Goodness not change by the evil of our malice.
155. Never! It was not and it cannot be thus,
156. for our malice the flea to conquer the Power that holds all things together.
157. What is the malice of demons and men compared to your mercies?
158. Or evil itself of all creation before your forgiveness?
159. Your pity is greater than the creatures that have come into being from you,
160. and your compassion cannot be compared to the work of your hands.
161. My thoughts, who love wandering, looked at the target of your mercies,
162. and began to take aim at the target of the greatness of your mercies.
163. You established the target of your mercies between the verses of the Scriptures,
164. and they are less than six thousand,[5] and it does not change.
165. Your Will has journeyed compassionately with every age,
166. and it has never diminished from what it was, until the very end.
167. You decreed the judgment of death upon Adam on the day that he sinned [Gen 2:17],
168. and Adam lived, after he sinned, for over nine hundred years [Gen 5:5].
169. You determined seven punishments of seven tortures for Cain,
170. and you did not complete them exactly as you determined [Gen 4:11–15].
171. You said, "I will erase all I have made, without forgiveness,"
172. and lo, the covenant: the whole creation with all that is.[6]
173. You cursed Canaan to be a slave and a slave of slaves,
174. and from him you brought about harsh kings who dominated the nations [Gen 9:25; 10:19].
175. You descended, without descending, to fight the Babylonians,
176. and you transformed them into vessels of your armor for the sake of peace [Jer 51:20].
177. You decreed that the land of the Philistines would have no man remaining,

178. and tens of thousands of its inhabitants remained without chastisement.[7]
179. You raised your hand against the Egyptians and punished them,[8]
180. and there was no chastisement that did not have a bit of mercy mixed into it.
181. You vowed that the Israelites would be destroyed in a terrible war,[9]
182. and after you vowed, you provided for them lovingly.
183. We see that you journey lovingly everyplace you journey,
184. and there is no chastisement with which you do not mingle sweetness.

VIII. God as Merciful Father and Teacher

185. We have been tested and we are being tested by your Sweetness,
186. and we never cease from pleading on behalf of our debts.
187. We take refuge in your great love at every time,
188. like children who take shelter with their parents at every hour.
189. We study your Fatherhood, O Father alone,
190. and we call you Father who begot us lovingly.
191. We do not know of another father besides you,
192. for there are no fathers whose love resembles your Fatherhood.
193. You alone are Father, and Lord, and Judge,
194. who has all of them with your Being without beginning.
195. Without beginning, you possessed everything you possessed divinely,
196. and there is nothing in you that did not exist permanently.
197. It is right, therefore, for the eyes of all to lift up to you,
198. and from you they ask for daily sustenance and forgiveness of sin.
199. Forgive our lives, O Fount of Immortal Life,
200. and grant us a time filled with peace and sustenance of life.
201. We have sinned greatly, and our evil has passed above our heads,
202. and we are close to drowning in the abyss of our debts.
203. The number of our disgraces has exceeded numbering,
204. and our debt cannot be measured by any known measure.
205. But we have also swallowed many intense punishments,

206. and yet our inclination has still not refrained from intimacy with evil things.
207. The measure of our great punishment has outweighed our vices,
208. and yet we have not tried to hate our malice—not at all.
209. If our malice witnesses to us, O Lord, as it is written,[10]
210. may you have pity and forgive, because of your immeasurable mercies.
211. Your compassion cannot be measured by any measures,
212. and if that is so, what is our malice, a miserable gnat?
213. Our malice is a miserable gnat, as large as it is;
214. toss it like a pebble into the great sea of your Sweetness.
215. Do not requite us according to our sins, as we are sinners;
216. for you, O Kinder than all, persuade against the way of our sinfulness.
217. You know us before our forming and after we came to be,
218. and you persuade our evil inclination that is so stubborn.
219. You formed it, and you led it to education,
220. and therefore, it learned to consider good and evil from you.
221. So if you are the Teacher, and it is the student of your teaching,
222. perfect your student according to the will of your Teacher-ness.
223. Take the load upon yourself for your young student who was enrolled with you,
224. and recite before him the study of words that make him wise.
225. Write the letters of the Name of your Being upon his mind,
226. and let him read with intelligence, and keep his life's works in order.
227. Repeat and write for him another verse of the love of man,
228. that he may bind his love to the *alap* of being and the *taw* of humanity.[11]
229. When a man is taught to read well,
230. it is easy for him to write and meditate on the freedom of his soul.
231. You filled the soul with freedom of soul when you formed it,
232. and it is quite capable to distinguish two things distinctly.
233. Discern, O discerning one,[12] that discernment that is placed in your nature,
234. and know your nature and your Fashioner who placed two within you.
235. Two are in you, O soul, mistress of good and evil,

236. judge justly which is just between the two of them.
237. With a palate of flesh, you distinguish sweet from bitter;
238. distinguish your nature as you distinguish what is not yours.
239. It is beautiful[13] for you to see the beautiful if you are beautiful,
240. and when your own beauty is beautiful to you, your perception is just.
241. Just is the perception of every man who has a soul,
242. and it is easy for him to distinguish the ugly from the beautiful.
243. Well, therefore, do the mute natures judge us,
244. and we owe them since they do not call our debt to account.
245. Indeed, the divine commandment led us justly,
246. and the times have changed outside the order of their changes.

IX. God's Justice and Our Debts

247. Just is our scourging, and right is the punishment of our insolence,
248. and we indeed deserve to be punished with double punishments.
249. Our inclination deserves to be punished with double punishments,
250. for it knows it has sinned, and does not remember the vengeance of judgment.
251. It heard that there is a judgment at the end of times,
252. and did not fear the torture of the name of Gehenna.
253. Woe to us: our opinion is more tyrannical than a tyrant,
254. and is true to us, while the vengeance of judgment is not.
255. If it is true to us, why is the evil inclination not ashamed?
256. And why does it make light of something true and clear?
257. Your judgment is true, O Head of Judges who judges all,
258. and what will we do who have made your judgments a lie?
259. Deceitfully we have heard the reputation of your just judgment,
260. and if we had heard it truly, we would not have sinned.
261. We have sinned as we have sinned, since our nature is inclined to sin;
262. O Lord of natures, pity our nature, lest it be indebted.
263. We have feared our debts for our entire lives,

264. and lo, we make up opportunities to beg for the absolution of our debts.
265. Absolve our debts, O Lord with authority over our debts,
266. and erase them from the memory of the book of your judgments.
267. Take them out of the archives of your courtroom,
268. and tear them up before the eyes of angels and men.
269. May there not be any note written by Adam left before you,
270. lest the haters of Adam take pride over the debts of Adam.
271. He had written a promissory note in Eden in eating the fruit,
272. and when he did not pay it, Satan rejoiced at the debt of his debts.
273. The interest of that commandment increased for his sons,
274. and they gave their bodies as pledges to greedy death.
275. Death retained their bodies for himself like pledges,
276. and lo, he swallows them savagely in the caves of Sheol.

X. Christ the High Priest, Overcoming Death and Sin

277. Swallowing Sheol swallows the sons of earth,
278. and there is no earthly one who reflects on the earth of his companions.
279. O Former of our earth: forgive our earth that became earth,
280. and resurrect our earth from mortality and from our debts.
281. We die two deaths, one worse than the other:
282. in the rotting of death, and in the disgraces of our evil inclination.
283. O Lover of our lives, resurrect our lives from both of them,
284. and open to us a door to mortality and forgiveness of sin.
285. Death and sin closed the door of their lies in our faces,
286. and lo, they plot to drown us without resurrection.
287. Show us the path of resurrection and the forgiveness of debts,
288. and teach us that death is eradicated and sin is silenced.
289. Through One from our race, you trod the path of the renewal of our race:
290. grant us to journey to the lovely promise of the renewal of our lives.
291. In the life of his life, he completed the gift of our lives,

292. and we trust that you will not lie in the promises of your words.
293. You provided, from our debt-filled race, a Pledge of peace,
294. and lo, he is extolled with the glories of your Divinity.
295. You made the Principal of our lives glorious above all, with you;
296. honor our lives for the sake of the life of the One you have chosen.
297. You have shown to him a great and indescribable love,
298. in that you lifted him to the great height of your Name.
299. May the One at the right hand of your Divinity plead to you,
300. that he may pacify you since we enraged you with our sinfulness.
301. It is said that he offers prayer to you on behalf of sinners [Heb 7:25];
302. lo, it is the time to claim the order of prayers.
303. He always prays on behalf of his beloved lovingly,
304. accept his words in the love that becomes your Sweetness.
305. Lovingly, you love him in the station of your own Name:
306. complete in deed the pleading of his words for our sake.
307. The Head of our race prays with us;
308. O Lover of our race, hear the Son of our race, and forgive our race.
309. Attend to our supplication, which the Son, the Son of our race, offers you,
310. and give us the hand of the forgiveness of debts that we beg from you.
311. Hear us, O Kind One, to whom the supplication of our words is heard,
312. and plead to yourself if our pleading is small before you.

XI. Our Finitude, God's Infinity

313. Our pleading is small compared to the greatness of our guilt,
314. and if we do not plead to you, even this is [because] of our guilt.
315. We are embroiled in a contest of passions over our debts at every hour,
316. and for us to plead is terrifying, and not to plead is doubly so.
317. It is terrifying to plead, since you do not need us to plead to you,
318. and it is a terror of terrors for us not to plead for our foolishness.
319. The pleading of the words of those who plead is not useful to you,

320. for the pleading of all was heard before they pleaded to you.
321. The sin of every age was seen by you before all creation,
322. and why would I even say "ages and times" in front of your Being?
323. You uphold the boundaries of limited things with your Being,
324. and there is nothing in creation that exists, which does not exist in you.
325. With you is the memory of writings that were and are,
326. and there is nothing made that is hidden from your Knowledge.
327. Our sins, and the justice of watchers and men, are unveiled to you,
328. and the reward and repayment of the good and evil are weighed by you.
329. If it is indeed the case that everything that is and will be is in you,
330. it is impossible for us not to beg on behalf of our debts.
331. We beg on behalf of our sins before your Greatness:
332. forgive our debts, and erase the great bond of our sin.

XII. Earthly Sins and Punishments

333. O Pitying one, forgive our evil, which has greatly increased,
334. and which has made us near companions of those in Sodom.
335. Do not allow time for our sin to dwell within us,
336. for if it does dwell in us, the least of our judgment is that of Sodom.
337. Let us not, O Lord, become companions in judgment with those of Sodom,
338. lest the name of our evil become like theirs.
339. Prevent the punishment like that of Sodom from us,
340. and do not paint a hateful image in our land like that of theirs.
341. When it burned, the land of Sodom became formless and void,
342. and deserted and desolate, without the possibility for seeds or fruits.
343. Let us never then see its chastisement, or any of it,
344. nor remember the name of its deeds in the course of our lives.
345. Our men live a short and debt-filled life,
346. O Lover of man, forgive our debt-filled lives.

347. May you not demand of us the debt of our debts,
348. for we have paid little of our debts with our punishments.
349. It is enough that you have led us, who are unjust, with visible things;
350. do not add double punishments to us, lest they destroy us.
351. Lift away your staff from the beatings of our bodies and our lands,
352. and chastise the heavenly assemblies, lest they condemn us.[14]
353. Pacify them, lest they show us a face of wrath,
354. and may they pacify the air which is troubled because of our sin.
355. Signal the ruler that controls the course of the months of the year
356. to lift the bridle of his movement in a troubled time.
357. Call and awake the spirit that holds power over wind
358. to hold back the rushing movements of air from severity.
359. Place order upon the orderer of silent times,
360. that he may teach them to keep the order of their changes.
361. In their disordered changes, everything has diminished,
362. and nothing has remained that is not less than it was before.
363. The dwelling of man has decreased and become lacking in all good things,
364. and the provision of the body and conversation of the soul is cut short.
365. Leisure of body and mind has run away from us,
366. and our society has grown like a tree in the days of winter.
367. The course of the months of the year is like a gloomy winter,
368. and there is no comfort to give us hope in anything decent.
369. There is no memory at all of anything restful or peaceful,
370. but rather the sound of disgraces thunders upon earth.
371. The sound of sin thunders alone among the earthly,
372. and the sound of good things is silent like a dead man without life.
373. All kinds of good things have died like a dead man without a shroud,
374. and have lost their operations like a dead man.
375. Good things have died, and varieties of shameful things live:
376. woe to us who have become dead to the truth and alive to sin.

XIII. Spiritual Sins and Punishments

377. We have resurrected dead sin through our sinfulness,
378. and in our cursedness, we have killed the children of righteousness.
379. We have made righteousness barren of children,
380. and have not let it grow fruits of love.
381. Our accursedness from the truth is like Pharaoh,
382. and perhaps the curse of our lack of peace is worse than the Egyptians.
383. Pharaoh choked the bodies of children in the river's water,
384. we have drowned the life of the soul in the flood of sin.
385. Men have killed the life of the immortal soul,
386. not that it dies, but rather that it becomes dead in sin.
387. The death of sin is worse than any death,
388. and the sound that resurrects the dead witnesses, which explains this:
389. "Death is not that which kills the body alone,
390. but that which destroys body and soul together."[15]
391. It destroys the body and soul together on the day of judgment;
392. woe to us who have approached the day of judgment, which does this.
393. Woe to us who have destroyed our body here through starvation and wounds,
394. and are preparing to be tortured in body and soul.
395. Woe to us who have been consumed by poverty in the temporal dwelling,
396. and have lost the inheritance of all good things in the one to come.
397. Woe to us who have been, and have not been, good in the work of life,
398. and will be resurrected but not be worthy of our resurrection.
399. We dwelt on earth, and were not successful in its journey;
400. how can we be successful in the manners of the heavenly?
401. We have, therefore, no place to be our place of work,
402. except Gehenna alone, where no man can work [John 9:4].
403. Woe to us who will have our life's dwelling there,
404. with that work that is filled with crying and gnashing of teeth.

XIV. The Final Judgment

405. May what I said not be the case for our debts,
406. and may we not lose our good inheritance here or there.
407. May we not leave this world naked,
408. and go to be lacking in glory in that building.
409. May we not be estranged from that glory which glorifies the good,
410. nor leave like the one who left the banquet [Matt 22:1–14].
411. You have promised good blessings to our race, through the Son of our race;
412. may the promise of your words not become a lie through our weakness.
413. We have become too weak and left off the work of truth,
414. and are too lazy to labor even a little in noble things.
415. The inheritance of immortal life is great and enormous,
416. yet we do not wish to take a single cent of it.
417. The judgment that will happen then at that government is terrible,
418. and it will not leave behind a single penny of our sins [Matt 5:26].
419. It will require of us even the word which goes unheard [Matt 12:3],
420. yet we never consider, and do not consider, that trial.
421. That trial entered my mind as it tended its words,
422. and it was shaken and stunned and began to compose words of pleading.

XV. Prayer and Good Works Contrasted

423. I wanted my ignorant mind to compose a pleading,
424. for I knew it was too weak to compose in many ways.
425. Pleading is easier than works for those who plead,
426. and because of this, my mind chose the easier one.
427. It is not desirable for the lazy man to proceed in works,
428. for he knows that the way of spiritual life is vexing.
429. My mind also fled from spiritual works,
430. and sewed for itself a garment of words to hide in.
431. Nakedly, it saw itself naked,

432. and it took words and spread them over itself out of shame.
433. It chose to hide its uncoveredness with words,
434. for it heard that it covered those who were like it.
435. It heard the voice of the wise man embarrassing the lazy,
436. and awakening the weak as if from sleep to work.
437. Till when will the wise cry out to the lazy:
438. "Have you slept and stepped from the work of justice?"
439. It painted the image of an ant for the weary one, too lazy to work,
440. and in it proved that his mind should awake to work.
441. "See the ant" [Prov 6:6], it speaks to him with a heavy heart,
442. "and learn from him the ways of industry and wakeful soul.
443. See how wakeful is the soul of the miserable thing toward its work,
444. and wake your powers to the work of noble things.
445. See that he prepares the provision of his life ahead of time,
446. and you also prepare yourself victual for the land prepared for you.
447. See that there is no one among them to command or obey,
448. and plead to yourself before another pleads for your work."
449. My thoughts, which hate work, heard these words,
450. and raised a hand to the work of pleading words.
451. The pleading of words set a foundation for the builders of works,
452. so that perhaps from words they may build buildings of works.
453. I wished to show the builders of works a building of words,
454. that they may become builders of works, more than my words.
455. O builders of the building of spiritual works,
456. build upon my words, working labors of your way of life.
457. Come to plead for forgiveness for all kinds of sin,
458. and add my word with your words in contrition and tears.
459. Come those who have completed your works as much as possible,
460. sprinkle your works like forgiveness upon sinners.

XVI. Supplication as the Medicine of the Sinner

461. Come, O sinners who have sinned and erred like sinners,
462. journey with words filled with study for sinners.

463. My reason studied a study of words about sinners,
464. that I may teach them the path filled with pity and mercies.
465. My mind added pity and mercies with the medicine of words,
466. that through words, men may drink pity and mercies.
467. I added the medicine of the forgiveness of sins to the spring of words,
468. and I longed for everyone to drink of it and have his sins erased.
469. I placed a sign to indicate this sign with the name "supplication,"
470. to supplicate and plead on behalf of my own debts and those of my friends.
471. Come, my friends, become my friends in the begging of words,
472. and let us plead together to the One who does not need to seek pleading.
473. One who seeks pleading—he does not seek it, as I said—
474. rather he teaches those who plead how to plead to him.
475. His command stands above our head like a teacher,
476. and makes us wise, without our soul's innocence being lost.
477. O One who makes man wise: forgive men who are hard of heart,
478. for they have torn up the life-filled books of your teaching.
479. See that our nature is weak with many weaknesses,
480. and do not requite what he owes from his enticements.

XVII. Human Misery

481. You are the One who formed it from dirt, as it pleased you,
482. and with its clay, you mixed the enticements of a weak inclination.
483. Your command added a weak inclination to its dirt,
484. and it is not able to gird up the weakness of its clay without you.
485. Vexing passions vex its life for its entire life,
486. and do not allow him to be girt up in the work of his life.
487. They always stand behind his back like flies,
488. and they disturb him from the consideration of noble things.
489. Night and day, he is crushed by crushing annoyances,
490. and there is no time when he is self-composed in his mind.
491. Summer and winter, he works and is smitten by his neediness,
492. and he always works, but his neediness is never filled.
493. Like a beggar, he begs for alms for his own life,

494. and knocks every hour upon the door of every craftsman.
495. He springs up every day looking for new work,
496. that perhaps he may find temporal provision for the time of his life.
497. He labors a labor when he tries new kinds of work,
498. and as much as he labors, his poverty only increases.
499. O poor one, son of the poor, who is poor and ignorant,
500. who does not consider keeping the order of his poverty!
501. O beggar who is always begging, summer and winter,
502. and the needs of whose soul are never filled by alms!
503. O laborer who hires his life out in labors,
504. who works every day and whose pay is defrauded by ignorance!
505. Ignorance has made him defrauded and a beggar,
506. and as much as he begs, his labor increases and his pay diminishes.
507. The dirt of Adam is diminished and consumed in drudgeries;
508. O Fashioner of his dirt, forgive his dirt before he perishes.
509. A few crumbs are kept in his storage,
510. and the winds of passion move them from (one) place to another.
511. A whirlwind of passions surrounds him as in a sandstorm,
512. and stands up against him like a rocky shore against the sea.
513. His passions, full of suffering,[16] are like water and wind,
514. and when they pass by him, he becomes like dust before feet.
515. The foot of passion passes by the sandstorm of his mortality,
516. and does not leave his dust to rest anywhere.
517. The clay of our clay is overwhelmed and scattered in every place,
518. and there is no place in creation not sown with our dust.
519. Lo, we are scattered like seed in the womb of the earth,
520. and have been made food for bugs and birds.
521. All that is left for the evil of our inclination, our bitter inclination,
522. is for our dirt[17] to remain in the earth and become a vessel of dirt.

XVIII. God's Saving Love

523. No, O Pitying One, let what I said not come to pass,
524. and may the word bearing this vain illusion not come to pass.

525. May our great hope in your Greatness not be vain,
526. nor the truth of your Name be made a lie in our deceitfulness.
527. You are true, and in you the truth of your Name stands,
528. and our deceitfulness does not lower you in any way.
529. Remain, therefore, in the promise of your words to our race,
530. and give us a hand, that we may stand quickly from our fall.
531. We fall much in our innumerable disgraces,
532. and if your help did not embrace us, we would fall forever.
533. You are forever, Lord God, Lord of ours and of all,
534. and in you stand heaven, earth, and all that is in them.
535. No, O Lord, may our great evil not be imputed to us,
536. but rather give your Name the honor due to your Name.
537. Honor your Name through the salvation that you accomplish for us,
538. lest the demons deride your Name due to our sin.
539. Because of our sin, the demons derided your great Name;
540. cut off the excuse of those looking for excuses by forgiving our sin.
541. Forgive our sin, and let its name never be remembered,
542. and then the excuse of those looking for excuses will be cut off.
543. Cut off also the fact that we offer you pleading at every hour,
544. for lo we weary you with the weariness of our words (though you are not wearied).
545. Burn up and prevent our speech also from composing,
546. and let it be unable to compose various supplications.
547. Lo, rational speech has wearied of bearing words,[18]
548. and it does not want to participate with the conscience.
549. Even the conscience remains with its conscience,
550. and does not want to meditate on a conversation of words.
551. Lo, there are no words left unsaid about forgiveness,
552. and as much as he may say, whatever he says, he says the same things.
553. Lo, they are said, and they are repeated by every mouth,
554. and what benefit, if there is no benefit from their weariness?
555. Lo, our entire race has raised a finger[19] from everything;
556. O Lord of natures, pity our nature, filled with debts.

NOTES

INTRODUCTION

1. See Aaron Michael Butts, "Narsai's Life and Work," in BHK, 1.

2. A *memra* (plural *memre*) is a metrical sermon. I will capitalize the word when referring to a specific work.

3. Greek being, from this perspective, a Western language. See, for example, the Synod of Isaac in 410 CE, referring even to Antioch as "the Church of the West," *Syndicon*, 3, 27.

4. In referring to Narsai's written language, as well as the linguistic milieu of his church, I will use the name of the language, Aramaic, rather than the name of their particular dialect of Aramaic called "Syriac" by scholars, unless the difference of dialect is relevant. For an account of philosophical texts translated from Greek to Aramaic, see John W. Watt, *The Aristotelian Tradition in Syriac* (New York: Routledge, 2019), 1–8; "Syriac Philosophy," in *The Syriac World*, ed. Daniel King (New York: Routledge, 2019), 422–437; Christoph Baumer, *The Church of the East: An Illustrated History of Assyrian Christianity* (New York: I. B. Tauris, 2006), 18, 156–158.

5. Acts 2:9. All biblical quotations taken from the Revised Standard Version unless stated otherwise.

6. An Aramaic honorific, literally meaning "lord" or "sir," but here signifying sainthood.

7. See Samuel Hugh Moffett, *A History of Christianity in Asia*, vol. 1 (San Francisco: Harper, 1992), 25–36; Baumer, *The Church of the East*, 14–30.

8. Moffett, *A History of Christianity in Asia*, 46–55.

9. That is, a quotation of the Last Supper. A volume of studies in commemoration of the tenth anniversary of the famous Common Christological Declaration between the Assyrian Church of the East and the Roman Catholic Church was edited by Cesare Giraudo, *The Anaphoral Genesis of the Institution Narrative in Light of the Anaphora of Addai and Mari: Acts of the International Liturgy Congress, Rome 25–26 October 2011* (Rome: Edizioni Orientali Christiana, 2013).

10. See, for example, Moffett, *A History of Christianity in Asia*, 443–462; David Wilmshurst, *The Martyred Church: A History of the Church of the East* (London: East and West Publishing, 2011), 234–276; Matteo Nicolini-Zani, *The Luminous Way to the East: Texts and History of the First Encounter of Christianity with China* (Oxford: Oxford University Press, 2022); Hidemi Takahashi, "Syriac Christianity in China," in King, *The Syriac World*, 625–652.

11. See *Sources*, 3; also Adam Becker, *Fear of God and the Beginning of Wisdom: The School of Nisibis and the Development of Scholastic Culture in Late Antique Mesopotamia* (Philadelphia: University of Pennsylvania Press, 2006), 163–168; Gianfranco Fiaccadori, "Cassiodorus and the School of Nisibis," in *Dumbarton Oaks Papers* 39 (1985): 135–137.

12. Wilmshurst, *The Martyred Church*, 459–461.

13. See Moffett, *A History of Christianity in Asia*, 136–144; Wilmshurst, *The Martyred Church*, 14–22; Sebastian P. Brock, "Christians in the Sassanian Empire: A Case of Divided Loyalties," in *Religious and National Identity: Papers Read at the Nineteenth Summer Meeting and the Twentieth Winter Meeting of the Ecclesiastical History Society*, Studies in Church History 18, ed. Stuart Mews (Oxford: Blackwell, 1982), 1–19.

14. It was once a common misconception, probably propaganda pushed by Protestant missionaries in the nineteenth century, that the Church of the East does not make use of iconography or is against it in principle. This is easily proven false when one looks at its own liturgical texts. See also Eva M. Rodrigo Gomez, "Painting Metaphors as a Means of Theological Expression in Narsai," in BHK, 191; Hendrika Lena Murre-van den Berg, *Scribes and Scriptures: The Church of the East in the Eastern Ottoman Provinces (1500-1850)*, Eastern Christian Studies 21 (Louvain: Peeters, 2015); Baumer, *The Church of the East*, 164–168.

15. For an educated appreciation, see Robert Taft, SJ, "The Assyro-Chaldean Office," in *The Liturgy of the Hours in East and West*, 2nd ed. (Collegeville, MN: Liturgical Press, 1993), 225–237.

16. Especially since there are no non-Syriac Aramaic Churches to distinguish them from, and Syriac is "by far the best-documented Aramaic dialect" in the first place. See Aaron Michael Butts, "The Classical Syriac Language," in King, *The Syriac World*, 222. As early as 1887, the Chaldean Patriarch Putrus Eliya XII consistently called the language of his church and people "our Aramaic language" [*lishanan Aramaya*], and he was followed in doing this by Assyrian prelates, such as Metropolitan Toma Darmo in 1960 and Patriarch Eshai Shim'un XXIII in 1961. See the *Chaldean Breviary* (Rome: Congregation for the Eastern Churches, 2002), 7–10 and *Ḥudhra*, 1–6, i–iv.

17. A similar critique is made by William F. Macomber, "A Theory on the Origins of the Syrian, Maronite and Chaldean Rites," *Orientalia Christiana*

Periodica 39 (1973), 235–236: "I would simply deny that the Chaldean rite is Antiochene"; as well as "A History of the Chaldean Mass," in *Worship* 51 (1997): 108: "Much more commonly, liturgists and ecclesiastics have called this rite by the compound names, East Syrian and East Antiochene. Such names, however, create the erroneous impression that the Chaldean rite is merely another branch of the rite of Antioch, an impression that is without solid foundation in fact and should be discarded today." See also Baumer, *The Church of the East*, 20: "it is certain that the diocese of Seleucia-Ctesiphon—that is, the nascent Church of the East—was never subordinated to Antioch."

18. Though somewhat anachronistic, the adjective describing the tradition of the Church of the East that seems most respectful to the fullness of its history and current life is something like "Assyro-Chaldean." This understanding goes back at least to 1860, when Fr. Joseph Gabriel discusses the Chaldean nation (*umtha*) and says other cultures received their sciences "first from the Chaldeans, or Assyrians, which means the same thing;" Adam Becker, *Revival and Awakening: American Evangelical Missionaries in Iran and the Origins of Assyrian Nationalism* (Chicago: University of Chicago Press, 2015), 316. Similarly Hurmizd Rassam, in *Asshur and the Land of Nimrod* (1897), says all the Christians of Mesopotamia have "the same Chaldean or Assyrian origin"; Becker, *Revival and Awakening*, 305. The term "ChaldoAssyrian" was promoted and popularized by military leader Agha Putrus (1880–1932); see Yasmeen Hannosh, "Minority Identities Before and After Iraq: The Making of the Modern Assyrian and Chaldean Appellations," in *The Arab Studies Journal* 24.2 (2016), 29. See also John Joseph, The Modern Assyrians of the Middle East (Boston: Brill, 2000), 1–32.

19. See Wilmshurst, *The Martyred Church*, 461.

20. *Synodicon*, 3–36.

21. See Becker, *Fear of God*, 17–18; 126–154.

22. Butts, "Narsai's Life and Work," 3–4.

23. Becker, *Fear of God*, 117; Frishman, part 3, 40; this idea goes at least as far back as 'Abdisho' of Nisibis in the thirteenth century—see Wilmshurst, *The Martyred Church*, 274.

24. See Moffett, *A History of Christianity in Asia*, 217–220.

25. A great deal of scholarship affirms the christological orthodoxy of the Church of the East historically speaking. See, for example, Sebastian Brock, "The Nestorian Church: A Lamentable Misnomer," *Bulletin of the John Rylands Library* 78, no. 3 (1996): 23–35; Baumer, *The Church of the East*, 7–8.

26. Narsai seems to draw most from Theodore, especially in his soteriology and Christology when it is polemic, and from Ephrem when he is engaging Arian ideas and in his poetic style. There is abundant literature on this topic, but see, for example, Frederick McLeod, "Narsai's Dependence on Theodore of

Mopsuestia," *Journal of the Canadian Society for Syriac Studies* 7 (2007): 18–38; Nathan Witkamp, "A Critical Comparison of the So-called 'Lawsuit' in the Baptismal Rites of Theodore of Mopsuestia and Narsai of Nisibis," *Vigiliae Christianae* 65 (2011): 514–542; T. Jansma, "Narsai and Ephraem: Some Observations on Narsai's Homilies on Creation and Ephraem's Hymns on Faith," *Parole de l'Orient* 1 (1970): 49–68; Judith Frishman, "Type and Reality in the Exegetical Homilies of Mar Narsai," *Studia Patristica* 20 (1989): 169–175; Frishman, "Type and Reality," part 3, 34–42; 180–182; for examples of Aphrahat's influence see Erin Galgay Walsh, "Holy Boldness: Narsai and Jacob of Serugh Preaching the Canaanite Woman," *Studia Patristica* 78 (2017): 85–98; Kristian S. Heal, "Joseph as a Type of Christ in Syriac Literature," *BYU Studies* 41, no. 1 (2002): 29–49.

27. *Sources*, 150.

28. In this volume, *Man* will be capitalized in reference to Christ for the sake of clarity. See John 8:40, Acts 2:22.

29. See Moffett, *A History of Christianity in Asia*, 175; Baumer, *The Church of the East*, 42–50.

30. See, for example, Simeon of Bet Arsham, quoted in *Sources*, 38; see also Becker, *Fear of God*, 43–45.

31. The text can be found at https://www.vatican.va/content/john-paul-ii/en/speeches/1994/november/documents/hf_jp-ii_spe_19941111_dichiarazione-cristologica.html.

32. *Sources*, 53 lists several possibilities in note 47.

33. *Sources*, 49.

34. *Sources*, 53–55.

35. *Sources*, 63.

36. *Sources*, 5, points out that the Robber Council of Ephesus in 449 names Armenians, Syrians, and Persians each having their own schools in Edessa.

37. Vööbus, 8, finds this unlikely, arguing that if it were true, no later biographer of Ephrem "would have deprived him of that merit had it rightfully been his." However, the later fall from grace of the School of the Persians into "Nestorian" ideology would be enough for at least some of Ephrem's admirers to want to separate him from the school as far as possible.

38. Vööbus, 14.

39. Vööbus describes his picture of this on 15–24. Becker is more restrained in *Fear of God*, 127–128. So also Daniel King, *The Earliest Syriac Translation of Aristotle's Categories* (Boston: Brill, 2010), 3–8.

40. *Sources*, 91.

41. *Sources*, 55.

42. *Sources*, 57–58.

43. *Sources*, 58.

44. *Sources*, 62.

45. *Sources*, 65.

46. Becker, *Fear of God*, 87–97.

47. Arthur Vööbus, *The Statutes of the School of Nisibis* (Stockholm: Etse, 1962).

48. *Sources*, 152.

49. Translated and discussed in Corrie Molenberg, "Narsai's Memra on the Reproof of Eve's Daughters and 'Tricks and Devices' They Perform," *Le Muséon* 106 (1993): 65–87; this incident is also discussed in "As If From Another World: Narsai's Memra 'Bad is the Time,'" in *All those Nations...Cultural Encounters within and with the Near East. Studies Presented to Han Drijvers*, ed. H. L. J. Vanstiphout (Groningen: Styx Publications, 1999), 101–108. See also Vööbus, *History*, 116. Barḥadhbshabba seems to count these years when claiming, in the *Cause*, that Narsai was head of the School of Nisibis for forty-five years rather than the forty he mentions in the *Ecclesiastical History*. The most significant dating problem regarding Narsai and Barṣawma is that the Council of Laphat, which would have allowed Barṣawma to marry Mamai, was not until 484. Either Mamai was Barṣawma's wife before the Council, or Barḥadhbshabba is projecting her future status back into the past, or our dating schema is at least two decades off.

50. *Sources*, 67–68.

51. *Sources*, 68–69.

52. Persian king from 459 to 484. *Sources*, 70.

53. *Sources*, 70–71.

54. See *Sources*, 8.

55. See McLeod, 3–8. The value of this distinction is seriously questioned, for example by Frances M. Young, *Biblical Exegesis and the Formation of Christian Culture* (Peabody, MA: Hendrickson, 2002), 161–216.

56. See also Frishman, "Type and Reality," 171–175.

57. Younan, Memra 14.

58. Younan, Memra 62.

59. Younan, Memra 49.

60. For the strict spiritual asceticism and community life of the School of Nisibis, see *Sources*, 8–9; Vööbus, 96–99.

61. Younan, Memra 62.

62. Discussed by Jansma, "Narsai and Ephraem," 11–12; Adam H. Becker, "The Comparative Study of 'Scholasticism' in Late Antique Mesopotamia: Rabbis and East Syrians," *AJS Review* 34, no. 1 (2010): 106–107. Frishman, part 3, 18–19. See also Younan, Memra 16, 221–260.

63. Younan, Memra 14.

64. See Christ's own explanation of his use of parables in Luke 8:9–10: "And when his disciples asked him what this parable meant, he said, 'To you it has been given to know the secrets of the kingdom of God; but for others they are in parables, so that seeing they may not see, and hearing they may not understand.'"

65. Younan, Memra 62.

66. Younan, Memra 62: 253–264; Memra 5: 13–42.

67. See Younan, Memra 49: 297–306; discussed by Lucas Van Rompay, "Humanity's Sin in Paradise: Ephrem, Jacob of Sarug, and Narsai in Conversation," in G. A. Kiraz, ed., *Jacob of Serugh and His Times: Studies in Sixth-Century Syriac Christianity* (Piscataway, NJ: Gorgias Press, 2010), 213; Alison Salvesen, "Without Shame or Desire: The Pronouncements of Jesus on Children and the Kingdom, and Early Syriac Attitudes to Childhood," *Scottish Journal of Theology* 59, no. 3 (2006): 319–320.

68. English translation in Frishman, part 2, 3–20.

69. Discussed in two memre translated in Frishman, part 2, 23–70.

70. Frishman, part 3, 73–90.

71. For Joseph, see Kristian S. Heal, *Genesis 37 and 39 in the Early Syriac Tradition* (Leiden: Brill, 2023); for Moses see Frishman, part 2, 93–122; Robert A. Kitchen, "Which One Is He? Narsai of Nisibis on Moses and the Divine Name and Essence and a Few Plagues," *Journal of the Canadian Society for Syriac Studies* 18 (2018): 15–23.

72. Younan, Memra 14: 213–244. Discussed by Robert A. Kitchen, "Winking at Jonah: Narsai's Interpretation of Jonah for the Church of the East," in *The Old Testament as Authoritative Scripture in the Early Churches of the East*, ed. Vahan S. Hovhanessian (New York: Peter Lang, 2010): 51–56.

73. Younan, Memra 49.

74. While Narsai affirms the natural equality of the sexes (for example, in Memra 49: 18, 25, and 39), he has moments of severe misogyny (such as in Memra 7: 435–504). See also Erin Galgay Walsh, "'How the Weak Rib Prevailed!' Eve and the Canaanite Woman in the Poetry of Narsai," in BHK: 199–226; Corrie Molenberg, "Narsai's Memra on the Reproof of Eve's Daughters"; Sergey Minov, "'Serpentine' Eve in Syriac Christian Literature of Late Antiquity," in D. V. Arbel and A. A. Orlov, eds., *With Letters of Light: Studies in the Dead Sea Scrolls, Early Jewish Apocalypticism, Magic, and Mysticism in Honor of Rachel Elior* (New York: Walter de Gruyter, 2010), 92–114.

75. See McLeod (Memra 4), 39.

76. See J. Edward Walters, "Where Soul Meets Body: Narsai's Depiction of the Soul-Body Relationship in Context," in BHK: 227–253, especially 233.

77. McLeod, *The Image of God*, 71.

78. See, for example, Younan, Memra 62: 91–94.

79. McLeod distinguishes the "vertical" binding in human nature through body and soul from the "horizontal" imaging that allows creatures to love God through it. McLeod, *The Image of God*, 72.

80. For example, Younan, Memra 16: 57–58; 141–148.

81. See Younan, Memra 5: 41–42.

82. Younan, Memra 5: 63–74.

83. See McLeod (Memra 6), 73.

84. See Walters, "Where Soul Meets Body," 234.

85. "Discernment" is discussed by Craig E. Morrison, "'The Faculty of Discernment in Narsai," in BHK: 161–173; "inclination" by Adam Becker, "The 'Evil Inclination' of the Jews: The Syriac *Yatsra* in Narsai's Metrical Homilies for Lent," in *The Jewish Quarterly Review* 106, no. 2 (2016): 179–207.

86. Younan, Memra 16: 173–206.

87. Younan, Memra 16.

88. Younan, Memra 49: 57.

89. Younan, Memra 49: 291–306.

90. Heb 12:5–11; see Younan, Memra 16: 275–284.

91. See, for example, Younan, Memra 16: 125–140.

92. Romans 6:23. See McLeod (Memra 6), 87. For an insightful discussion, see Gary A. Anderson, "*Christus Victor* in the Work of Ephrem, Narsai, and Jacob of Serug," in Verna E. F. Harrison, ed., *Suffering and Evil in Early Christian Thought* (Grand Rapids: Baker Academic, 2016), 57–80, especially 67–68.

93. Younan, Memra 5: 95–154.

94. Younan, Memra 5: 133–136.

95. Younan, Memra 5.

96. See McLeod (Memra 4), 45.

97. Younan, Memra 5: 202.

98. See McLeod (Memra 6), 93–95; (Memra 36), 107–109.

99. Matt 3:17; Younan, Memra 21: 1–34.

100. Younan, Memra 21: 141. See Sebastian Brock, "Greek Words in Ephrem and Narsai: A Comparative Sampling," in *ARAM* 11–12 (1999–2000): 439–449, especially 444–446.

101. Younan, Memra 21: 224, 310, and 449.

102. McLeod, *Narsai's Metrical Homilies*, 107.

103. McLeod, *Narsai's Metrical Homilies*, 139–143.

104. Younan, Memra 5.

105. Younan, Memra 16: 237–248.

106. McLeod, *Narsai's Metrical Homilies*, 135; Younan, Memra 16: 141.

107. Younan, Memra 81.

108. Cf. Heb 9:1–5.

109. See, for example, McLeod (Memra 4), 49.

110. *Functional* is a term used by McLeod, for example, on 29.

111. Younan, Memra 81. See also McLeod (Memra 4), 37.

112. McLeod (Memra 4), 43.

113. Younan, Memra 81: 77–86; Arius is mentioned by name in line 149.

114. See, for example, Younan, Memra 81: 133–136.

115. McLeod (Memra 45), 177.

116. See, for example, McLeod (Memra 36); (Memra 36), 117; (Memra 45), 173.

117. McLeod (Memra 4), 51, 67. It is also argued that Narsai is more tolerant of the *communicatio idiomatum* than expected. See, for example, Judith Frishman, "Narsai's Christology according to His Homily 'On the Word Became Flesh,'" in *The Harp* 8–9 (1995–1996): 289–304, especially 296–297.

118. McLeod (Memra 36), 125–127. Christ's Body in the tomb is even itself called "the vivifier of the dead" on 127.

119. For example, Narsai says that the child Christ is the fashioner of the Magi who presented him with gifts, in McLeod (Memra 4), 59; (Memra 36), 131; (Memra 45), 163. Several citations are also in McLeod, 28.

120. McLeod (Memra 4), 65.

121. See, for example, McLeod (Memra 4), 63, 65, 69; Frishman, "Narsai's Christology," 298–299; Ibrahim Ibrahim, "La Doctrine Cristologique de Narsai" (PhD diss., Pontificia Studiorum Universitas A. S. Thoma Aq. in Urbe, 1975), 345–350.

122. Memra 72: On Moses, in M.2, 291. My translation.

123. Younan, Memra 13: 109–120. See Adam Becker, "Names in Fervent Water," in BHK, 32–35.

124. Younan, Memra 16.

125. Younan, Memra 5: 33–42.

126. This is discussed by Paul M. Pasquesi, "*Qnoma* in Narsai: Anticipating *Energeia*," in *Studia Patristica* 92 (2017): 119–126; Francis Kanichikattil, *Divine Liturgy in the Vision of Narsai* (Bangalore, India: Dharmaram Publications, 2003), 23; Frishman, part 3, 13; Baumer, *The Church of the East*, 46–47.

127. For example, see the hymn *Brykh Ḥannana* attributed to Babai the Great, in the *Ḥudhra*, vol. 1, 118; my translation is in *Emmanuel* (El Cajon, CA: Chaldean Media Center, 2013), 137.

128. Younan, Memra 62.

129. Younan, Memra 62.

130. Younan, Memra 62.

131. Frishman, part 3, 51.

132. Connolly.

133. Discussed by Connolly, xii–xx.

134. See S. W. Sunquist, "Narsai and the Persians: A Study in Cultural Contact and Conflict" (PhD Diss., Princeton Theological Seminary, 2000), 18.

135. Connolly (Memra 39), 33–45.

136. Connolly (Memra 39), 33.

137. McLeod (Memra 6), 79, 89; (Memra 40), 155.

138. For example, Connolly (Memra 38), 52, 60, (Memra 59), 62, 67. Narsai also uses fire imagery to describe baptism: see Amir Harrak, "Memra 33 of Narsai: The Sacramental Nature of the 'Church of the Nations,'" *Parole de l'Orient* 41 (2015): 181–203, especially 198–199. See also Kanichikattil, *Divine Liturgy*, 86.

139. Connolly (Memra 38), 55; (Memra 59), 62.

140. Connolly (Memra 39), 36.

141. Connolly (Memra 59), 69.

142. Connolly (Memra 38), 48; see also Marcia A. Kappes, "The Voice of Many Waters: The Baptismal Homilies of Narsai of Nisibis," *Studia Patristica* 33 (1997): 534–547, especially 539–540.

143. Connolly (Memra 59), 64; Frank H. Hallock, "Aphrahat, Demonstration VII: On Penitents," *Journal of the Society of Oriental Research* 16 (1932): 43–56.

144. Connolly (Memra 38), 55.

145. Narsai has at least one full Memra, number 78, whose topic is a chastisement of priests. An English translation by Adam Becker is forthcoming.

146. Discussed in Kristian S. Heal, "Narsai and the Scriptural Self," in BHK: 133–143; Frishman, part 3, 24.

147. See Adam Becker's forthcoming volume on Chastisement Memre.

148. See Becker, "Evil Inclination," 197–198.

149. Younan, Memra 16.

150. See Corrie Molenberg, "As If from Another World: Narsai's Memra 'Bad is the Time,'" in H. L. J. Vanstiphout, ed., *All Those Nations…Cultural Encounters Within and With the Near East: Studies Presented to Han Drijvers at the Occasion of His Sixty-Fifth Birthday by Colleagues and Students* (Groningen: STYX Publications, 1999), 101–108.

151. *Sources*, 69.

152. *Sources*, 66–67.

153. Both the Assyrian and Chaldean Churches sing, for example, Memra 16 each year during the liturgical service called the Supplication of the Ninevites. *Ḥudhra* vol. 1, 411–423.

154. Most recently Philip Michael Forness, "The Construction of Metrical Poetry in the Homilies of Narsai of Nisibis and Jacob of Serugh," in BHK: 93–115; Judith Frishman, "The Style and Composition of Narsai's Homily 76, 'On the Translation of Enoch and Elijah,'" in René Lavenant, ed., *Symposium*

Syriacum Katholiek Universiteit, Leuven, 29–31 August 1988 (Rome: Pontifical Institute of Oriental Studies, 1988), 285–297.

155. Discussed in Forness, "The Construction of Metrical Poetry," 96–97.

156. A full recording of Memra 16 can be found at https://younan.blog/2022/09/05/narsai-memra-16-recording/. For a discussion on syllabic stress, see, for example, Takamitsu Muraoka, *Classical Syriac: A Basic Grammar with a Chrestomathy* (Wiesbaden: Harrassowitz, 2005), 16: "here also differ ES [Eastern Syriac] and WS [Western Syriac]: ES always stresses the penultimate vowel, whereas WS stresses the final syllable when it is closed, but the penultimate when it is open."

157. For example, Sebastian Brock, "'Syriac Dialogue'—An Example from the Past," in *The Harp* 15 (2011): 305–318; J. F. Coakley, "Syriac Exegesis," in *The New Cambridge History of the Bible*, vol. 1 (Cambridge: Cambridge University Press, 2016), 705; Frishman, part 3, 15–16.

158. *Ḥudhra*, vol. 1, 92–93.

159. *Ḥudhra*, vol. 1, 105–106.

160. BHK.

161. Aaron M. Butts, Kristian S. Heal, and Sebastian P. Brock, *Clavis to the Metrical Homilies of Narsai* (Louvain: Peeters, 2021).

162. Variously translated by others as "nod," "hint," "gesture," "sign," "wink," or "command"; it means a gesture given by one in authority that relays his will. Narsai sometimes uses it to refer to God's will, or even God himself. See Kitchen, "Winking at Jonah," 53–55; Kitchen, "Which One Is He?," 20; Frishman, part 2, 83.

CHAPTER 1

1. A word referring to an individual example of a nature, difficult to translate into English. In Church of the East theology, there are two *Qnome* in Christ (human and divine) and three *Qnome* in the Trinity (corresponding to the three Persons). In some cases, "self" works as a translation, but in others it has theological implications absent in the Aramaic. "Individual" or "individuality" have also been proposed as translations, but these can imply independent subsistence, which again is not present in the Aramaic. With this clarification in mind, I will translate it as "individual." See Introduction.

2. In these verses Narsai deliberately uses the first word of Genesis, *brashyth*, which itself imitates the Hebrew.

3. Gen 2:23. The word for both "wife" and "woman" is the same in Aramaic (*ḥawa*).

4. *Raza*, which can also mean "symbol."

CHAPTER 2

1. Gen 3:7. The tradition here is that Adam and Eve ate a fig (not an apple, or any other fruit), which makes sense given the textual context here. A similar tradition is found in Church of the East documents such as the *Life of Adam and Eve*, *The Book of the Bee*, and the *Cave of Treasures*.

2. A paraphrase of Gen 3:17–19, with the added embellishment of Divine Sarcasm.

3. *Ḥawa*, "Eve," is in Narsai's eyes a cognate of *hayya*, "life."

4. *Qa`en*, "Cain," is here interpreted as cognate with the verb *qna*, "to gain or possess."

5. The probable meaning here is that the first gift that God gave, Cain, was considered by Eve (a representative of our nature) to still be God's possession.

6. *Hawel*, "Abel," is here interpreted as cognate with the word *hewla*, "vanity or emptiness."

7. Cain is deceptive because his will was not with his offering.

8. Though not in the text of Genesis, the idea that fire consumed the offering of Abel is found at least as early as Aphrahat's *Demonstration IV: On Prayer*.

9. Perhaps implied by Gen 4:10.

10. Narsai interprets Gen 4:12, when God calls Cain a "restless wanderer," as meaning that Cain's body would tremble, probably following the text of the *Pshyṭta* (the Aramaic Bible), which says that Cain would *za`a' w-na`ad*, "tremble and wander," on the earth.

CHAPTER 3

1. "Peoples" here refers to the non-Jewish nations of the world, "the people" refers to the Jews.

2. Broadly, "Babylonia," the region where "Ur of the Chaldeans" would have been located. See Gen 11:31.

3. Or "symbolically."

4. Because ancient Chaldeans were known for astrology, their name also took on the meaning of "astrologer" for some periods of history.

5. Narsai is noting that Abraham's addressing the three men in the singular *lord* is a prefigurement of the Persons of the Trinity who share one Divinity. See Gen 18:3.

6. "For himself" could also be translated "himself."

7. Cf. Matt 1:1, where Christ is called "Son of Abraham."

8. That is, Christ on the cross.

9. This is explicitly liturgical language—"mystery"/*raza* and "served"/*shammish* are the words used for the eucharistic liturgy and the act of ministering to it, respectively.

CHAPTER 4

1. *Raza*, which will variously be translated "mystery" or "symbol" here.
2. Or "the nations," referring to non-Jews.
3. Or "he who was," possibly referring to Christ, who was to be born from the seed of Abraham.
4. "The people" in this memra (and quite often elsewhere) ordinarily refers to the Jews, the Chosen People. This will be nuanced by the end of this memra.
5. Jonah 4:2. These verses anticipate the ending of the book of Jonah.
6. This seems to mean that Jonah is resisting God's call because preaching to the nations would lessen the superiority of his own people, given to them by their possession of the Law.
7. Here "life" means salvation.
8. "Ministering to a mystery" is a liturgical phrase referring to the Eucharist.
9. An angel.
10. That is, so that Jonah would not remain in the fish more than three days.
11. Here the word *people* is used for the Ninevites, which up until now has been used exclusively for the Hebrews.

CHAPTER 5

1. A term for an angel found in the book of Daniel and common in the literature of the Church of the East.
2. Or: jealousy.
3. Moses, the traditional author of Genesis.
4. These verses seem to follow the genealogy in Luke 3:23–38.
5. The hidden pun here is that "consented to" and "was completed" are the same word, *shilmath*.
6. *Parṣopa*.
7. See memra 37, line 351 (included in this volume), where Narsai associates Eden with Sheol.
8. There are three extra syllables in this verse, in the word "in his nature."
9. *Parṣopa*.

CHAPTER 6

1. *Dinḥa*, most literally "dawn," but also an "epiphany" and the liturgical feast of the Epiphany, which in the Church of the East celebrates the event of Christ's baptism and extends for an entire season (until the beginning of Lent or *Ṣawma Rabba*).

2. Or "ruins."

3. Or "him." Cf. 1 John 1:1.

4. The etymology of John is "God has pity."

5. Not that John's parents did not have a sexual union, but that John's supernatural conception (in his parents' old age) prefigured Christ's.

6. That is, John's mind was not interested in earthly glory.

7. That is, greater than a human can have by nature.

8. There appears to be a line missing here.

9. Cf. Gen 6:4. Narsai may be interpreting "daughters of men" as "daughters of Cain."

CHAPTER 7

1. That is, John the Baptist.

2. This section is paralleled by a long hymn in the *Ḥudhra* for Christmas attributed to Narsai. See vol. 1, 562–565, as well as the Introduction.

3. That is, the angels in Luke 2:14.

4. Narsai seems to be imagining that Satan appears to Christ in human form.

5. That is, Christ fasted for the same number of days as Moses and Elijah. Cf. Exod 34:28; 1 Kings 19:8.

6. Luke 4:9.

7. Ps 91:11–12.

8. Referring probably to Adam's nakedness in Gen 3:10.

9. It appears that a line is missing here.

CHAPTER 8

1. Cf. Heb 12:2. "Son of man" can also simply mean "human."

2. For example, in Luke 7:15.

3. Or: crucified.

4. That is, a funeral home.

5. That is, the melodies of his lamentations.

6. Perhaps "masked his face."

7. Cf. Luke 16:24; "Gift" can also mean "grace" here and is a term that can refer to the Eucharist.

8. Cf. Luke 15:15.

9. Luke 13:24.

10. Perhaps referring to Gospel accounts of Christ raising the dead, though unclear.

11. That is, who led you astray from your straying?

12. Literally "life."

13. Mingana I.337 adds a footnote explaining the anti-Nestorian content of these verses.

14. Luke 23:43.

15. Similar to Narsai's understanding of Enoch and Elijah. See Frishman, 3–20.

16. Gen 3:24.

CHAPTER 9

1. "God" here translates *El*, the ancient Aramaic, Hebrew, and Akkadian word for God.

2. Luke 15:15, the first of many references to the parable of the Prodigal Son in this memra.

3. This could also translate to "tighten our knot, lest it loosen…."

4. From here to line 74, the grammatical object is (human) "nature," or "our nature," but this becomes conceptually untenable. It is clear that, eventually, Narsai is talking specifically about Christ from line 69 onward (at the latest), and I have therefore translated all pronouns with this referent "him" rather than "it."

5. The next two sections are a commentary on the parables of the Lost Sheep and the Prodigal Son (Luke 15:3–32); in the following section, the angels represent the older son who was embittered by the younger son's rebellion.

6. 2 Sam 12, as well as many of the "penitential" psalms attributed to David.

CHAPTER 10

1. There is an earlier English translation of this memra by Erin Galgay Walsh in *The Cambridge Edition of Early Christian Writings*, vol. 4: *Chalcedon and Beyond*, ed. Mark DelCogliano (Cambridge: Cambridge University Press, 2022), 194–213.

2. Poetic paraphrase of John 1:1.

3. Walsh posits this as Cyril of Alexandria (Walsh, p. 203), but Arius is named explicitly in line 149.

4. This line is missing in the published edition but helpfully reconstructed from a manuscript by Walsh, p. 208.

5. That is, the example of soul and body.

CHAPTER 11

1. That is, will in time or change its will.
2. That is, the sun, moon, and stars.

CHAPTER 12

1. *Ḥawba* can mean "debt" or "wrongdoing" or "sin."
2. An interest this steep would have been seen as absurd in Narsai's time.
3. Exod 3:14. Narsai seems to be stressing the present tense of God's Name "I am."
4. That is, God has created us without the use of any preexisting matter.
5. Presumably Narsai is saying that the Bible has around six thousand verses according to the division made at his time. There are around 23,000 by today's counting.
6. Referring to the flood at the time of Noah in Gen 6:13, and the rainbow in Gen 9:12–13.
7. One reference is Gen 26:3.
8. Namely, the plagues described in the book of Exodus.
9. Perhaps Deut 29:23.
10. Perhaps Rom 2:15.
11. *Alap* and *taw* are the first and last letters of the Aramaic alphabet.
12. That is, the soul.
13. *Shappyr*, which could mean "noble" as well.
14. The following verses assume an angelic role in the workings of nature.
15. Matthew 10:28; Narsai is positing that Christ here refers to sin, not God, which destroys both body and soul.
16. "Passion" and "suffering" both translate the same word, *ḥassha*.
17. That is, our body.
18. See Rom 8:26: "Likewise the Spirit helps us in our weakness; for we do not know how to pray as we ought, but the Spirit himself intercedes for us with sighs too deep for words."
19. Presumably a sign of weariness.

SELECT BIBLIOGRAPHY OF WORKS IN ENGLISH

A comprehensive and relatively up-to-date bibliography on Narsai scholarship can be found in Aaron M. Butts, Kristian S. Heal, and Sebastian P. Brock, *Clavis to the Metrical Homilies of Narsai* (Louvain: Peeters, 2021). Below is a list of works for further reading. Most important is the recent major work *Narsai: Rethinking His Work and His World*, ed. Aaron M. Butts, Kristian S. Heal, and Robert A. Kitchen (Tübingen: Mohr Siebeck, 2020) ("BHK"). There is a current project to translate and publish all of Narsai's works in English from Peeters in the coming years.

Anderson, Gary A. "*Christus Victor* in the Work of Ephrem, Narsai, and Jacob of Serug." In Verna E. F. Harrison, editor, *Suffering and Evil in Early Christian Thought*, 57–80. Grand Rapids: Baker Academic, 2016.

Arickappallil, I. "The Folly of the Cross and the Glory of Resurrection in Mar Narsai." In *The Folly of the Cross: Festschrift in Honour of Prof. Varghese Pathikulangara, CMI*, edited by P. P. Kochappilly, 18–30. Bangalore: Dharmaram Publications / Kottayam: Denha, 2000.

———. "The Holy Spirit in Narsai of Nisibis: A Theological Synthesis." PhD diss. Rome: Pontifical Oriental Institute, 1992.

———. "Mar Narsai, The 'Charismatic': A Study Based on Mar Narsai's Homily on Pentecost." *The Harp* 13 (2000): 125–134.

———. "The Pneumatological Vision of Mar Narsai." *The Harp* 8–9 (1995–96): 195–208.

Baumer, Christoph. *The Church of the East: An Illustrated History of Assyrian Christianity*. New York: I. B. Tauris, 2006.

Becerra, D. "Exegesis, Askesis, and Identity: Narsai's *Mēmrā on the Parable of the Ten Virgins*." In BHK, 9–23.

Becker, Adam. "The 'Evil Inclination' of the Jews: The Syriac *Yatsra* in Narsai's Metrical Homilies for Lent." In *The Jewish Quarterly Review* 106, no. 2 (2016): 179–207.

———. *Fear of God and the Beginning of Wisdom: The School of Nisibis and the Development of Scholastic Culture in Late Antique Mesopotamia.* Philadelphia: University of Pennsylvania Press, 2006.

———. *Sources for the Study of the School of Nisibis.* Liverpool: Liverpool University Press, 2008.

Brock, Sebastian. "A Guide to Narsai's Homilies." *Hugoye* 12, no. 1 (2009): 21–40.

———. "God as the Educator of Humanity: Some Voices from the Syriac Tradition." In *Jewish Education from Antiquity to Ages: Studies in Honour of Philip S. Alexander,* Ancient Judaism and Early Christianity 100, edited by George J. Brooke and Renate Smithuis, 236–251. Leiden: Brill, 2017.

———. "Greek Words in Ephrem and Narsai: A Comparative Sampling." In *ARAM* 11–12 (1999–2000): 439–449.

———. "The Nestorian Church: A Lamentable Misnomer." *Bulletin of the John Rylands Library* 78, no. 3 (1996): 23–35.

———. "'Syriac Dialogue'—an Example from the Past." In *The Harp* 15 (2011): 305–318.

Butts, Aaron M. "Narsai's Life and Work." In BHK, 1–8.

———. "Reclaiming Narsai's Mēmrā of the Feast of the Victorious Cross." *Hugoye: Journal of Syriac Studies* 23 (2020): 3–30.

Butts, Aaron M., Kristian S. Heal, and Robert A. Kitchen, eds. *Narsai: Rethinking His Work and His World.* Tübingen: Mohr Siebeck, 2020.

Butts, Aaron M., Kristian S. Heal, and Sebastian P. Brock. *Clavis to the Metrical Homilies of Narsai.* Louvain: Peeters, 2021.

Childers, J. W. "In Search of Jesus: Performative Christology in Narsai's *Mēmrē* on Baptism." In BHK, 69–91.

Coakley, J. F. "Syriac Exegesis." In *The New Cambridge History of the Bible,* vol. 1. Cambridge: Cambridge University Press, 2016.

Connolly, R. H. *The Liturgical Homilies of Narsai.* Cambridge: Cambridge University Press, 1909.

Darling, R. A. "Narsai of Nisibis. On the Expression, 'In the Beginning,' and Concerning the Existence of God." In *Biblical Interpretation,* edited by J. W. Trigg, 203–220. Message of the Fathers of the Church 9. Wilmington, DE: Michael Glazier, 1988.

Forness, Philip Michael. "The Construction of Metrical Poetry in the Homilies of Narsai of Nisibis and Jacob of Serugh." In BHK, 93–115.

Frishman, J. "Narsai's Christology according to His Homily 'On the Word Became Flesh.'" *The Harp* 8–9 (1995–96): 289–303.

———. "The Style and Composition of Narsai's Homily 76, 'On the Translation of Enoch and Elijah.'" In *Symposium Syriacum. Katholieke Universiteit, Leuven, August 29–31 1988*, edited by Rene Lavenant, 285–297. Rome: Pontifical Oriental Institute, 1988.

———. "Themes on Genesis 1—5 in Early East-Syrian Exegesis." In *The Book of Genesis in Jewish and Oriental Christian Interpretation: A Collection of Essays*, edited by J. Frishman and L. Van Rompay, 171–186. Traditio Exegetica Graeca 5. Louvain: Peeters, 1997.

———. "Type and Reality in the Exegetical Homilies of Mar Narsai." *Studia Patristica* 20 (1989): 169–175.

———. "The Ways and Means of the Divine Economy: An Edition, Translation and Study of Six Biblical Homilies by Narsai." PhD diss., Universiteit Leiden, 1992.

George, D. E. "Narsai's Homilies on the Old Testament as a Source for His Exegesis." PhD diss., Dropsie University, Philadelphia, 1972.

Harrak, Amir. *Mar Narsai: Homily 33 on the Sanctification of the Church.* Texts from Christian Late Antiquity 54. Piscataway, NJ: Gorgias Press, 2018.

———. "Memra 33 of Narsai: The Sacramental Nature of the 'Church of the Nations.'" *Parole de l'Orient* 41 (2015): 181–203.

Heal, Kristian S. "Construal and Construction of Genesis in Early Syriac Sermons." *Studia Patristica* 78 (2017): 25–32.

———. *Genesis 37 and 39 in the Early Syriac Tradition*. Leiden: Brill, 2023.

———. "Joseph as a Type of Christ in Syriac Literature." *BYU Studies* 41, no. 1 (2002): 29–49.

———. "Narsai and the Scriptural Self." In BHK, 133–143.

———. "Tradition and Transformation: Genesis 37 and 39 in Early Syriac Sources." PhD diss., University of Birmingham, 2008.

Jansma, T. "Narsai and Ephraem: Some Observations on Narsai's Homilies on Creation and Ephraem's Hymns on Faith." *Parole de l'Orient* 1 (1970): 49–68.

———. "Narsai's Homilies on Creation: Remarks on a Recent Edition." *Le Muséon* 83 (1970): 209–235.

Kanichikattil, Francis. *Divine Liturgy in the Vision of Narsai*. Bangalore: Dharmaram Publications, 2003.

Kappes, Marcia A. "The Voice of Many Waters: The Baptismal Homilies of Narsai of Nisibis." *Studia Patristica* 33 (1997): 534–547.

King, Daniel, ed. *The Syriac World*. New York: Routledge, 2019.

———. *The Earliest Syriac Translation of Aristotle's Categories*. Boston: Brill, 2010.

Kitchen, Robert A. "The Ascetic Narsai: Ascetical and Monastic Practice and Theology in the *Mēmrē* of Narsai." In BHK, 145–159.

———. "Three Young Men Redux: The Fiery Furnace in Jacob of Sarug and Narsai." *Studia Patristica* 78 (2017): 73–84.

———. "Which One Is He? Narsai of Nisibis on Moses and the Divine Name and Essence and a Few Plagues." *Journal of the Canadian Society for Syriac Studies* 18 (2018): 15–23.

———. "Winking at Jonah: Narsai's Interpretation of Jonah for the Church of the East." In *The Old Testament as Authoritative Scripture in the Early Churches of the East*, edited by Vahan S. Hovhanessian, 51–56. New York: Peter Lang, 2010.

Kochuparampil, J. M. "Syriac Fathers on Mary and the Eucharist." *The Harp* 22 (2007): 283–297.

Kollamparampil, A. G. *From Symbol to Truth: A Syriac Understanding of the Paschal Mystery*. Bibliotheca Ephremerides Liturgicae, Subsidia 110. Rome: Edizioni Liturgiche, 2000.

Komban, P. "Second Reading about Joseph by Narsai." In *The Folly of the Cross: Festschrift in Honour of Prof. Varghese Pathikulangara, CMI*. Edited by P. P. Kochappilly, 313–324. Bangalore: Dharmaram Publications / Kottayam: Denha, 2000.

McLeod, F. G. "Man as the Image of God: Its Meaning and Theological Significance in Narsai." *Theological Studies* 42, no. 3 (1981): 458–468.

———. "Narsai's Dependence on Theodore of Mopsuestia." *Journal of the Canadian Society for Syriac Studies* 7 (2007): 18–38.

———. *Narsai's Metrical Homilies on the Nativity, Epiphany, Passion, Resurrection, and Ascension*. Patrologia Orientalis 40, no. 1. Turnhout: Brepols, 1979.

———. *The Soteriology of Narsai*. Rome: Pontifical Oriental Institute, 1973.

McVey, K. E. "The Mēmrā of Narsai on the Three Nestorian Doctors as an Example of Forensic Rhetoric." In *III Symposium Syriacum, 1980. Les contacts du monde syriaque avec les autres cultures (Goslar 7–11 September 1980)*. Orientalia Christiana Analecta 221. Edited by R. Lavenant, 87–96. Rome: Pontifical Oriental Institute, 1983.

Minov, Sergey. "'Serpentine' Eve in Syriac Christian Literature of Late Antiquity." In *With Letters of Light: Studies in the Dead Sea Scrolls, Early Jewish Apocalypticism, Magic, and Mysticism in Honor of Rachel Elior*, edited by D. V. Arbel and A. A. Orlov, 92–114. New York: Walter de Gruyter, 2010.

Moffett, Samuel Hugh. *A History of Christianity in Asia*. Vol. 1. San Francisco: Harper, 1992.

Molenberg, Corrie. "As If from Another World: Narsai's Memra 'Bad Is the Time.'" In *All Those Nations...Cultural Encounters within and with the Near East: Studies Presented to Han Drijvers at the Occasion of His Sixty-Fifth Birthday by Colleagues and Students*, edited by H. L. J. Vanstiphout, 101–108. Groningen: STYX Publications, 1999.

———. "Narsai's Memra on the Reproof of Eve's Daughters and 'Tricks and Devices' They Perform." *Le Muséon* 106 (1993): 65–87.

Morrison, Craig E. "The Faculty of Discernment in Narsai." In BHK, 161–173.

Muehlberger, E. "Extraordinary Conceptions: Insemination and Theories of Reproduction in Narsai's Thought." In BHK, 175–185.

———. "Narsai, On the Symbols of the Church and on Baptism." In *The Cambridge Edition of Early Christian Writings*, vol. 2. Edited by E. Muehlberger, 306–320. (Cambridge: Cambridge University Press, 2017).

Muraoka, Takamitsu. *Classical Syriac: A Basic Grammar with a Chrestomathy*. Harrassowitz Verlag: Wiesbaden, 2005.

Murre-van den Berg, Hendrika Lena. *Scribes and Scriptures: The Church of the East in the Eastern Ottoman Provinces (1500–1850)*. Eastern Christian Studies 21; Louvain: Peeters, 2015.

Nicolini-Zani, Matteo. *The Luminous Way to the East: Texts and History of the First Encounter of Christianity with China*. Oxford: Oxford University Press, 2022.

Papoutsakis, E. "United in the Strife That Divided Them: Narsai and Jacob of Serugh on the Ascension of Christ." *Δελτίο Βιβλικῶν Μελετῶν* 32 (2017): 45–77.

Pasquesi, P. M. "Qnoma in Narsai: Anticipating Energeia." *Studia Patristica* 92 (2017): 119–128.

Payngot, C. "The Homily of Narsai on the Virgin Mary." *The Harp* 13 (2000): 33–37.

Popa, C. S. "Adam's Instruction on Full Knowledge: An East Syrian Theological Issue according to Narsai and Gīwargīs I." In *Adam and Eve Story in Jewish, Christian and Islamic Perspectives*, edited by A. Laato and L. Valve, 171–183. Studies in the Reception History of the Bible 8. Åbo: Åbo Akademi University, 2017.

Salvesen, Alison. "Without Shame or Desire: The Pronouncements of Jesus on Children and the Kingdom, and Early Syriac Attitudes to Childhood." *Scottish Journal of Theology* 59, no. 3 (2006): 319–320.

Satyaputra, A. G. "Reexamining Narsai's Christology: On the Two Natures of Christ." *Stulos Theological Journal* 6, nos. 1–2 (1998): 23–32.

Sunquist, S. W. "Narsai and the Persians: A Study in Cultural Contact and Conflict." PhD diss., Princeton Theological Seminary, 1990.

Taft, Robert, SJ. *The Liturgy of the Hours in East and West.* Collegeville, MN: Liturgical Press, 1993.

Thumpeparampil, T. "Mar Narsai and His Liturgical Homilies on Christian Initiation." *Christian Orient* 13 (1992): 123–134.

Van Rompay, L. "The Christian Syriac Tradition of Interpretation." In *Hebrew Bible/Old Testament. The History of Its Interpretation.* Vol. 1, *From the Beginnings to the Middle Ages (until 1300)*, edited by M. Sæbø, 612–641. Göttingen: Vandenhoeck & Ruprecht, 1996.

———. "Humanity's Sin in Paradise: Ephrem, Jacob of Sarug, and Narsai in Conversation." In *Jacob of Serugh and His Times: Studies in Sixth-Century Syriac Christianity*, edited by G. A. Kiraz, 199–217. Gorgias Eastern Christian Studies 8. Piscataway, NJ: Gorgias Press, 2010.

Vööbus, Arthur. *History of the School of Nisibis.* Louvain: Peeters, 1965.

———. *The Statutes of the School of Nisibis.* Stockholm: Etse, 1962.

Walsh, E. G. "From Sketches to Portraits: The Canaanite Woman within Late Antique Syriac Poetry." In *Syriac Christian Culture: Beginnings to Renaissance*, edited by A. M. Butts and R. D. Young, 66–82. Washington, DC: Catholic University of America Press, 2020.

———. "Holy Boldness: Narsai and Jacob of Serugh Preaching the Canaanite Woman." *Studia Patristica* 78 (2017): 85–98.

———. "'How the Weak Rib Prevailed!': Eve and the Canaanite Woman in the Poetry of Narsai." In BHK, 199–226.

———. "Sanctifying Boldness: New Testament Women in Narsai, Jacob of Serugh, and Romanos Melodos." PhD diss., Duke University, 2019.

Walters, J. Edward. "Where Soul Meets Body: Narsai's Depiction of the Soul-Body Relationship in Context." In BHK, 227–253.

Wilmshurst, David. *The Martyred Church: A History of the Church of the East.* London: East and West Publishing, 2011.

Witkamp, Nathan. *Tradition and Innovation: Baptismal Rite and Mystagogy in Theodore of Mopsuestia and Narsai of Nisibis. Supplements to* Vigilae Christianae 149. Leiden: Brill, 2018.

———. "A Critical Comparison of the So-Called 'Lawsuit' in the Baptismal Rites of Theodore of Mopsuestia and Narsai of Nisibis." *Vigiliae Christianae* 65, no. 5 (2011): 514–542.

SCRIPTURE INDEX

TOPICAL INDEX